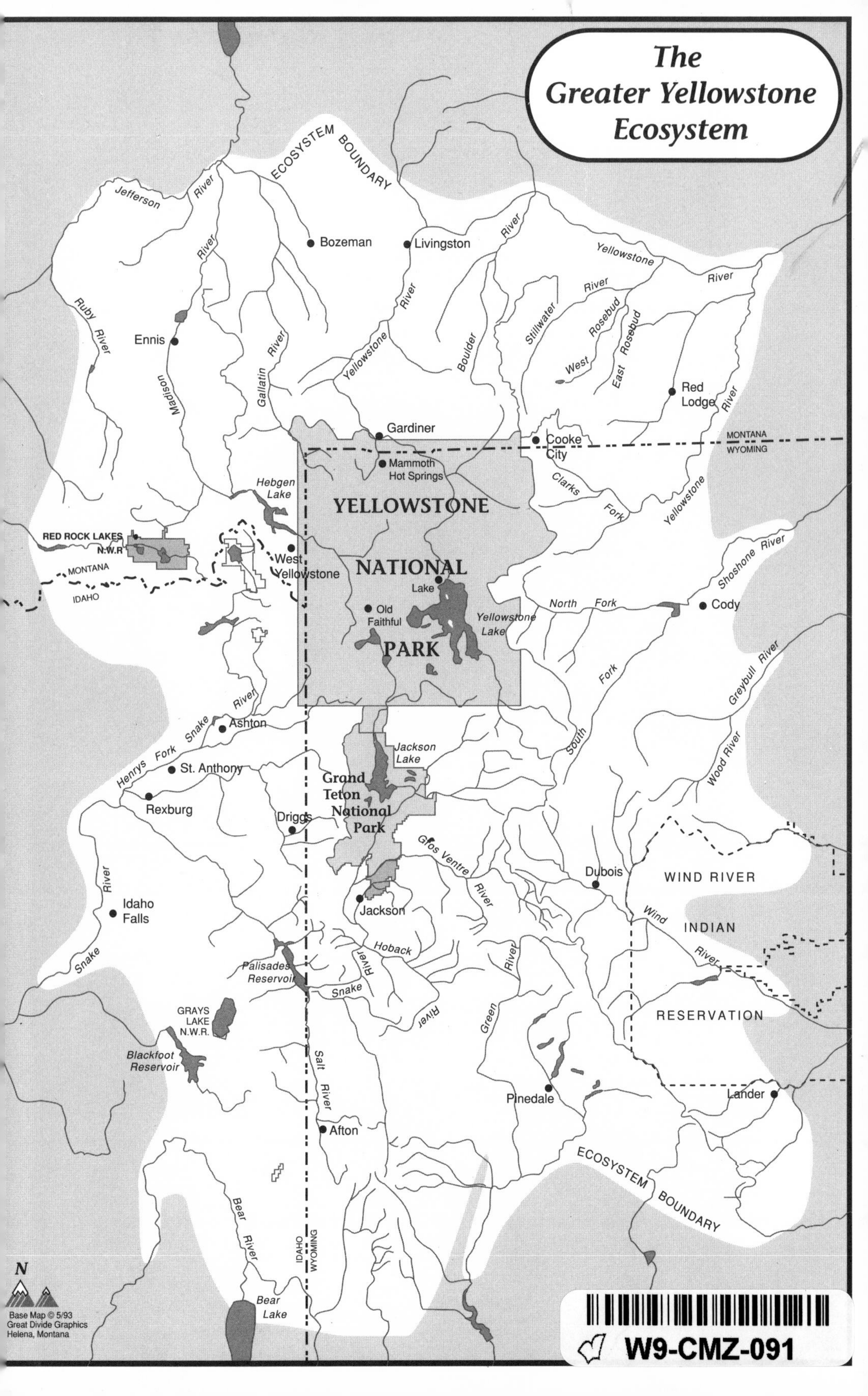
The Greater Yellowstone Ecosystem
ECOSYSTEM BOUNDARY
Jefferson River
Ruby River
Madison River
Gallatin River
Ennis
Bozeman
Livingston
Yellowstone River
Boulder
Stillwater River
West Rosebud
East Rosebud
Red Lodge
Gardiner
Cooke City
MONTANA
WYOMING
Mammoth Hot Springs
Clarks Fork
Hebgen Lake
YELLOWSTONE NATIONAL PARK
RED ROCK LAKES N.W.R.
MONTANA
IDAHO
West Yellowstone
Lake
Old Faithful
Yellowstone Lake
North Fork
Shoshone River
Cody
South Fork
Greybull River
Wood River
Henrys Fork Snake River
Ashton
St. Anthony
Rexburg
Jackson Lake
Grand Teton National Park
Driggs
Gros Ventre River
Dubois
WIND RIVER INDIAN RESERVATION
Wind River
Snake River
Idaho Falls
Jackson
Hoback River
Green River
Palisades Reservoir
Snake
GRAYS LAKE N.W.R.
Blackfoot Reservoir
Salt River
Pinedale
Lander
Afton
Bear River
IDAHO
WYOMING
Bear Lake
N
Base Map © 5/93
Great Divide Graphics
Helena, Montana

LAST REFUGE

LAST REFUGE

The Environmental
Showdown in
Yellowstone and the
American West

JIM ROBBINS

WILLIAM MORROW AND COMPANY, INC.
NEW YORK

It is the policy of William Morrow and Company, Inc., and its imprints and affiliates, recognizing the importance of preserving what has been written, to print the books we publish on acid-free paper, and we exert our best efforts to that end.

Library of Congress Cataloging-in-Publication Data

Robbins, Jim.
Last refuge : the environmental showdown in Yellowstone and the American West / by Jim Robbins.
p. cm.
Includes index.
ISBN 0-688-11178-5
1. Yellowstone National Park. 2. Public lands—West (U.S.)
3. Environmental protection—Yellowstone National Park.
4. Environmental protection—West (U.S.) 5. West (U.S.)—
Description and travel—1981- I. Title.
F595.3.R63 1993
333.73'16'0978—dc20 93-9426
CIP

Printed in the United States of America

First Edition

1 2 3 4 5 6 7 8 9 10

BOOK DESIGN BY LISA STOKES

With Love

For my mother, Betty, and father, Jim,
For my children Matthew and Annika, in hopes they'll know some of the West that I have known.
And especially for Chere. If along the way I have forgotten to say thank you, I hope this will do.

Acknowledgments

Thanks first to all my sources. And thanks to all those who thoroughly read and commented on the draft: Dayton Duncan, Tom Dyja, Chere Jiusto, Ed Lewis, Steve Van Mouwerik, and Sandy Tolan. Also those who reviewed portions of the book, including John Varley, David Lageson, Diane Boyd, Chris Hunter, and Phyllis and Jeff Dorrington.

Howard Berkes of National Public Radio has always been an inspiration and sounding board for a lot of the stories and ideas in this book. Jim Coates of the *Chicago Tribune* and Bill Schmidt of *The New York Times* have also helped me to form some of my ideas. Thanks to the editors at *The New York Times* who helped me first see what makes the West interesting to the rest of the country and taught me a great deal about journalism. Thanks to *The Boston Globe* for their interest in the West as well.

Thanks to the staff of the Greater Yellowstone Coalition for their time, especially Dennis Glick, Bob Ekey, and Louisa Willcox. Thanks to the staffs at the Lewis and Clark Library and the State of Montana Library, for their research help and to Anna Nordell, who kept me from drowning in paper by keeping my files. Thanks to Martha Moutray and Susan Leon for getting me started, and to my agent, Lisa Bankoff, and my editor, Bob Shuman, for picking up the reins.

Contents

Introduction

In the summer of 1988 I drove from my home in Helena, Montana, south to Yellowstone National Park to spend some time reporting on the incredible fires there for *The New York Times.* I checked in with officials at park headquarters in Mammoth Hot Springs to find out where the fires and fire fighters were. The best bet, they said, was Old Faithful, the geyser and tourist complex in the southern half of the park.

The place was jumping. Bombers were flying overhead through smoke-filled skies, radios were crackling, fire trucks racing, and hundreds of people were being hustled out of the area. Officials at Mammoth thought the fire would move to the east of the Old Faithful area. When I got there, I found out predictions had changed: the fire, officials said, was headed straight for Old Faithful. Indeed it was. It roared to the edge of the parking lot where I stood, and surrounded it with a wall of flames and a blast-furnace-like heat that was suffocating.

I stood in the parking lot with other journalists and fire fighters, consumed by mixed feelings of fear and awe as the unbridled forces of nature swirled around us. There was nothing we could do but wait for the fire to burn itself out.

I spent a great deal of time around the wildfires of Yellowstone those weeks, and each time the feelings were the same—an incredible urge to watch the spectacle, and at the same time a sense of fear, a sense that these fires were so much bigger than anything I had encountered before. It took effort, at times, to remain calm.

Though I had covered Yellowstone and other environmental issues for a decade, the fires brought something home to me. When I came to Montana from the East, I was captivated by the wildness of the place. I had hiked, skied, rafted, climbed and camped in Montana, and enjoyed it. I had never felt overwhelmed by it, though, until the fires in Yellowstone.

The American West is fast leaving an era when nature was the great variable. The primary components of the Old West, logging and mining and agriculture, constitute the West in which nature was battled and forced to give up a living. Sometimes it didn't work that way. A storm or a fire or a cold snap wiped it all out. Or lives were lost.

Those occupations are fading in the West, and instead people who work in the cities and towns have the choice of going out into nature or staying home. Nature is important, but not largely an integral part of existence anymore. Fewer people have to battle nature for their living. Or fear it. This new view of nature is the view from the New West, the urban West, the West of tourism and adventure and national parks. The new view is a luxury and it is dramatically changing the way people relate to the landscape.

Last Refuge is about how both the Old West and New West affect public forests and parks and other publicly owned resources, such as wildlife and rivers. When the West was first settled, the lands that fell into public domain were considered worthless. A century later, as America's environment deteriorates and other places fill with people and roads and buildings, the open spaces of the West are fast becoming invaluable.

Now a protracted land war is being fought over these millions of acres of public domain. *Last Refuge* is about the battle between New West and Old, about two different ways of seeing the world, and about a new kind of vision that seeks a middle ground that might preserve the best of both.

Yellowstone, the park and surrounding lands, works well as a paradigm for the American West. There are the obvious similarities. Bigness, for example. The mountains themselves, the canyons and rivers: topography and how it affects life here, physically and emotionally. And Yellowstone, like much of the West, is characterized by large tracts of empty land with small or medium-sized settlements in between. The ways of life are similar. Many people in and around the park, like those of much of the West, still make their living in largely the same way, directly off the land, public and private. Ranching. Farming. Logging. Mining. Outfitting and guiding. Tours.

There's more to the comparison than just the physical. Yellowstone, like the West, holds a unique place in contemporary American mythology. The western myths, many of the stories America holds dear, dwell in the mountains and the plains. The West is a "visionshed," a place where mystery and adventure and beauty are stored like the water the mountains harbor.

So the book starts in Yellowstone. But since the park is bigger than its borders, the book moves on to the Yellowstone ecosystem and from there to the rest of the West to see how the region is impacted by change, and what the answers to the problems arising from that change might be.

A definition of "the West" is in order. In a broad sense the West is often defined as that part of the United States west of the hundredth meridian, where the amount of rainfall is considerably less than that to the east and where behavior changes dramatically by dint of a parched landscape. The West of this book is somewhat smaller. It is primarily about those states where the Rocky Mountains are: Montana, Idaho, Wyoming, Utah, Colorado, New Mexico, Arizona and Nevada. Oregon, Washington and California are included because of their substantial acreage of public lands, though growing numbers of people and development, in my opinion, have drastically changed their western character.

J.R.
Helena, Montana

Heaven and Earth unite
To send down the sweet rain
Without being commanded by the people
It falls evenly by itself

—Lao-tzu

1
The Soul of Fire Mountain

THE EXPEDITION THAT WOULD VISIT THE DARKEST HEART OF the Yellowstone Plateau in 1870 and bring back the concept of a national park did not get off to a smooth start. The party of adventurers—led by thirty-eight-year-old former Montana territorial governor Nathaniel Pitt Langford—packed up tents, cigars and food and lashed them to their horses on Main Street in Helena, Montana Territory.

Adversity was not far off. Three hundred yards after starting out, gear and food tumbled off the packhorses. By the time the horses were repacked, expedition members grumbled about how it was getting late and how they might as well just wait until tomorrow; so they adjourned to a bar called Nick Greenish's Halfway House for the rest of the evening. Departure the next day, it turned out, was a staggered one. "Several of the party," a reporter for the *Helena Herald* wrote, "were under the weather and tarried in the gay Metropolis until night drew her sable curtain down when they started off in search of the expedition."

Hangovers weren't the only problem. Crow Indians, whose reservation bordered the park, were restless; a member of the crew got lost and nearly died; an army lieutenant had a painfully infected thumb; and a dog called Booby came up lame with sore feet and needed to have little moccasins made. But the party eventually made its way to the wilderness of the Yellowstone Plateau.

Once in the area that would become the park, the men set the standard for a visit to Yellowstone. They climbed mountains, hiked to the base of waterfalls and broke through the wilderness to gaze open-mouthed on the spectacle of a skyrocketing stream of hot water. They named the geyser Old Faithful.

One night the party sat swatting gnats and smoking cigars in their camp, alongside the steaming-hot springs where the Firehole and Gibbon rivers come together to form the Madison. They chatted about how they might divvy up this fine piece of real estate that had deeply impressed them all and which would, they were sure, "eventually become a source of great profit to the owners." But one of the party, Cornelius Hedges, shook his head in disagreement. "Mr. Hedges said there ought to be no private ownership of any portion of that region," Langford wrote in his journal, "but [that] the whole ought to be set apart as a great National Park, and that each of us ought to make an effort to have this accomplished."

For having produced what would become an enormous idea, Hedges' mind, according to his own journal entry that day, was actually on more mundane matters—his stomach. "No fish in river. Grub getting very thin."

The party returned to Helena by stagecoach from Virginia City, Montana, on the twenty-fifth and twenty-sixth of September. All except Truman Everts, who had to be fetched back by rescuers on October 6. The adventure of the Yellowstone Plateau proved a little too rugged for Everts, who got separated from the party and thoroughly lost, and was found crawling along the ground near Blacktail Deer Creek in the north of the park, making strange sounds. "It did not look like an animal I had ever seen," wrote a British soldier of fortune named John Baronett, who rescued Everts, "and it was certainly not a human being. I went up close to the object; it was making a low groaning noise, crawling along upon its knees and elbows, and trying to drag itself up the mountain." Everts recovered.

The expedition's idea for the park was not the only one, but the long-bearded N. P. Langford was among those who picked up the torch to have the Great Geyser Basin set aside as a federal reserve. He did not carry the idea alone—he had help from a formidable ally. Langford's nickname was "National Park" Langford, but he could have been dubbed "Northern Pacific," for he made the trip to Yellowstone as a scout for the Northern Pacific Railroad, which saw hauling visitors to a newly created tourist attraction on what was otherwise worthless acreage as another way to cash in on its vast empire of western lands.

On March 1, 1872, President Ulysses S. Grant signed the bill that made Yellowstone the first national park. However mercenary the reasons for its creation, America's first natural reserve soon became a worldwide example of the selfless preservation of natural wonders, of farsighted social policy and a gift to humanity.

Times change. Now, more than a century later, there is increasing opinion that Yellowstone the park is an anachronism, a grand idea made obsolete by the passage of time and the accumulation of scientific knowledge, a remarkable place that is sinking fast into serious trouble. Just as the park was the product of a new way of seeing resources at the time, some are now calling for a new frame of reference for Yellowstone.

The call for a new kind of Yellowstone is controversial. Some think the park is fine like it is. One thing that is agreed on is that Yellowstone is still one of the world's most unusual places.

In the deep blackness of night, a thunderstorm, full of sound and fury but no rain, passes over the Yellowstone Plateau and shakes the earth. Instead of moisture, the sky offers fire in the form of a lightning bolt that zigzags to the parched ground, illuminates the forest for an instant and then is gone. A smoldering limb drops into the duff, the dry accumulation of partly decayed vegetation on the forest floor. The next day the coolness of morning wears off and the forest dries out; by afternoon there is a faint trail of smoke. Then the warm afternoon winds blow up. Before long a towering column of muscular black clouds rises high in the air.

Several hot dry days go by. The fire grows so large that it creates its own weather, sucking in tremendous amounts of oxygen to fuel itself and causing winds of eighty or a hundred miles an hour or more.

Smoke takes over the sky. On the edges of the fire, in the bizarre midday darkness, bison and deer graze, unaware of the flames. As smoke swirls in front of the afternoon sun, different opacities and colors of the smoke create a kaleidoscopic effect. The light has a luminescent orange cast one minute, then pink, or red the next.

Suddenly an eerie kind of silver twilight or near dark shrouds everything. Glowing coals the size of marshmallows drop out of the sky. Tiny pieces of silver ash swirl through the air like snowflakes. Funnel-shaped dust clouds driven by tremendous winds spiral through the air.

The sound overwhelms all. There is the crackling of the burning wood, the wind through the trees. Near the heart of the fire, however, is a roar, a screaming roar that fills the air without ceasing, the sound of nature unmitigated as fire consumes the forest. Judgment Day, it seems, has descended.

Capriciously the fire skips across the landscape, its pattern dictated by swirling winds, changing weather, topography and different kinds of fuel. Trees a hundred feet tall go up like flash paper, and burn ferociously like giant torches. On the grassland the fire forms a sheet of flames several miles wide. It appears to be a rhythmic, living thing, moving with the wind faster than a deer can run. Hugging the ground, the fire flows uphill, then down, again and again. Occasionally it hits a small island of trees and downed timber and explodes in a flash of flames.

The fires continue until an early snow smothers them.

Left behind in the ash are nitrogen, potassium and other fertilizers. A fire is a powerful pulse of nutrients for the species that survive. The next spring, lush green grass as high as an elk's belly and bouquets of wildly vibrant flowers are jolted into existence in the blackened meadows. Trees stick up like a forest of huge burnt matches for as far as the eye can see, and the ground is baked dark and hard.

The Yellowstone landscape, like most of the mountain West, is the product of fire, thousands of years of repeated fires. The elk and antelope, lodgepole pines and fescue grasses, are all species adapted to fire. But Yellowstone has been shaped by an even bigger fire, a fire that dwarfs the forest fires that sweep the landscape, a fire that lies below the ground.

Beneath the more than two-million-acre park that covers portions of Idaho, Montana, and Wyoming lies a giant hidden and active subterranean volcano. Vast chambers hold red-hot molten and partly molten rocks, like a stew that ponderously swirls, bubbles, and convulses. This igneous material sits at the top of a 125-mile column of molten rock that spikes up from the Earth's interior and reaches to just a mile or so below the surface of the park. The Earth's crust above the heat has collapsed and forms a shallow oval depression—a caldera—forty-five miles long and twenty-eight miles wide, entirely within Yellowstone.

The force of the first eruption here some 2.2 million years ago was almost unimaginable—one of the largest volcanic eruptions ever on Earth. For thousands of years the subterranean volcano had simmered and roiled, and lava oozed out intermittently. Then, with a force that dwarfed the Mount St. Helens explosion, perhaps by a factor of one thousand, fragmented material in the magma chambers exploded. All life within two miles of the blast was annihilated by a huge *nuée ardente*—a glowing, superheated cloud of gas and ash of enormous proportions. Wildlife of the time, including fifteen-foot-tall camels, giant bison, horses, shovel-tusked mastodons, saber-toothed tigers, giant tortoises, tapirs, wolves, and lions, were wiped out. Where the glowing lava didn't smother the forests, it triggered dozens of fires.

A giant ash cloud emerged from the volcano, and ash and pieces of rock rained down on such faraway places as Saskatchewan and Louisiana. Animals throughout the region starved, as grass was covered with ash. In Kansas, almost a thousand miles to the southeast, the ash is thirteen feet thick in some places and was mined in the 1930s to make household cleanser. Life on the whole planet was drastically altered, as a cloud of remnants encircled the planet and blotted out the sun. A volcanic winter descended on the Earth, a winter that lasted for decades.

A million years passed in relative quiet. Ice ages came and went, leaving behind rounded boulders, large and small, debris called glacial till. Then a second explosion occurred, somewhat less violent than the first.

When the first two explosions in the Yellowstone Caldera took place, it was actually the Idaho Caldera. The Earth's continents sit like pats of butter on a bowl of porridge, and are slowly drifting apart. North America moves roughly three inches to the west each year; the Atlantic Ocean is more than one hundred feet wider now than when Columbus first crossed it. The magma spike is stationary, a blowtorch directed upward on the North American continental plate. As the plate has moved slowly over the heat from northeast to southwest, the magma has left a plume trace on the land. It begins in Idaho and arcs to Yellowstone. So the first caldera explosion was in what we call south-central Idaho, the second one to the east of Island Park, Idaho.

Some 600,000 years later a third cataclysmic blast took place, this one in Yellowstone and apparently during an ice age, for there is evidence to show that torrid, three-hundred-foot-thick lava flows rumbled along the ground until they met the mammoth sheets of ice and were literally stopped cold. One place where this likely happened was Obsidian Cliff, a sheer bluff made out of volcanic glass in the northern part of the park. Because it fractures well and holds a clean, sharp edge, Indians who occupied the area found the jet-black obsidian invaluable for crafting knife blades and arrowheads. The Teton and Madison ranges, which now begin on the northern and southern boundaries of the park, were at one time probably a continuous range. The seventy-five miles of mountains that once connected them were simply atomized by the blast.

Existence of the caldera was unknown until the 1950s. It wasn't until the mid 1980s when a park geologist was comparing black-and-white aerial photographs of Yellowstone Lake in the center of the park, taken just a decade apart, that clues to the enormous movement of the caldera began to emerge. The pictures didn't add up. Why had the lake inundated grassy banks along its southern edge in the span of just a few years? Why had small islands in the Southern part of the lake been submerged in just a few years? Why were pine and spruce trees several hundred years old suddenly dying at the edge of the lake's southern end? The water level was rising, the pictures indicated, but only at one end of the huge lake. It didn't make sense.

Finally, geologists hit on an explanation. For reasons that remain a mystery, the caldera, which sits under the northern portion of the lake, was rising. It pushed up the end of the giant lake, causing water to run down to the southern end, the same way that lifting up one end of a bathtub would cause the water to slosh to the other end. Deepening water was drowning the trees and submerging the banks. Yellowstone Lake became a kind of huge spirit level; with it, one can note the movement of the caldera. The magma spike is not far beneath the lake. In fact, though the water temperature at the lake bottom has been measured at 38 degrees, just thirteen feet below the bottom, the mud is a steaming 220 degrees.

* * *

The seething and churning subterranean volcano is part of the reason that Yellowstone is one of the most seismically active regions of the country. That and the fact that it is also crossed by four major fault lines, which are stress points in the Earth's crust where earthquakes are focused. The geology in and around the park is shaken and jiggled by hundreds of small temblors each year and occasionally racked by a big one. The most violent of recent Yellowstone quakes occurred on August 17, 1959, when some eighty million tons of rock—half a mountain—was jarred loose by a quake measuring 7.5 on the Richter scale. The slide buried twenty-five unfortunate campers at a national forest campground on the western edge of the park and stopped up the Madison River, creating Quake Lake.

The massive flows of lava that oozed out of the subterranean volcano more than a half million years ago piled up to create the Yellowstone Plateau, what naturalist John Muir called Fire Mountain, a rise more than eight thousand feet in altitude, a much higher topography than any land forms around it. The Yellowstone Plateau is actually a group of five plateaus—Madison, Central, Mirror, Pitchstone and Two Ocean.

As the glowing lava flowed out of the volcano, it smothered trees, creating in Yellowstone an extraordinary collection of petrified redwood forests. After the trees were buried, water carrying silica percolated through the porous rock and replaced each living cell with a stone replica. Some of these petrified giants have been exposed by erosion; one such place is Specimen Ridge.

The column of red-hot magma that spikes up so close to the surface in the park is the engine that drives the park's remarkable array of thermal features, which in places make the park look like, as one trapper put it, "a place where hell bubbled up." These ten thousand geothermal features are nearly two thirds of the world's total, the largest intact collection in the world, and the primary reason Yellowstone was made America's first national park in 1872. One of the ten major geothermal areas in the world, only two have not been destroyed or damaged, and one of them is Yellowstone.

A labyrinthine network of rock chambers above the subterranean volcano filled with pressurized, superheated, slowly moving water is responsible for Yellowstone's hot-water display. There are four kinds of geothermal features in the park. The best known feature is the geyser, which is an underground column of water that periodically erupts. The tube holding the water connects either to chambers alongside or to water-bearing porous rock. The water at the bottom of the column is heated by volcanic rock to well above the normal boiling point (199 degrees at this altitude, more than a mile above sea level) but does not boil, because it's under so much pressure from the weight of the water above it. When the superheated, pressurized water gets hot enough and finally does boil, it expands, and some of the water at the top of the column is expelled. The sudden reduction of pressure on the remaining water causes it to boil and vaporize instantly. The resulting steam furiously explodes into the air in a tall jet. Sometimes, however, the pressure underground in these features is too much to bear and they violently self-destruct; there are explosive craters in the park up to four thousand feet across.

There are some three hundred geysers in the park, and most of them only splash a little, reaching a height of ten feet or so. Six are grand geysers, which erupt to a height of a hundred feet or more and whose eruptions can be predicted. The tallest jet is that of Steamboat Geyser in the Norris Geyser Basin, which sometimes erupts in intervals measured in days, and then lies dormant for decades. It rises to a height of 380 feet.

Old Faithful is the most famous geothermal feature in the park. It erupts to a height of 180 feet at intervals ranging from forty minutes to two hours, winter and summer, at a temperature of 199 degrees. When the surface temperature at Old Faithful drops to 30 or 40 degrees below zero—the record is 60 below—and the geyser roars into the sky, the water freezes in the air and cascades back to earth making a sound like tinkling glass.

Where there is an opening but not enough pressure for an eruption, a fumarole is formed, a hole in the earth that roars and hisses as steam and other gases rush up its throat. The water that feeds these features is heavily laden with silica and other minerals, and as water splashes out, the minerals often form small white volcano-shaped cones around the opening. There are also mudpots, filled with plastic, moiling mud that looks like hot gray or brown paint and makes a *fwap, fwap* sound as it simmers. Some mudpots are so loud the Langford expedition likened the noise to "reports of distant artillery." Hot springs, the fourth kind of geothermal feature, are pools where hot water surfaces from below, but where pressure is very low. Silica in the water in hot springs forms sinter, or geyserite, a lightweight rock that forms the beautiful and delicately scalloped edges of rock around some pools. Silica particles sometimes adhere to air bubbles in the water, collecting one particle after another, until the bubble becomes too heavy to float and sinks to the bottom to become one of many tiny gray globes that look as if they were fashioned by a silversmith.

Clusters of geothermal features in the park are geyser basins, and these landscapes in the park look bizarre, surreal, even postapocalyptic. "Thank you," wrote an editor for *Lippincott's Magazine* when explorer C. W. Cook submitted a description of the geysers in 1869, "but we do not print fiction." The ground in some places is so hot that petroleum in the soil has been naturally refined and sits in steaming black pools on the surface. Elk wallow in the greasy, warm substance. There are places in the park where the earth seems eerily alive, as boiling water beneath the ground causes it to tremble and the sultry stink of sulfur fills the air. Some fields hold every feature, from tiny, steaming holes in the ground to vats of bubbling gray mud to swimming pool-sized craters filled with violently boiling crystal-clear turquoise water that seems to have no bottom.

The earth seems like it is straining to speak here. Or perhaps sing, a ghostly-sounding geyser choir—throaty roars, sputters, rumbles, hissing and deep gargles emanating from the holes in the ground. Geyser fields are also oddly colorful. Different communities of algae live in different temperatures of water, and as the water splashes out of a geyser, the algae in it change color as they get farther from the source. Red algae that look like some kind of horrendous industrial effluent, peculiar to hot springs, line the sides of the hot pots and streak the ground. Other water is blue-green, red, yellow or the orange color of a Creamsicle. Ghost trees stand in the geyser fields, killed by the chemicals in the hot water, and the curling tendrils of steam are specters that haunt all geyser basins. There are boiling rivers where hot springs pour into streams that a few hours ago were still snow. There is a famous place along Yellowstone Lake where a fisherman can catch a trout on his line and, without touching it, swing it over to a scalding fumarole, and boil the fish for dinner, just like the early trappers did. However, with all of the naturally occurring chemicals in the water, the cooked trout wouldn't taste very good.

* * *

Once the lava from the subterranean volcano had finished its grand ooze and had cooled, life wasted no time in beginning the journey back to the vacuum of the plateau. Lichen, a symbiotic arrangement of algae and fungus that comes in green, gray, black or brown, moved in to cling tenaciously to the hardened lava and begin the process of soil restoration. It wedged into the cracks and gathered there. Rain fell, froze and made the cracks a little larger. When water falls on the carbon dioxide produced by the lichen it creates carbonic acid—which is what makes the bubbles in soda pop—and dissolves limestone. The lichen expanded its territory and attracted other organic material. Eventually a stray seed, perhaps brought by a bird or borne on the wings of the wind, fell into the pile and took root. Small plants, a shrub or a tree now find an ecological toehold. They grow and, in turn, die and create a more fertile seedbed, paving the way for the next generation. In as short a span as two or three centuries, forest is growing again.

Forest predominates in Yellowstone now. Three quarters of the park is covered with different kinds: towering, black-green Douglas fir and spruce fir. Forests of thin, tall lodgepole pines growing in such numbers and so close-set that they are called doghair and are too thick to walk through. There are stands of quaking aspen, with their heart-shaped leaves that shimmer in a breeze.

Grassy meadows cover much of the rest of the park. Studded with gray-green sagebrush, they are what give life to the herds of elk, deer and bison that have earned Yellowstone the name "America's Serengeti." After a rain the smell of sage in these meadows is thick and fragrant. Deer and grouse browse its leaves. In the spring and summer the purple of lupine and the flaming red of paintbrush shine. Larkspur, Queen Anne's lace and bluebells grow. The meadows are broken by lakes and swamps, decorated with pond lilies, water hemlocks and snow-white swans.

Up in the high country, above the timberline, which occurs at ten thousand feet here, are Yellowstone's alpine areas. Glacier lilies sprout impatiently as soon as the snow recedes, often next to the lip of diminishing snowbanks. Soft blue alpine forget-me-nots follow. Sky pilots, elephant's-head and Parry's primrose grow here as well. Bumblebees and flies go flower to brilliant flower pollinating each in return for the nectar. Tiny, stunted, wind-twisted bonsai-like pines carpet the high country with a dwarf forest called krummholz, survivors in a brutal environment.

* * *

One of the alpine areas here is the Two Ocean Plateau. It is a carpet of green, a treeless meadow that rolls along for several miles. A single creek starts here and then splits to flow into two boulder-dotted waterways that take off in different directions—Pacific and Atlantic creeks—narrow enough at this point to step over. Eventually each of these creeks sends its water into a different ocean, on an opposite side of the United States.

Because Fire Mountain juts into the sky, the Yellowstone Plateau is a magnet for passing storms and water is abundant in Yellowstone. As the eastward-moving storm systems pass over, they drop moisture. Often rain, but more often snow—twenty feet on average. Thus Yellowstone's high country acts like a giant sponge, soaking up water in the winter, and squeezing it out in the spring, summer and fall. Much of the water finds its way into the hot rocks beneath the geothermal features. The plateau is also a nursery for dozens of creeks, lakes, bogs and swamps. But some four trillion gallons of water flows out of the park each year. Three of the West's great rivers get their start in the park: the Yellowstone, which roars through a stunning 1,200-foot canyon, eventually flowing into the Missouri; the Missouri, two of whose three major sources—the Madison and the Gallatin—start here; and the Snake, which, a thousand miles downstream, empties into the Columbia.

This is cold clear water, so thick and sweet it is a kind of mountain nectar. Where you have water like this, you have fish, and Yellowstone has one of the finest fisheries in the Lower Forty-eight. Rainbow and brown trout, both well-established ecological interlopers, and native cutthroat trout—so named because of a slash of red on their white throats—are abundant.

The park's fish serve as a critical food source for another of the park's species—the grizzly bear. Grizzlies, of which there are some 250 in the Greater Yellowstone area, are omnivores, which means they eat almost everything and anything, though 70 percent of the diet is vegetation. Come spring the bears eat the onion-like roots of glacier lilies and spring beauties—meadows where bears have torn the ground for the tiny roots look like they've been disced by a tractor. In summer bears gobble whitebark pinecones; in the fall, plump, sugar-sweet huckleberries. But when cutthroat trout swim out of Yellowstone Lake to spawn in the narrow, meandering tributaries that feed it, the bears waddle up the streams, seizing fish after fish in their massive paws and eating them, a bear's version of heaven.

Grizzlies also feed on the elk that swarm through the park. One morning as the sun began to creep up over the horizon a sow grizzly and three cubs emerged from a forest and wandered out into a meadow. As the mother loped along, her light brown fur rippling in a steady breeze, the three cubs bounded along with her, swatting each other or playfully snapping at her neck. As the ursine procession neared an island of pine trees in the midst of the sea of grass, loud mewing shrieks began to echo in the air, timorously at first, then rising in volume and intensity. The grove was an elk nursery. Dozens of elk had recently given birth to flimsy-legged calves in the sheltered area. The elk cows were forced to flee the approaching bears. Some of the calves could walk well enough to go with the cows; but others too weak yet to stand lay trembling in the grove. Maybe they would be lucky and the bears would pass them by. The fleeing mothers seemed to be shrieking for the ones they were forced to leave behind.

Grass squeaks loudly as a bison yanks it with its teeth from the ground near the park's geothermal features. The animal moves around like an eating machine, snorting, chewing and darting out its long tongue—as thick as a forearm—never taking its mouth off the ground. A thick mat of black, frizzy hair sits on its head like a cheap wig. A big, brown eye in the side of its head blinks occasionally. Bison have huge heads, massive, truck-sized shoulders, a high-arching backbone and an improbably small rear end. In the spring, rubber-legged fuzzball calves try to stand. They are a centerpiece of a Yellowstone visit.

The last free-roaming herd of bison in the United States grazes these foothills and meadows, and wanders along—sometimes in—park roadways, oblivious to humans. Come winter the buffalo wander through the mists and fog that shroud the geothermal fields and look like prehistoric apparitions. They wade in naturally warmed waterways, their backs covered with frost and snow. Their faces are often covered with snow, since they use their heads to push it away to get at dried grass beneath. Or they feed on green grass fooled by geothermal springs into thinking it's summer all year. Sometimes they feed a little too close. Bison, especially young ones, occasionally tumble into the boiling hot springs, and for several weeks, says one ranger, "it smells like someone's cooking a big pot of soup." By summer the bison is a pile of bleached bones at the bottom of the spring.

There is no shortage of ruminants in the park. One of the largest herds of elk in the world grazes the grass of Yellowstone. There are eight distinct herds of elk, with a total number of more than 35,000. These are among the last of the great migratory elk herds that once roamed as far east as New York and Georgia. Come early September the big bulls will leave their bachelor groups and begin gathering their harem of cows, anywhere from six to twenty of them. This collection is not uncontested, and the bulls, which can weigh up to one thousand pounds each and stand five feet at the shoulder, will engage in combat, with the larger bull usually the victor. The neck of the bull becomes engorged with blood in the fall, hard as a tree trunk, rendering the antlers a powerful weapon. Very few of these contests, however, end in death. Later in the fall, the fires of passion fully stoked, the elk are seen in the Park Service town of Mammoth, peering into windows, grunting and shrieking loudly as they feverishly and shamelessly seek to couple anywhere, even on the front lawn, during the annual season of lust, the rut.

Coyotes prowl the Yellowstone landscape, feeding on the dead and the wounded, hunting mice and rabbits. Mule deer and white-tailed deer graze the slopes. Bighorn sheep cling to the cliffsides. Moose wallow in the swamps. Pronghorn antelope gallop with blinding speed.

These are the "charismatic megafauna" in the park, the animals that people come from Minneapolis, Tokyo, Denver, Hamburg and Bozeman to see. But there are other species, smaller but no less necessary for keeping the wheels of the ecosystem turning, each providing its own kind of spectacle. The slow, graceful glide of the white pelican, massive white birds with wingtips the color of coal. The large and long-legged sandhill crane, with its tremulous and haunting call. The black oily sheen of the raven. The occasional beaver that drops trees and dams streams. The brown and silver heather vole that lives in huckleberry patches. The blotched tiger salamander. The prairie rattlesnake.

Most people know Yellowstone in its fleeting summer season. However, winter is the natural state of Yellowstone, a season that descends in October, often in a matter of hours and without preamble, and is worked loose finally by the June sun. Even then it is not deterred from making occasional unannounced visits throughout the summer. The metabolism of the park as a whole slows down in the winter, a state somewhere between wakefulness and sleep.

Yellowstone during the short days of mid-December is like a place above the Arctic Circle. The sun makes a poor showing. In the high country, fierce, blinding squalls force wildlife to slowly descend to low-lying ranges. The same steady gales that keep pregnant steel-gray storm clouds scudding through park skies sweep winter grasses clean of snow. This is make-or-break season, for winter is the Great Predator in Yellowstone, and death rides with each winter storm.

Grizzly and black bears, having completed a fall frenzy of eating, have waddled off to some dark cavity sequestered by heavy snow, and hibernate until roused by the warm sun of the spring. As the brunt of winter descends, the long, serpentine herd of elk cows, calves and antlered bulls makes its final descent from the higher elevations, according to some ancient, unseen call of nature. The elk, some people say, are indicators of the weather and seem to know when change is coming. One morning a few years ago several thousand elk moved down out of the mountains and into the National Elk Refuge near Jackson, Wyoming. By the next afternoon twenty-six inches of snow had fallen.

Waterfalls, like the 130-foot Tower Falls in the park's interior, become entombed in cylinders of glass-like ice of their own making, as water vapor freezes. While the falls can't be seen through the ice, the muffled plunge of the water can be heard.

Sunlight dapples the snow-shrouded landscape, glaring through hastily moving clouds and casting shifting, mottled patterns on rolling hills and forest valleys. At its most brilliant, the sun, cutting sharply through clean, crisp air makes the snow glitter as if encrusted with thousands of sparkling diamonds.

In the midst of winter come respites called chinooks. In a matter of hours the icy fingers of winter are pried loose, and warm begins. After thirty below zero for three weeks, the warmer breezes feel downright tropical. It may be thirty below in the morning, yet by midafternoon the temperature is in the fifties and the snow is melting. Not always a blessing, for if the snow melts and refreezes, it creates an icy surface that makes life difficult for grazing animals that have difficulty breaking through the ice to find grass.

N. P. Langford was among those stunned by what he saw on the plateau. "Your memory becomes filled and clogged with objects new in experience," he wrote. "It is the new phase in the natural world; a fresh exhibition of the handiwork of the Great Architect; and while you see and wonder, you seem to need an additional sense fully to comprehend and believe."

Before whites came to the West, the Yellowstone country was split among several different tribes of Native Americans. In the period just before the Europeans descended in full force, the Blackfeet held the territory north of the Yellowstone River, the Crows the land to the south. To the West the Shoshones. A small group of Shoshones, the Sheepeaters, were the only inhabitants of the Yellowstone Plateau. While most of the Shoshones adopted the horse and the gun, the Sheepeaters clung to the old way of Indian life. They lived in small bands, traveled on foot, kept large dogs, gathered berries and herbs and hunted small animals, fish, elk and especially bighorn sheep. The Sheepeaters never signed a treaty, but as the other Shoshones around the park were packed off to reservations, they became isolated. In 1871, a year before the area was designated a park, they joined Chief Washakie's Shoshones on the Wind River Reservation in Wyoming.

Trappers were the first whites to make their way into Yellowstone country. Early French trappers called the area Roche Jaune, after the yellow rocks along the river, which was probably a continuation of the Indian name for the area. John Colter, a trapper who served with Lewis and Clark, was one of the first white men to penetrate deep into the heart of Yellowstone, in 1806, and his stories of "rivers that ran so fast the bottom got hot" convinced many people that Yellowstone was a figment of his imagination.

Once reliable reports confirmed the unusual features, interest in setting aside this extraordinary landscape began to grow. The idea of a park was such a new concept that, for fourteen years after it was created, the park existed in a kind of bureaucratic limbo. The United States had created the world's first national park, but was clueless on how it should be administered. There were superintendents appointed—Langford was the first—but with little staff and funding they could not bring bureaucratic order to the chaos of more than two million acres of wilderness thousands of miles from

Washington, D.C. Some wagon roads had been built, along with a hotel, a store and a post office at Mammoth Hot Springs.

A chronic problem for the inchoate park was raiding parties of poachers. It was difficult country to patrol, especially without much staff. The poachers raided the wildlife mecca at will, mowing down buffalo, elk and beaver. On August 17, 1886, Captain Moses Harris and M Company of the 1st Cavalry marched into Yellowstone to take command from the civilian superintendent, David Wear. But the army was not there solely because of the problem of market hunters. Inadvertently, Congress had never authorized the $20,000 that was going to pay the superintendent and his people. When some representatives tried to correct the oversight, they ran into the railroad and concession interests that did not like Wear's management of the park. These interests managed to block funding. To keep the park from falling prey to the "local vandals," there was no choice but to call in the troops. They held the plateau until 1918.

Since the government came to Yellowstone, one of the predominant themes has been wrong yet generally well-meaning management (with these good intentions occasionally pushed off track by the forces of profit and politics). That was the case in 1917, for example, when acting superintendent Chester A. Lindsley wrote: "Timber wolves were reported from several different sources during the month, and while not numerous they are a menace to other animals as they kill often. Two were killed during the month of December by Steve Elkins, who is working by day with his trained dogs, hunting mountain lions." These days park officials say the lack of predators is one of the park's big problems, and they are battling to bring wolves back to Yellowstone.

The boundaries of the park pose a similar problem. In 1872 Congress drew a line around Yellowstone's most salient and obvious features for protection, making zigs here and zags there, based on political considerations and not on biological ones. No one knew about the caldera at the time. Or the fact that elk need grass in the winter outside the boundaries. The park may be 2.2 million acres—the size of Rhode Island and Delaware combined—but in the last two or three decades or so, the embryonic science of ecology has begun to show the shortcomings of even that much ground. The park itself is a fragment, a small part of a larger ecological system that, depending on how you define it, may be as large as eighteen million acres—more than 28,000 square miles.

Yellowstone the park is roughly fifty miles from northern border to southern. The entire ecosystem, as biologists define it, is 150 miles or more from north to south. The ecosystem is more than twice as wide as the park, as well.

The Greater Yellowstone Coalition (GYC), a Bozeman, Montana-based environmental group dedicated to protecting the whole ecosystem and not just the park, defines an ecosystem as "a dynamic collection of plants, animals and their physical environment interacting through a variety of processes and operating as a unit." It works something like this: The sun provides energy for plants, which make carbohydrates, which a bear eats for energy. The bear defecates, and microorganisms turn the waste into usable nutrients for the plants. And the process begins again. A large ecosystem like the Yellowstone is the collection of many small ecosystems, with many of these processes taking place together.

The problem in the Greater Yellowstone ecosystem is that not all the pieces are intact or available. Yellowstone the park is like a plant, and the land that surrounds it, the roots. A grizzly bear can't live solely in the high country of the Yellowstone Plateau. When it emerges from hibernation, its stomach is growling and the park is still locked in winter. It needs the succulents that grow in the spring at low levels, and the carcasses of winter-killed elk revealed by the retreating snow. Bears may wander out of the park as far east as Cody, Wyoming, more than fifty miles from the park boundary. Groundwater that recharges the geysers and hot springs of Yellowstone lies under private and government land north and west of park boundaries. In the wintertime, elk migrate across Yellowstone boundaries in almost every direction, and park bison have been trying to colonize land to the north of the park for many years.

Things were fine as long as there were not many changes in the land around the park. However, land management is extremely splintered, and each owner of the land manages for different goals. Within the ecosystem there are seven national forests, two parks (Yellowstone and Grand Teton National Park), three wildlife refuges, state land, county land, an Indian reservation and private land. On this mosaic all manner of activity is taking place. Trees have been stripped from the land on the eastern border of the park, creating massive clear-cuts visible from satellites. Subdivisions are constructed along rivers and streams and other important wildlife habitat. Gold mines are operated on Bureau of Land Management (BLM) and Forest Service land, and toxic-waste piles from past mining are leaching into streams that flow into the park. Drilling for oil and gas or hot water to the south of the park could upset the delicate balance of hot water and pressure that creates the park's geothermal features. Cattle are run on state and federal land, competing with wildlife. Activities on all this land outside the park—but important to park features—are carried out in much the same way they have been for 120 years or more. The difference is that there is a great deal more of it now, and people now know these activities are either damaging the region's natural features, or have that potential.

The Rocky Mountain West is a gathering of ecosystems like the Yellowstone ecosystem; different sizes and different components, but each functioning in essentially the same ways. In the language of ecologists, a collection of ecosystems (some that would fit on a tabletop) make up a landscape, while ecosystems are composed of communities of individuals along with their physical and chemical environment. The eight Rocky Mountain states could be called a landscape, a landscape consisting of hundreds of ecosystems, alpine to desert to forest, all of which overlap and interact with each other. And these natural systems are more complete in the West than almost anywhere else. Many, however, are slowly being torn apart.

One attribute most of the ecosystems of the West have in common is critical to bear in mind. They are extremely dry and extremely fragile. Damage done to the western landscape does not heal. Wounds suffered by the land, a century ago or more, are still visible. Rifle pits dug by Custer's 7th Cavalry in 1876, for example, can still be seen on the bluffs overlooking the Little Bighorn River.

Some say the people of the West have unwittingly painted themselves into an ecological corner. The ability to measure impact from change has always lagged behind mankind's ability to inflict change. Now the knowledge is catching up and it poses new problems: adjusting resource practices in ways that reflect ecological reality conflicts with long-established, traditional ways of doing business in the Rocky Mountains. The economic triad that supports many western communities—logging, minerals (including oil and gas) and agriculture—is a way of life that is at the heart of the culture and character. It is the Old West. Ecological knowledge also conflicts with burgeoning newer activities, the so-called New West—real estate development, urbanization and tourism.

So the West, like Yellowstone, is in the middle of an ecological conundrum, caught between two paradigms. The Old West and the New West on one side, both presently carried out in a way that reflects short-term profit first and foremost; and on the other side, what environmentalists hope will be the Next West, one that takes long-term costs into account, which means keeping not only the economy healthy, but the environment as well. Supporters of the Next West want to redefine the term *progress.*

It is an enormous gap. There is a great deal invested in the established economy and culture, the status quo, in terms of both money and emotion. Yet the real, and often hidden, ecological and economic cost of this status quo is becoming clearer all the time. And that damage, critics point out in a loud and insistent voice, is being subsidized by the federal government.

Both sides see it as a battle for survival, and in a nutshell, this conflict is what lies at the heart of the contentious and angry West.

There is a concerted effort to change this situation. When it was set aside, Yellowstone was the global prototype of the national park idea, the DNA for the idea of a park, and it has been replicated in many other countries. The Yellowstone area is considered by the United Nations as one of the last great intact temperate ecosystems. Playing on the park's prominence, the GYC—which is two groups in one actually, a coalition of more than ninety local and national environmental groups and a freestanding organization that has its own staff and agenda—want to make the Yellowstone ecosystem the prototype, a paradigm, for sustainable ecosystem management. That is, to manage the entire ecosystem in an intelligent way that doesn't cause irreparable, ongoing damage to the species and natural features and that doesn't end with the crash of the natural systems. To create an economy, they say, that lives off the interest rather than the principal.

Yellowstone, the GYC says, is the place to do it. The park is a symbol for nature at its finest. Yellowstone is the place to chart a new course for the relationship between humans and nature in the American West. Many of the conflicts playing out in the West these days are playing out in the Greater Yellowstone ecosystem. If the change is accomplished here, they argue, it could provide a blueprint for the rest of the West.

2
Water the Color of Red Wine

MUD CAKED ON HER BLUE JEANS UP TO HER KNEES, A WILLOWY Louisa Willcox stands surrounded by the ruins of a vanished civilization—dilapidated houses, huge, rusted cylinders, planks, a sluice box, thousands of nails crumbling with rust and corrosion. Out of the mouths of several old mine tunnels, from deep beneath the mountain, run tiny streams the color of red wine. A marmot scampers from behind a pile of wood and runs to a more distant refuge.

This is what's left of the Glengarry Mine, a gold and silver mine that, until the 1950s, operated near timberline in the Beartooth Mountains, a range of granite mountains that cover a great deal of Montana and Wyoming north and east of the park. The cold, trickling streams are carrying iron, cadmium, manganese and other heavy metals out of the hillside and into Fisher Creek, a stream narrow enough here to jump across.

This is high alpine country, above ten thousand feet in altitude and inhospitable to all but the hardiest. Grizzly bears wander through here. And moose. Mountain goats and bighorn sheep. Nine months of the year it is covered with snow—many feet of snow. To get here requires a climb on a steep, rutted, crater-filled two-track road, a road intimidating even for four-wheel-drive vehicles. Navigating several miles of road takes over an hour.

That the Glengarry Mine is here at all is testimony to the incredible tenacity of miners and mining companies, and their single-minded commitment to finding and extracting the mother lode. In spite of that determination, the miners who built and occupied these structures, who dug out the ore with pick and shovel and pushed small metal railcars from deep within the earth by hand and hauled the ore down the treacherous road with horse and wagon, may have missed most of the gold and silver. What they missed may be so much, in fact, that a new kind of mining civilization is rising again.

This time things will be done differently. Instead of men scratching at the earth with picks and shovels, drills will bore tunnels big enough to drive trucks in. Huge house-sized machinery will literally pick up pieces of the mountain and cart them away. The pieces of mountain will be reduced to dust so as much of the gold as possible can be extracted.

A company called Crown Butte Mining, Inc., which is owned primarily by the Canadian mining giant Noranda Minerals, is working on a mine that will sit high in the mountains that tower over Yellowstone in a gold, silver and copper complex that Crown Butte claims is among the richest in the region. It is called the New World Mine.

This new world on the horizon makes Willcox nervous and angry to no end. "It's everywhere you don't want a mine to be," Willcox says. "It's perched at ten thousand feet at the head of three drainages. It's in alpine area above timberline. And it's a major corridor for the grizzly bear." Willcox is the program director for the Greater Yellowstone Coalition, a bureaucratic title for a kind of environmental warfare specialist who travels to the different hot spots in the ecosystem, organizing local groups and researching threats. The thirty-seven-year-old Willcox, with a graduate degree in environmental science from Yale, fits the job. When asked why she moved to the West years ago from Philadelphia, she answers with one word: "Mountains." Now, she says, she will do her damnedest to keep the mountains from being ruined. Armed with facts, she is a hard-nosed, take-no-prisoners type of environmentalist. She rapidly fires off facts about leach pad liners and the mating habits of moose, which use the Noranda mine site part of the year. Many people admire her tenacity, her feistiness, her commitment. Others, including a few on her own side, find her abrasive and alienating as she fights for the cause. "I'm not too much of a hard-ass," she says. "When you look at how isolated the park is, how fragmented the habitat is, we really don't have much left. I'm not too much of a hard-ass."

As she stands among the ruins of the Glengarry, you can almost see her anger beginning to well. "We've got pictures of even worse mining sites that we pass around at meetings," Willcox jokes, as she picks her way through the rusting junkyard. "We call it eco-porn." The Glengarry Mine is on the flank of Henderson Mountain, a mountain above the three line that is scarred with small, open pits and roads that cut back and forth to the top, located near the remote northwest corner of the park, just outside the park's borderline. This is Yellowstone's most dramatic alpine country, with towering mountain peaks. Most of the mountains in Yellowstone were vaporized by the volcanic explosions, and so most of the park is low-lying, rounded mountains, ridges and rolling meadows.

The peaks of the Beartooths are battleship gray, etched by growing and receding glaciers. Narrow ribbons of waterfalls hang over the sides of the peaks, and the mountains are covered with blankets of pines and spruce. They are the kind of dramatic, sudden mountains more characteristic of Glacier National Park or the Canadian Rockies.

The problem—here as well as throughout the West—is an ineluctable law of physics: everything flows downhill. Mining is so disruptive, and the by-products are so toxic, that environmentalists say it is all but impossible to mine without serious disruption to the environment. It would be especially difficult to mine in the clouds above Yellowstone without doing damage to the park and surrounding wildland that lies below. On patented land—land owned by the mining company—the New World Mine is squeezed in among some of the choicest publicly owned land in the country. High above them all.

Miller Creek flows out of this alpine area to the southwest, into Yellowstone Park's Soda Butte Creek, which flows in turn into the Lamar River. Fisher Creek tumbles into the Clarks Fork of the Yellowstone River in Wyoming, a federally designated Wild and Scenic River. And the Stillwater River flows out of here into the Absaroka-Beartooth Wilderness Area. "Even people in the Forest Service call it the mine from Hell," says Willcox. "It's a real nightmare."

A nightmare, that is, depending on who is doing the dreaming. For Noranda Minerals, the New World could be a bonanza—ten times as rich as the ore in open-pit gold mines now operating in Montana, producing as much as a hundred thousand ounces of gold per year. All told, a billion dollars' worth.

David Rovig, president of Crown Butte Mining, Inc., in Billings, Montana, is confident his company can mine with minimal environmental impact. "Absolutely," he says. "We're not taking apart a mountain. Ninety percent of our reserves are deep in the mountain. There are two small pits involved in the plan, two very small pits. When we're done, the area will look better than it does now. People are making statements that have no basis in fact."

As the abandoned Glengarry Mine indicates, this part of the Yellowstone ecosystem has had experience with gold mines before. The town of Cooke City was founded as a mining town in the 1880s. The area boomed and at one time had a thousand year-round residents. But the mines played out and the miners drifted away, to be replaced by businesses catering to tourists who were discovering Yellowstone by automobile. There are some seventy year-round residents now.

The mine sits high above the town of Cooke City. If the mine is permitted, some locals fear things in this tiny town would change, dramatically and, many residents say, for the worse. More than 300 workers would flood in during the construction stage, and 140 workers would be needed year-round.

Trucks would rumble up and down the two-lane highway to haul ore to a mill or supplies to the mine. A new, sixty-eight-mile-long, sixty-nine-kilovolt transmission line would be constructed. A large impoundment would be needed to hold mill tailings, and administration buildings, warehouses, toolsheds and other structures would be built. And hundreds of people would come in to the area to live. "It would take away our high-mountain hideaway," says Ralph Glidden, owner of the historic Cooke City Store and an opponent of the mine. "We really don't need that kind of change here."

Chemical change overshadows most concerns. Waste piles from the old McLaren Mine, which sit just above the town, still drain red, iron-laden water into Soda Butte Creek, despite efforts to stem the flow. This acidic water has sterilized several miles of Soda

Butte Creek in the park, killed the trout and insects and plants that once lived there. A century after the mining took place, the stream is beginning to recover. Slowly.

Even though the New World Mine may affect the nation's first and largest park, the federal agencies that are responsible for giving the go-ahead on the mine say they are powerless to deny the company permission. Powerless before the General Mining Law of 1872—a law passed the same year Yellowstone Park was established—which has been interpreted to give miners who are seeking gold, silver, platinum or other precious metals carte blanche on land owned by the public. Meant to spur development of the West by pick-and-shovel-toting miners, the law these days primarily serves large corporations. It is a core issue of the vitriolic debate over public lands.

A different kind of New World brought the first of the Old World visitors to North America, though the goal was the same: gold. Spanish myth had long held that in the eighth century, seven Catholic bishops had fled Spain ahead of an invasion by the Moors. They sailed off to an island to the west where each man founded a city, and each became wealthy beyond measure. Driven by dreams of unbridled wealth, Spanish explorers for years feverishly sought out the Seven Cities of Cibola. The discovery and conquest of the Aztecs, who were rich with gold and jewels, only convinced them the myth was true, and whetted their desire for more.

In the sixteenth century, after the conquest of Mesoamerica, Spanish eyes turned to the vast unexplored territory to the north. A Spanish holy man by the name of Fray Marcos de Niza was sent from Mexico to scout for the seven cities. In what is now New Mexico, Fray Marcos came upon a Zuni pueblo, the town of Hawikuh. The black robe pulled up outside the town and sent a guide in, who was killed and mutilated by the tribe. No matter. Fray Marcos had what he needed. Or thought he did. As he looked down on the adobe city from a distant hill in the shimmering sun of the desert, he saw what he wanted to see—a city made of gold. He hurried back with his report.

A large-scale expedition of a thousand men was mounted to follow Fray Marcos's directions, led by Francisco Vásquez de Coronado. But when the soldiers and priests and Fray Marcos entered the village, they were stunned. By Aztec standards the village was impoverished, no gold or jewels to be seen. Instead of a city made of gold, they found a city of mud.

The hunt for gold often renders everything else mere distraction, and the Spanish remained undaunted. They heard tales of other, much wealthier pueblos. Hawikuh became a base, and soldiers were sent to check out other stories. But there was no gold. No silver. Nothing of importance to the Europeans except a few souls to convert.

The Spanish wintered in the pueblo. As the thaw came, they heard from an Indian called the Turk, who spoke of yet another place far off that was, finally, one of the fabled cities of gold. Quivira was its name; golden bells, the Turk said, hung from trees and played lullabies for the Quivirian king. Coronado and his men saddled up and rode across the plains to what is now Kansas, in the frenzied search for Quivira. What Coronado discovered instead were Wichita Indians living in houses made from prairie grass. No gold. Turk was killed where he stood, and a disgusted Coronado rode with his men back to Mexico City.

Forty years later the Spanish returned. In 1610, on the banks of a tiny stream that tumbled down out of the Sangre de Cristo Mountains, they built the beginnings of the outpost of Sante Fe—"holy faith"—which became the capital of their territory, New Mexico.

For two centuries after the Spanish made their first inroads into New Mexico, the West would still be the domain of those who had called it home for thousands of years. England and France claimed portions, but neither country moved to settle or develop the remote and far-flung region. In 1805, Lewis and Clark came and explored the West for the administration of Thomas Jefferson, looking for a water route to the Pacific. But even after they blazed their trail, the traffic in the Rocky Mountain region was limited primarily to trappers and adventurers. Settlers began to filter through the Rockies to the Pacific coast on the Oregon Trail in the 1840s, but few came to the intermountain West to live.

Mining is primarily responsible for the first permanent settlement of whites in most of the mountain West. It started in 1849 when gold was discovered in California. Would-be miners in the East sailed to Panama and from there up to California. There were far more miners than the diggings could support, and in the spring of 1859, rumors of discovery lured droves of miners over the Sierras to Nevada, where the Comstock Lode had been discovered. At about the same time, gold was discovered in Colorado, near what is present-day Denver. From these two places miners swarmed over other parts of the West, in search of gold.

The first miners who came to the western goldfields were individuals who prospected their way through the mountains, camping alongside streams and panning for gold. If "color" was found, miners would stake claims and set up sluice boxes—wooden boxes with a series of ridges on the bottom. Water and gravel from the stream bottom would wash over the ridges, and the gold, much heavier than the sand gravel, would be caught in the crevices. Miners who developed surface deposits of gold were called placer miners—cream skimmers, essentially, who took the gold that was easiest to locate. They descended on a find and wasted little time on amenities such as housing. They threw up tents or log cabins and spent their time working the dig. This was the seed of a mining town—sometimes the seed took root, other times it perished.

If a dig was rich—such as the Comstock Lode in Nevada or Alder Gulch in Montana—larger companies followed. They used hydraulicking to separate gold from the ground, a destructive technique in which high-pressure hoses were trained on a mountainside, turning the soil and gravel into slurry, from which the gold was removed. Underground mining was used where the gold was in ore. Narrow, dank tunnels were sunk into hillsides. It was an extremely dangerous occupation. (And still is.) Cave-ins and explosions were commonplace. In the 1890s, dredging was developed: a barge would float on a river or pond, scooping out river gravel for processing in an on-deck sluice.

If the gold deposits held out for any length of time, a town might achieve critical mass, with support services. A long way from a city, great money could be made by enterprising haulers who brought eggs, liquor, and fresh meat into the mining camps. Towns began to take form from the camps, with stores, saloons and hotels. Some survived to become cities. Some didn't. Alder Gulch, Bannack, Virginia City, Montana; Idaho City, Idaho; Granite, Montana; Park City, Utah; Telluride, Colorado; Silverton, Colorado; Atlantic City and Encampment, Wyoming—all were once bustling mining towns with hundreds or thousands of inhabitants. The ore played out and they either became ghost towns or survived by moving on to another economy. The architectural and industrial skeletons of these places still dot the mountainsides of the West.

Only a few mining towns went on to become real cities, cities far out of proportion to the wilderness of the West. These metropolises looked like something from the East, plunked down by tornadoes, with monumental buildings and opera houses and polluted skies. Places like Denver; Helena, Montana; Boise, Idaho; Leadville, Colorado; and Bisbee, Arizona.

One of the most famous mining towns in the West, and certainly one of the richest, was Butte, Montana. Butte is in southwest Montana, and about forty miles to the north of the Yellowstone ecosystem boundary. But there is no better example of what mining had done to some parts of the West, and how the real costs of development are often hidden or deferred.

Butte became a stage that hosted an astounding half-century-long drama, the unbridled, rough-and-ready frontier capitalism unique to the American West. Corrupt, bawdy, wide-open and for a long time the driving force in the fate of the Treasure State, Butte was known as the "black heart of Montana."

A small creek meanders down out of the mountains and into the Clark Fork River (not to be confused with the Clarks Fork tributary of the Yellowstone River) along the continental divide in southwest Montana. In 1863 miners called the creek Silver Bow for the bow-like meanders the glistening water made. Earlier that year a gold rush had occurred at Alder Gulch. Before long the camp was overcrowded. Miners spread out from there, scouring other streams in the territory. In 1864 a party of miners came to Silver Bow Creek, some sixty miles from Alder Gulch, threw down their packs and panned for gold. Yellow glistened in their pans and word quickly spread.

In a few months Silver Bow City sprang up, seven miles from what would later be Butte. Placer miners clogged the stream, usually working in groups of four on two-hundred-foot lengths, the size of a claim. In the winter of 1864–65, 150 lived in the inchoate town. In 1867 the population reached 5,000; rough-cut-lumber buildings lined a mud street, and honky-tonks and gambling dens gave the miners somewhere to spend their money.

By the time the census takers came around in 1870, the town had dwindled to 241 people—142 whites, 98 Chinese and one Negro. The placer gold had all but played out. There was a good deal of silver in the rock, but liberating it was beyond the ken of most of the miners. So people left, following rumors of riches elsewhere.

By 1872, just a few hardy optimists were still working their claims at Butte when William A. Clark paid a visit to the mining camp. A prospector who had sold his claim on Horse Prairie Creek, near the boomtown of Bannack, Montana, he had pocketed the substantial sum of $2,000. With it he bought up several claims from the miners working the Butte hills. Shortly thereafter he went to New York, where he took cram courses on mineralogy and geology. A small, wiry, mustachioed Scotsman from Iowa, described as cold, crafty and shrewd, Clark came to play a pivotal role in the transformation of Butte from a mining camp to one of the premier cities of the West.

Also to play a crucial role in Butte's future was Marcus Daly, a very different man from Clark, a friendly, salt-of-the-earth Irish peasant, with a white droopy mustache and white, thinning hair. His mining acumen was so great that people said he could see into the ground farther than anyone else. After emigrating to New York from Ireland, he took a ship to Panama, and another up to California, where he worked as a ranch hand and miner. He was part of the rush to Nevada's Comstock Lode, and then moved on to a mine in Utah, where he worked his way up to mine foreman at the Emma Mine in Alta. Daly had heard of the Butte diggings and came to inspect them for his employers in 1876. Impressed with what he saw, he stayed on to open a silver mine of his own. He brought to Butte the first ability to extract silver from the rock, and the first stamping mill, which was used to crush ore. It was the first outside capital and expertise in Butte, and would prime the pump for other outside financiers to provide the money to pull apart the Richest Hill on Earth. Butte was achieving critical mass.

Butte followed the standard pattern of mineral development in the West. The small miner came in and took what he could from his claim. But it required real money to get the ore out of the mountain, and to ship it somewhere for milling. Financiers from Boston, New York and San Francisco bankrolled the big, money-making mines, and so controlled the destiny of towns and even whole states, as in Montana.

In 1866, a New Yorker named Michael Hickey came to what was then called Butte City and located a claim on a hill. In a *New York Tribune* article by Horace Greeley during the Civil War, Hickey had read a description of how General McClellan's army would "wrap up" General Lee's forces like an anaconda. He named his claim after the giant snake, and sold the property to Daly in 1880 for $30,000.

In 1885, with most of the Butte area staked out, Daly drove to a spot twenty-six miles west of Butte, to Warm Springs Creek in the Deer Lodge Valley. There he laid out the site for a giant, state-of-the-art smelter and a town to surround and service it, a town that took the name of his company, Anaconda.

Several factors came together that would play into the fantastic growth of Butte and environs, and keep it from becoming another western ghost town. First, there were huge reserves of copper in the hill, in addition to the gold and silver. In the 1870s the telephone and incandescent lights were invented, and the demand for copper exploded as telephone and power lines were strung across the country. Copper mines flourished in Globe, Ajo, Jerome and Bisbee, all in Arizona, and at Bingham Canyon in Utah. But none of the western copper camps were a match for the production at Butte. In 1881, the steel ribbons of the railroad reached blossoming Butte, and the scent of boom was in the air like never before.

Copper reigned as king through the 1890s, and Daly's newly formed Anaconda Mining Company was the largest. To keep the copper-producing engine running smoothly, the company grew horizontally. Vast amounts of wood were needed for fuel, for construction and for timbers to shore up the miles of tunnel for the mines. Anaconda formed a logging company and began to strip trees at breakneck pace. In a few years the mountains near Butte had been denuded. The company turned to publicly owned land for its timber. This in spite of the fact it was illegal, for in 1878, Congress had passed the Timber and Stone Act, which forbade this kind of logging. But the frontier was a long way from Washington and the law was largely ignored. Anaconda also hired dummy entrymen to file claims on wooded land, which entitled the "homesteader" to buy it for $2.50 an acre. The company then bought it from them. Anaconda and its suppliers would eventually be caught, prosecuted and fined for their massive despoliation and multimillion-dollar theft, but the fines amounted to nothing more than a slap on the hand. "Viewed in perspective," wrote historian Michael Malone in 1981, "the whole ugly episode seems a monumental miscarriage of justice, a disgrace to American jurisprudence."

The Anaconda Mining Company also moved into coal and power generation to supply its furnaces. It bought up real estate: farmland, hotels, rails, water and electrical works and sundry other commercial holdings. In 1895, Daly's company became the Anaconda Copper Mining Company, and by that name it would dominate the state well into the twentieth century. It was known to most Montanans simply as "The Company."

In 1889, Montana became a state. Four years later Congress and President Cleveland voted to end the U.S. government's purchase of silver bullion, an act that yanked the economic rug out from under mining communities around the West. Overnight, many mining towns were left to the ghosts. Often high in the rugged mountains with six months of winter and hundreds of miles from any major cities, there was little reason besides mining for miners to stay. In Granite, Montana, a mining engineer, upon hearing the news of silver's collapse, tied down a steam whistle so it emitted a continuous wail, the mournful sound of a town dying. Some twenty-four hours later, three thousand miners were gone.

For those like Clark, Hickey and Daly, who had invested in copper, it was the beginning of the real boom. It was also the beginning of the clash of these metal millionaires.

As copper turned into money, Butte came into a heyday, the glory days of a Rocky Mountain empire steeped in contradiction. It was filthy and beautiful, wealthy and dirt poor. Tall, elegant buildings went up. Turreted, many-roomed mansions were constructed. An opera house was built along with world-class hotels and theaters. Trolley cars climbed the streets. Famous performers and heads of state came. At the same time, head (or gallows) frames—black iron structures that lowered miner-filled elevators into the two hundred mines below the ground—dotted the urban landscape. Piles of ore were reduced to a concentrated form out of doors by setting fire to them—called heap roasting. A thick, pungent, acrid smoke, heavy with arsenic and sulfur from burning ore and from the smelters, would envelop the town for days. Streetlights had to be lit during the day, and people couldn't see across the street. A traveler had a difficult time navigating in the pall, and according to a writer of the time had to "follow the hacking cough of his forerunner." The smoke killed vegetation for miles around, and caused death and illness.

The mystery writer Dashiell Hammett spent time in Butte as a Pinkerton detective, and set a story there called *Red Harvest.* Butte, he wrote, is "an ugly city of forty thousand people, set in an ugly notch between two ugly mountains, that had been all dirtied up by mining."

But the people of Butte were a tough, rollicking bunch, and the streets of the mile-high town were filled with languages from around the world. Chinese, Cornish, English, Welsh, Norwegian and Finnish were all spoken. No language so widely as Irish Gaelic: the Irish were one of the largest ethnic groups in Butte, and combined with Daly's prodigious influence, they controlled the city.

With thousands of miners working three hard shifts and making good money, Butte had a vice industry of legendary proportion. At the end of their shift, hundreds of miners, their lungs and eyes black with soot, would make their way into uptown Butte. In 1893 there were 212 bars, many of them operating around the clock. At ceremonies on opening day they removed the lock from the front door or threw the key in the toilet. There was wide-open gambling, including faro, blackjack, crap, roulette and poker.

Butte was also famous for the hundreds of prostitutes, or "soiled doves," that plied their trade here, an occurrence in most mining towns. "They were like bees attracted to honey," wrote one miner. "Let a strike be made anywhere and before sunup the next day, there would be a dozen or more of them set up and ready for business."

Butte's East Galena Street and another thoroughfare called "Venus Alley," after the hundreds of prostitutes that worked in the small rooms or shacks there, were two of the famous avenues of sin. "It looked like a street leading into hell," wrote one journalist of Galena Street in its heyday. "Young men, boys, old men; hundreds of them wandering about. Girls in the doors and windows soliciting in honeyed words. Young girls, some looking as though they should be in school. Beauty, withered hags, Indian squaws, mulattos, Japanese, Chinese. Every race and color. Noise. Ribaldry. The shrill shrieks of a police whistle. The clang of the patrol wagon. Drunken cries. Maudlin tears. Bodies for sale."

The place was run by pimps like Diamond Tooth Baker, an obese purveyor who filled his dental cavities with diamonds. Madams like May Maloy and Belle Rhodes worked their way up through the ranks. There were cribs where a miner could spend a dollar for a "poke," or high-class places that advertised on theater and racetrack programs.

This was the backdrop against which the drama of the copper

kings, each extremely rich and powerful, would unfold. Daly, for example, in addition to his timber, coal, railroad and other holdings, owned the Montana Hotel in Anaconda, built in 1888 with a dining room that could seat five hundred and an extraordinary Victorian bar with a likeness of the head of Daly's favorite racehorse, Tammany, inlaid on the floor. Daly spent a good deal of his time at his twenty-thousand-acre stock farm in the Bitterroot Valley, where he lived in a twenty-five-room mansion. When he died, his estate sold 369 racehorses.

Clark, with capital from Boston and New York, had formed the B and M Copper Company and had built his own huge smelter and refining complex in Great Falls, Montana, near a hydroelectric dam that provided cheap electricity. Clark's company owned banks, retail stores, newspapers, lumber properties, coal mines and streetcar systems. Clark also owned the productive United Verde Mine in Jerome, Arizona.

The opening salvo in the war between Clark and Daly was over the fate of public land. The Democrat Clark was running for delegate to Congress from the Montana Territory. Though Daly was a Democrat, the Democratic administration of Grover Cleveland favored cracking down on illegal timber cutting on federal land. That would include Daly's operations and that made him nervous; he set out to steal the election for the opponent Thomas Carter.

The secret ballot system had not yet begun, and Daly's shift bosses were able to paste Carter's name over Clark's on many of the ballots cast for Clark. Meanwhile Daly's men voted early and often. Clark lost.

In 1889, Montana achieved statehood, and Clark, wanting to avenge his loss, ran for one of two Senate seats. This was before the popular vote, and members of the legislature chose the senators. Bribes running into the thousands of dollars were offered by both Clark's and Daly's men. Pinkertons were used to ferret out dirty laundry with which to blackmail legislators into voting a certain way. When the balloting had ended and the smoke had cleared, Clark fell three votes shy of the thirty-five needed. The governor appointed a Republican to the Senate. However, the U.S. Senate, controlled by Democrats, rejected the choice. For a year Montana had only one senator.

The next battle in the war of the copper millionaires was over which town—the banking capital of Helena or smelter town of

Anaconda—would be chosen state capital. Not surprisingly, Daly favored Anaconda, and Clark, with his political and banking ties, favored Helena. The two opposing machines went at it hammer and tongs. Newspapers owned or bribed by either side trotted out their rhetoric. The *Butte Miner*, for example, called Daly an "employee" of an "alien, soulless corporation" and cast Anaconda as a company town. Clark's men struck back and handed out thousands of tiny copper collars, a symbol of The Company's control over the state, a control they said would be extended if Anaconda were chosen capital.

Pro-Anaconda forces, meanwhile, assailed Helena as being the creature of the "Northern Pacific—the land-thieving octopus." The railroad had received a grant of millions of acres of valuable and controversial land, courtesy of the taxpayers.

There was also the usual campaign revelry. Each side staged parades, concerts and fireworks. They handed out free drinks and dollars. Sometimes many dollars. Some claimed as much as $50 was paid for a single vote. In the end, an estimated $1.5 million was spent by the two sides.

Helena became the capital. Clark had his revenge.

However, it was not enough. In 1899, still craving political power, Clark made his boldest try for a Senate seat. In the process he would turn himself and the state's political apparatus into a paragon of corruption.

Clark marshaled his forces and his war chest for the attack. "We'll either send the old man to the Senate," said his son Charlie, who was in charge of buying votes, "or the poor house." Clark offered a cool $10,000—ten one-thousand-dollar bills—to any legislator who would cast a vote for him.

A Democratic legislator, Fred Whiteside, found the offer repugnant, and after he threatened to expose Clark, the bribe was upped to $300,000. Then Whiteside was threatened. Unswayed, he testified before a legislative committee to what Clark had offered, which the committee in turn referred to a Helena grand jury.

But Clark gave new meaning to the word *tenacious* and the election moved ahead. On the first ballot, just seven legislators voted for Clark. But the balloting—along with the bribery, blackmailing and bullying—continued for eighteen days. Clark gained with each round of balloting until he and his opponent tied. The grand jury, meanwhile (amid rumors that they too had been offered $10,000 apiece), refused to indict Clark. At the same time, a Clark-dominated legislative election committee unseated Whiteside. The committee reviewed the ballots from his election win, and discarded all votes in which the X was marked after, rather than before, his name. The review threw the election to his opponent. Whiteside was forced to leave the legislature.

By the twenty-eighth of January, Clark had "convinced" enough legislators to vote for him. Fifty-four cast one for the copper magnate. Ebullient, and supremely arrogant, Clark crowed over the "magnificent victory." Helena's bars on Last Chance Gulch bubbled over with free champagne. Clark's bar tab came to $30,000—pocket change compared to the estimated $431,000 he spent on bribes to win the seat.

The tale does not end there. Clark went to Washington to assume his seat in the Senate, but before he was seated the Committee on Privileges and Elections investigated the affair and uncovered the fraud. The Senate gathered to expel Clark. Before they voted, however, the copper baron, with tears in his eyes, resigned his seat.

Clark returned to Montana, the will to power still burning inside. The old man had one more trick to gain him the Senate seat he coveted. The Republican governor of the time, Robert B. Smith, was a Daly supporter. The lieutenant governor, however, was a Clark man. Under the pretense of examining mining property, Smith was taken by a friend of Clark's to California. A code telegram was sent to Lieutenant Governor A. E. Spriggs, who was in South Dakota: "Weather fine, cattle doing well." That was his signal to return to Helena, where he immediately appointed Clark to the Senate seat he had just been banished from. But the Senate refused to seat Clark.

In 1899, executives of Standard Oil, the famous Rockfeller trust, formed a holding company called the Amalgamated Trust and bought out Daly's Anaconda Copper Mining Company. It did not end the battles in Butte; in fact, the best was yet to come.

In 1893, the last of the copper kings had come to the diggings at Butte. A short, stocky fellow of German-Irish descent, F. Augustus "Fritz" Heinze was a charming mining engineer who loved to drink and gamble. He started as an engineer for Clark's B and M, and then returned to Germany in 1892 for a short course in geology. He became an expert on the Butte hills' geology and the labyrinthine ore complexes. The mining community claimed that Heinze, like Daly, had a sixth sense about what lay under the ground, a so-called magic pick. In 1893, he formed the Montana Ore Purchasing Company, and later opened a smelter in Meaderville, a town next to Butte.

The General Mining Law of 1872, which governed—and still governs—mining, held that whoever owned the portion of a vein of mineral ore that came closest to the surface—called the apex—owned the right to mine the entire vein, even if other claim owners were mining it. Amalgamated's Butte and Boston Company claimed that it owned the apex of a valuable vein that Heinze's Montana Ore Purchasing Company was mining, and took him to court. Heinze's attorneys mounted a strong defense, and portrayed Amalgamated as an out-of-state corporate evil empire. The jury decided in favor of Heinze.

With the help of a friendly judge or two and a staff of thirty-seven attorneys, Heinze—perfecting the act of "courthouse mining"—went on the offensive against the mammoth Standard Oil boys. The battle escalated as both sides threw lawyers and money at each other to get the other's mining properties. Heinze even took on a new partner: William A. Clark. Using the trust as a giant bogeyman, Heinze and Clark put together a powerful political coalition that came to control the state house, the state senate and several key judgeships. The coalition would finally award Clark his coveted prize: a legitimate seat in the U.S. Senate.

After he gained his Senate seat, Clark abandoned his coalition with Heinze and sold out to Amalgamated, to the boos and jeers of the anti-Amalgamated electorate. Heinze would fight on, at least for a while, both in court and beneath the Richest Hill on Earth.

There was a rich body of ore that both Heinze and Amalgamated would claim. They took the matter to court. Neither company could, while the court was deciding the issue, mine the ore. Heinze got worried. He was operating on a thin margin, and in order to keep his smelter producing and to pay his debts, Heinze needed access to the ore. Ever resourceful, he hit on an idea: he transferred his title to the vein from one of his companies, which was under the injunction, to another, which Heinze claimed was not subject to the ruling.

Surreptitiously, Heinze sent hundreds of men into his Minnie Healy Mine to seal off Amalgamated's tunnel to the disputed ore and to start digging around the clock. For a while Heinze operated undetected, but eventually men from the Amalgamated in nearby tunnels could hear muffled dynamite explosions. They snuck into the Minnie Healy, where, historian Malone writes, they saw "armies of men swarming like ants through the stopes hauling prize ores out."

The judge ordered Heinze's men to stop. They didn't. As the gears of justice slowly turned and Heinze continued to gobble up the ore, Boston and Butte sent its men into the shafts to physically stop the mining. An underground war in the tunnels erupted. As one side moved in to mine, the other would attack them, and there was hand-to-hand fighting. Chemical warfare was used: one side would burn garbage and rubber and fan it so the smoke would force the other side out. They threw smoke bombs. They trained fire-hoses on the other, dynamited tunnels and electrified the rails that mine cars moved around on. After two men were killed, both sides agreed to a truce and to let the courts decide. Once again Heinze won.

In 1906, the era ended. Heinze sold his company to the Amalgamated, the shouts of traitor from the people of Montana echoing in his ears. The state of Montana fell under the dominion of a single entity—the Anaconda Mining Company—until 1982, when the company closed its doors for good.

What remains of the once grandiose Rocky Mountain metropolis of Butte is a group of stately historic buildings—it is a national historic landmark, one of the largest in the country, clustered at the lip of a giant open pit. Mining, at one time the giver of life to southwest Montana, turned cancerous. In 1955, the company decided it could no longer make a profit with the labor-intensive blasting and hauling of ore out of the ten thousand miles of tunnels that laced the hill. It opened the mountain up, and turned it into a huge open pit, the Berkeley Pit.

Mining would have continued chewing up what remained of Butte had not Anaconda, absorbed by the Atlantic Richfield Company (ARCO), closed its operations in 1982. Much of Butte is gone, including the entire town of Meaderville, which was the Italian district, lined with small homes and shops and bars. Walkerville, another small enclave, is gone. Columbia Gardens, a beautiful amusement park built by William A. Clark, had a merry-go-round, a roller coaster, a Ferris wheel and a playground. There was a trolley that hauled Buttians to the garden, and a huge sylvan pond with white geese. It was a cool, green oasis to a city that worked in hot, dirty mines beneath the earth. It was consumed by the shovel in 1973. As Butte disappeared, so did the people. At its peak, Butte had about 100,000 residents. Today it has only some 33,000.

The boom-and-bust experiences of Butte are legend in the West, and are a part of what environmentalists fear in the Yellowstone ecosystem. Hundreds of workers will be hired for the Noranda mine alone, perhaps tripling the population of Cooke City. What if more mines are built? Decisions on what goes on there may suddenly be taken away from longtime residents, and be made by strangers or by a company based in Toronto. And what happens in twenty years when the ore plays out? What will the area be left with?

But there is another lesson that Butte holds, one the people who live in Cooke City fear most when they walk outside their shops and homes and picture the New World Mine high in the mountains above their town.

These days the problem in Butte is not what is gone, but what remains. After seventy-five years of binging, Butte is suffering a serious toxic hangover. The Richest Hill on Earth and the area around it has become the Most Toxic Hill on Earth, with mining-spawned waste so widespread that a scientist who studied the problems says that returning the area to a condition anything close to pristine might be impossible. "The only reasonable remediation response may be perpetual monitoring, or perhaps the creation of a National Environmental Disaster Monument that could illustrate the costs of past mistakes to future generations," wrote University of Montana geologist Johnnie Moore. The boom in Butte these days is in environmental remediation: some twenty eco-consulting firms have offices there and work at cleaning up the mess.

The 340-mile-long Clark Fork River—named after William Clark, of Lewis and Clark—has its beginnings a stone's throw from Butte in the tributaries of Silver Bow Creek, Mill Creek and Warm Springs Creek, which originate near the continental divide in an area riddled with enormous amounts of toxic waste from mining. Hundreds of miles of tributary creeks and the river itself are hazardous and off-limits to humans. There are four separate Superfund sites leaching toxic waste into the headwaters of the Clark Fork, each designated by the federal government as dangerous to human health. The Clark Fork Complex, as this constellation of toxic-waste sites is known, is a fifth of the size of Rhode Island. It is divided into twenty-eight small toxic tracts.

All but a small part of the city of Butte is a Superfund site, and around town there are three million cubic yards of old mine tailings, rocks, dirt, soil and other mining detritus, filled with high levels of such toxic elements as arsenic, lead, cadmium and mercury. These are heavy metals and pose an extremely serious threat to human health. Nineteen million cubic yards of toxic tailings sit in Warm Springs Ponds and along Silver Bow Creek—enough, according to the Clark Fork Coalition, an environmental group that rides herd on the cleanup, to fill a convoy of dump trucks that would line up head-to-tail from Butte to Miami to Albuquerque and back to Missoula. Some twenty-six miles of Silver Bow Creek's thirty miles are barren of fish. On the 1,200-site National Superfund Priorities List, which ranks the most serious sites according to the threat they pose to human health, the Silver Bow Creek unit is number twenty.

Part of the Silver Bow Creek unit is the Berkeley Pit—2,200 feet deep, 1.5 miles long and a mile wide—next to which the city of Butte is poised. When ARCO closed the mines, it stopped pumping water out, which it had done so it could mine. The hole has since been filling, at the rate of some seven million gallons a day, with water of a burnt red shade, highly toxic and full of floating mine timbers and other debris. As the groundwater continues gushing into the pit, the EPA estimates that within ten years the water level will reach the same level as groundwater in the area and will mingle with and contaminate the aquifer that lies beneath the town and the outlying area. Worse, the noxious brew may spill out the top of the quarry and flood the town. The only answer seems to be the use of huge—and expensive—pumps that will suck the water out and send it through a treatment plant. Since the water will continue to flow into the pit, it will have to be treated forever.

The six-thousand-acre site where the Anaconda smelter separated the metal from the ore for ninety-six years is number forty-eight on the national Superfund list. It is some twenty-five miles west of Butte. There are 185 million cubic yards of poisoned tailings here, and 27 million cubic yards of furnace slag, or waste, and 300,000 cubic yards of flue dust. A contaminated 585-foot-tall brick smokestack stands like a monument over all of it.

The Milltown Reservoir is ranked 321 on the priority list, and is loaded with 6.5 million cubic yards of thoroughly contaminated tailings and sediment. This is downstream from Mill Creek, a residential community of some thirty-five families that was permanently abandoned in 1980 because of high levels of heavy metals and other toxics.

The Montana Pole Treating Company chemically treated timbers for forty-six years to shore up the mining tunnels. The site is now 735 on the list of 1,200 Superfund sites. Diesel fuel and cancer-causing dioxin and PCB have seeped from it into Silver Bow Creek and into the groundwater.

Even worse, these poisons are fugitives, having migrated courtesy the rivers and streams, and are scattered along 120 miles of the Clark Fork. Over the more than a century in which wastes were dumped pell-mell into the streams and rivers, the toxic material was transported downstream. Large areas of the river's floodplain were contaminated, and in some places all living things were killed. In their stead, bright blue and green copper sulfates encrust the ground. There are also four dams on the river, and behind each have gathered tons of toxic sediment—six million cubic yards behind one dam alone. The sediment is full of such things as lead, cadmium and arsenic—a time bomb of sorts, one that could some day be loosed on the river.

Arsenic is also widely scattered across the countryside near Anaconda. When a new copper smelter went on-line there in 1902, the wind-borne poison began to settle on nearly two hundred square miles of land. Shortly thereafter, one rancher twelve miles downwind lost a thousand cattle, eight hundred sheep and twenty horses to arsenic poisoning in a single year. The arsenic is still on the ground, still toxic and still stunting the growth of vegetation. High levels of arsenic have been found in children in the area.

The Clark Fork watershed—the whole region drained by the Clark Fork and its tributaries—is so polluted that a thunderstorm will often fall on the watershed and cause toxic substances to wash into the river, killing fish for miles along the watercourse. In July of 1989, one such toxic pulse killed five thousand fish with acute copper poisoning. While a river the size of the Clark Fork—one of the largest rivers in the state—and with its diversity of habitat might be expected to have three thousand to five thousand trout living in each mile of water, most of the Clark Fork has less than 10 percent of that number, while in some places there are a paltry eighty fish per mile.

Humans have not escaped the effects of the mining waste either. A study of three thousand U.S. counties between 1959 and 1972 showed that Silver Bow County was among one hundred counties with the highest death rates for people aged thirty-five to seventy-four. In another study, Butte had the highest mortality ratio (the actual number of deaths versus the expected number) for any city in the nation in 1950–51 and in 1959–61, and the fifth highest in 1969–71. A National Cancer Institute study of the average mortality rate from lung, trachea and bronchial cancer showed that in Montana, Idaho, Wyoming and North Dakota the rate was 25 per 100,000 people, plus or minus 4 percent. In Deer Lodge County, where Anaconda is located, and Silver Bow County, where Butte is, the rate was twice that.

Under the Superfund law, the cleanup of the Clark Fork Complex, which may cost as much as $1 billion, will be paid for by ARCO, which inherited the site when it merged with Anaconda in 1977. The EPA has spent some $30 million of taxpayer money in the cleanup so far. A lawsuit will determine if and how much ARCO will pay for damage to the natural resources, amounts sure to run into many millions of dollars. However, those people who have suffered and continue to suffer health problems from the maze of exposures in Butte will probably go uncompensated.

Butte is not the only place where miners have been replaced with toxic-waste remediation workers. Toxic-waste sites can be found near any number of western mining towns, waiting, like huge, festering wounds, to be treated. Bunker Hill in the Silver Valley of northern Idaho. The Yak Tunnel on the headwaters of the Arkansas River near Leadville, Colorado. (Indeed, much of the town of Leadville.) The copper wastes near Miami and Globe, Arizona, east of Phoenix. Telluride, Colorado. The Bingham Canyon Mine, near Salt Lake City. It's estimated that twelve thousand miles of American rivers and streams have been polluted by mining.

There are some 400,000 abandoned mines in the United States—ranging from "glory holes," or small pits in the ground (which make up the vast majority), to huge open pits—and most of them are in the West. They total 281,581 unreclaimed acres. The U.S. inspector general estimates it will cost $11 billion to clean up the abandoned mines, and that is probably a low figure. Some estimates range as high as $50 billion. Who will pick up the tab has not been determined.

With large-scale mining all but a memory in southwest Montana, the city of Anaconda is hoping to kill off the aura of Old West that still clings to the town and build on its grave a monument to the New West. The Atlantic Richfield Company—responsible for much of the Superfund site—has hired golfer Jack Nicklaus's consulting firm, Golden Bear, Inc., to design a $1 million golf course to go right on top of the toxic Old Works, the rambling complex where Daly's smelter was located. Covered with soil and stabilized, the course will not be a health hazard, say officials.

Even these days the reclamation of mining sites in such fragile places as the alpine country of the Yellowstone ecosystem is more art than science. Putting the Beartooths back together again after they are mined is nearly impossible, Willcox believes. And she won't settle for a golf course.

Mining has changed dramatically since the days of the copper kings. No one expects the Noranda mine even to come close to the free-for-all of Daly and Clark. Mining has gone from an extremely labor-intensive business to one that is extremely capital-intensive. Although production isn't dwindling, the number of miners is. In Colorado, for example, the number of miners fell from 36,632 to 20,438 between 1980 and 1990. But the boomtown is still a western phenomenon. In the late 1980s, towns throughout the West started going through a new gold boom. None went through a rise as meteoric as that of Elko, Nevada, a small dusty cowtown in the north-central part of the state. During the peak in 1987, 1988 and 1989, Elko was growing at the respective annual rates of 16, 11 and 21 percent. Before the boom, growth was around 2 percent.

This kind of growth has not taken place in the Yellowstone ecosystem. But there has been a smaller boom in platinum in the northern part of the ecosystem, near Nye, Montana. And with seven thousand active mining claims in the ecosystem, and new technologies that make once-marginal gold deposits worth mining, there is fear that mining has potential for real problems.

These days in the West it's a big boom in little gold. Gone are the days when prospectors picked a nugget as big as a baby's fist out of a stream. In the past decade, gold particles smaller than bacteria, visible only with an electron microscope, have produced more money in today's dollars than all of the mining in Nevada since the days of the Comstock Lode. New extraction and exploration technology, in tandem with a plateau of gold prices at a level more than twice the cost of production, have fueled the boom. While there is some placer and deep mining, "no-see-um" gold is where it's at.

Numbers tell the boom story. In 1979, the total U.S. production of gold was 964,000 troy ounces. In 1987, it leapt to 4.9 million troy ounces, and in 1991 was 10 million troy ounces.

Newmont Gold Company, owned primarily by Newmont Mining, is the largest player in the crowded micro-gold game. There are dozens of companies, large and small, who are furiously digging and processing gold-bearing ore. The payoff can be rich beyond imagination—the General Mining Law of 1872 transfers precious metal deposits from public to private ownership at no charge. And unlike federally owned oil, gas and coal reserves, there are no royalty payments to the Treasury. State tax laws, a holdover from the old days, also treat the mineral industry lightly.

Newmont's Gold Quarry Mine, seven miles north of Interstate 80 near Carlin, Nevada, used to be the 223,000-acre T Lazy S cattle ranch, a patchwork of federal and private land. Now it is the most profitable gold mine in the country.

The Nevada boom began with Newmont in 1964, when it was called the Carlin Gold Mining Company. Newmont was the first one into the world-famous Carlin Trend, a geologic formation where windows of rich gold deposits have poked up through the mountains. Even at $35 an ounce, Newmont was making some money at the Carlin mine. In the fall of 1971, however, as controls collapsed and the free market roused the price of gold from its slumber at $35 per ounce, the intensity of exploration along the Carlin Trend rose correspondingly. Gold, buoyed by record high prices for oil and fears of inflation, spiked at $825 an ounce in 1980. Mining firms began to sit up and take notice.

From the lip of Newmont's open-pit mine near Elko, Nevada, the serious nature of earthmoving taking place here is apparent. A small mountain has literally been carted away and processed through crushers. In its stead is the huge pit that resembles an open-air amphitheater, where the rocks are predominantly a soft red color. Gusts of wind swirl across the ground where vegetation has been removed, sending dust devils spiraling high into the air.

Workers swarm over the landscape, dwarfed by huge shovels and numerous dump trucks the size of small homes grinding and roaring, and accompanied by the beeping of back-up alarms. Black diesel plumes float above the colossal $750,000 vehicles, as, grinding and roaring, they cart away 140 tons of rock per load, each ton bearing four hundredths of an ounce of gold. For every ton of gold-bearing ore Newmont takes from the ground, it must move a ton of overburden to get to it.

"I've been working for Newmont for fifteen years," says Alvin Randall, a driller, referring to the appearance of the ore, "and I never have seen any gold."

Drills are operating around the pit, meanwhile, searching for subsurface areas where the gold reserves are most promising and mapping where the jaws of the $3 million hydraulic excavators will move next.

Once the ore is loaded onto trucks, it's hauled less than a mile to one of two places, depending on its grade. Some of the better grades of ore go to a huge ball mill, where the ore is processed the old-fashioned way. The ore is mixed with water and pulverized to fine particles, and the resulting slurry is baked and treated with cyanide, which draws out the gold.

The rest of the ore goes to a mill that uses the heap leach method. Although the attraction of the heap leach method is that the ore doesn't need to be crushed, which is energy intensive, Newmont crushes its ore anyway. Newmont figures the crushing increases the return from the gold. "We're turning a mountain into dust," said one worker at the mine.

The heap leach method of processing ore, developed by the U.S. Bureau of Mines during the 1970s, helped fuel the rush in micro-gold. It was first applied by Newmont in 1981. In this method, the gold-bearing ore is toted to a series of conveyor-belt-linked crushers where the pieces of ore are reduced to roughly an inch across. The ore is then placed in huge, flat-topped piles atop a quarter-inch-thick plastic liner. Several irrigation sprinklers are spread across the top of each pile, and a water and cyanide solution is pumped through the sprinklers. The solution trickles down through the up to two hundred feet of rock, separating the micro-gold from the ore as it goes. The gold-bearing liquid runs off the plastic liner into a channel alongside and into a pond that holds the pregnant solution. The solution is forced through the series of charcoal filters, which collect the gold. The charcoal is then stripped of the precious metal, which is fashioned into gold bullion and shipped elsewhere. This activity takes place twenty-four hours a day, 365 days a year.

Newmont Gold owns other properties on the Carlin Trend, including the Genesis, the Blue Star, the Carlin and the Rain mines, all clustered within a few miles of each other. At the end of 1987, Newmont estimated it had fifteen million "proven and probable" ounces in the ground in the Tuscarora Mountains, while a more liberal company estimate places the reserves at more than thirty million ounces.

The cost of the heap leach process varies, but averages around $200 per ounce. One Colorado miner is heap leaching more than 100,000 ounces of gold annually for $165 an ounce. The older process of grinding the ore to powder and then baking it and extracting the gold with cyanide is energy intensive and more expensive. Deep mining, which means tunneling well beneath the surface, and the attendant processing cost more than $300 an ounce.

There are still deposits of gold to be found in the outback that rival the stories that lured prospectors west in the early days of the boom. The AMAX Sleeper Mine in the Slumbering Hills of northern Nevada, some forty miles northwest of Winnemucca, has become something of a legend among mining company geologists, for the bits of gold are visible in the ore there. It isn't much to see, but remember that mine employees usually can't see any gold at all in the ore. The Sleeper ore in some rare cases contains one hundred ounces of gold per ton of rock, which the company has mined and extracted at an extremely low $105 per ounce. Start-up costs at the Sleeper were $21 million, and the facility paid for itself in less than six months.

The center of world gold production is shifting from South Africa to the United States. In 1980, South Africa produced more than 70 percent of the world's gold, while last year it produced only 46 percent. The United States, meanwhile, produced a little more than 3 percent of the world's gold in 1980. In 1992, it produced 23 percent. The total world production in 1991 (excluding that of Russia) was 1,312 metric tons.

Where does all this gold go? Overwhelmingly into jewelry. In 1991, more than 2,100 metric tons of gold were turned into gold chains and other jewelry, far more than the total production. (Which means recycled gold and bank sales made up the rest.) There has been a meteoric rise in gold jewelry sales in the last few years, largely because the Japanese have discovered gold jewelry in a big way. "In 1985, the average Japanese woman owned zero pieces of gold jewelry," says Michael Brown, of the Gold and Silver Institute. "The average woman now owns nine pieces of jewelry." (The next largest uses of gold are for dentistry and coinage, which together accounted for 285 metric tons in 1991.)

Growth in gold jewelry sales have kept the price high and have sustained the gold boom in the western United States.

The gold finds have lured companies from the United States, Canada, Australia, China and South Africa to the American West. "It's overwhelming. The companies are backed up three deep trying to lease land" that individuals have staked claims on, says Walter Phelps, formerly of the Nevada office of the federal Bureau of Land Management, and now with the Utah office. "These old miners can call the shots."

Perhaps more than anyone, Phelps has a handle on just how widespread the scramble for gold is in Nevada. Anyone who filed a claim on federal land in Nevada—which accounts for 85 percent of the state—came to the office he managed on the outskirts of Reno and registered that claim. During the height of the boom in the late 1980s, a thousand claims a day were recorded. Even though things have cooled off some, ten thousand claims were recorded in Nevada between July and September 1992.

There have been other changes in the boomtowns, as Elko and other western cities find their fate inextricably bound to the price of gold. The 1980 census found eight thousand souls in the town of Elko. Ten years later census takers counted nearly fifteen thousand. The boom has been good for the butcher and the baker as well as the local sporting houses. Miners and prostitutes still maintain a symbiotic relationship.

"There's no doubt it's been good. A little bit rubs off on everybody," says Eddie Gammel with no hint of irony, as he sits at the small bar in Mona Lisa's, one of two brothels that Gammel's wife owns—though he actually runs them—and one of Elko's five legal brothels. Three girls are working down at the other end of the bar.

As a customer comes in, Mrs. Gammel, who works behind the bar, rings a bell, and the girls—two in nighties, one in a body stocking—parade out. Thirty dollars for fifteen minutes. Gammel estimates receipts are up 15 percent since the rush began. "We get business every day instead of just on payday and weekends," he says. "And so the girls stay longer, because they're making more money. Instead of two, three or six months, they're staying a year or more."

Aluminum in the hills near Elko must far outweigh the gold being mined. Trailer parks and developments of double-wide mobile homes are scattered in nooks and crannies throughout Greater Elko. At the peak of the boom, new homes and apartments bloomed crazily in the desert. Recreational vehicle parks went in. As a result of all the development, taxable valuation soared from $46.5 million in 1979 to almost $121 million in 1992. "We've approved more subdivisions in ten months during the boom," said then city manager Terry Reynolds, "than we did in the past ten years."

Newmont and other large gold companies have tried to help Elko keep up with the boom. American Barrick and Newmont provided $850,000 for water tanks and lines. Newmont built two hundred apartments for the help. Near Carlin, the company built huge aluminum dormitories—called a "man camp"—for several hundred construction workers. Newmont has also loaned money to contractors to build homes. Freeport McMoRan built three hundred homes, and also built a city park, made loans to the school district and bought portable classrooms. Newmont donated the salaries for two city policemen to Elko and bought prowl cars for the Elko County sheriff and the police department of the tiny town of Carlin, just south of the Newmont mine.

The mining companies are on their best behavior. Like Montana and other western states, Nevada began as a colony of the mining industry. So complete was mining interests' control here that the Nevada constitution to this day contains a prohibition on taxing minerals in the ground. There is a net proceeds tax that goes primarily to counties that can be as high as 5 percent. In 1991, gold and silver production was valued at nearly $2.4 billion. After the deduction of their operating costs, the value of taxable proceeds was estimated to be $585 million. Mining's total tax payment was $28 million, all of which went to counties. By contrast, the gaming industry in Nevada, which in 1991 grossed around $5 billion, paid about a 6 percent tax on that gross revenue, or $420 million.

* * *

Ron Glunt operated heavy equipment at a mine in Gabbs, Nevada, when he heard about the boom at Elko. More precisely, he heard about the pay at Elko. The average annual wage, with benefits, company officials say, is $36,000. And there's plenty of overtime, which can bring the annual pay up to between $45,000 and $50,000.

Glunt contacted Newmont, he says, and the company expressed keen interest. So he came north. But when Newmont conducted a physical and found out he had a serious back ailment, "they cut me off," he says. He'd already quit his job, so he decided to stay in Elko to look for work at the other mines, perhaps at one where the physical wasn't as thorough.

Nearly out of money, Glunt was sleeping in the back of a battered pickup truck on a dead-end dirt road in a hidden gulch just outside of Elko, one of many ad hoc campgrounds serving Elko's homeless. He shared the unimproved camp spot with Weeden Marchebanks, a heavyset, red-faced cowboy from Prescott, Arizona, who had pulled his tiny, ancient trailer to Elko in search of work. These two men, and others like them, go down to the Texaco truck stop for $1 showers and visit the restroom at the city park. The city park is off-limits to the homeless at night, but at first light, people who have spent the night in cars make their way to a picnic table where they spend their day.

Walking through the thick dust where Glunt camped was like walking through four inches of flour, a dust so fine it hung in the air for several minutes after it was disturbed, billowing through the shafts of light that stab through the pine trees. A big white "E" for Elko is painted on the hill above the campers. Around them are other trailers and tents, people who had come to Elko in search of a dream, a modest dream of hard and honest work that paid more than $30,000 a year, with decent fringes. Some of the people had found a job but were still unable to find a home. Many others had spent their savings to get to Elko, hearing somewhere the promise of work. But they lacked the skills to get hired.

This is a dim side of the Gold Rush. People still pull into Elko to live in a park or in the hills and look for work, though fewer of them now than the estimated three hundred or so people who were looking during the height of the boom. "This is Woody Guthrie stuff,"

Glunt says, taking a pull on a plastic milk carton full of water. "These people up here aren't bums. They're Americans. There's no winos or derelicts. They want to work and they're trying to hang on. This isn't what everybody said it would be, that you could pull in on a Wednesday and be working by Friday."

"There's a lot of people bumming," said Marchebanks. The red light of sunset shining through a pine tree casts a mottled pattern on his bare chest and ample stomach as he sits on the stoop of his tiny trailer in the heat. "They come up here with money and gamble it off and now they're living by the river."

As a result of the influx of people, the crime rate in Elko soared in the late 1980s. But arrests declined, as policemen no longer had time for investigative work. Criminal complaints filed by the district attorney during the boom were up 22 percent in one year, while county complaints went up 37 percent. Drunk driving arrests soared 50 percent.

Things have leveled off somewhat now, though growth still continues at a higher rate than before. Lorry Lipporelli, city manager, says that all told, he thinks Elko is better off. "It's not an itty-bitty community anymore," Lipporelli says. "I could [in the past] name everyone in town. I can't now. But amenities have increased. There are more doctors at the clinic. More family-oriented people, who put down roots and make a community better. I met a guy who works for Newmont who speaks seven languages. What an addition to the community. In my opinion it's good that Elko has changed."

While the days of the boom are not over, neither are the days of environmental problems. Environmental technology has come a long way since Butte's heyday, but given the amount of dirt being moved, and the kinds of chemicals being used, there is grave concern about the effects of mining. The mining industry generates 800 million tons of hazardous waste each year, waste that needs to be cared for, for many years. A whole new generation of problems is being created.

The waste from a mine is piled on the ground nearby, and for the next ten or fifteen or twenty years will leach cyanide and heavy metals like arsenic into the groundwater and into the river. With current technology, there is no way to prevent it.

The chemical central to the gold rush is cyanide, so toxic that a teaspoon of weak cyanide solution can be fatal to a human. Gold producers use about 100 million pounds of cyanide each year, and some of it inevitably finds its way into the environment. In addition to liberating gold from the rock, it extracts toxic metals such as arsenic and lead and carries them into the environment. When sulfide-bearing rock, which contains much of the gold being mined, is exposed to water, it oxidizes to become acidic. It then mobilizes other toxics and washes into streams and groundwater.

In Montana, several leach pad liners have leaked, contaminating precious groundwater supplies and streams with cyanide and affecting the drinking water of the mine's neighbors. Tens of thousands of ducks, geese and other waterfowl have been killed. In a single incident in Nevada, more than a thousand ducks and geese were killed when they landed on a gold mine settling pond laden with cyanide. In Colorado, acid mine runoff from the Clear Creek–Central City mining district into nearby streams has forced some residents to find alternative sources of drinking water.

Destruction also comes from the small mom-and-pop-type mining operations, which are exempted from reclamation requirements under a small miner exclusion. Montana state mining officials say the small miner has been a disaster for many streams and rivers, an opinion echoed by officials in other states. If the disturbance is under five acres, or less than 36,500 tons are moved annually, there is no reclamation provision. "They go in there and rip up five acres and leave," says one geologist with the Montana Department of State Lands, which oversees hard rock mining. "You can walk away from it. It's usually a placer operation in the middle of a creek and it completely destroys it."

Environmentalists say the federal Bureau of Land Management, which administers the lion's share of western mining because the mining occurs on its lands, is extremely lax in enforcing environmental laws. The U.S. Forest Service, which will govern the Noranda mine, has done better in regulating mining, they say, but in a place like the Beartooths near the park, there is no way to prevent possible problems. "If this mine goes ahead, the area will commit itself to wastewater treatment in perpetuity," says Willcox. "It will be a permanent Superfund site that will need perpetual care."

* * *

Of course there is no way to put a mountain that has been turned into dust back together. The giant holes in the desert where mountains once stood will be around a long time, perhaps forever, and there are probably three hundred to four hundred in the West now. Reclamation law requires that processing facilities be demolished, that roads be reclaimed and waste piles be reseeded. But the giant pockmarks on the landscape will remain. The only requirement is that the benches carved on the inside wall of the pits to prevent collapse be reseeded. Add to that that western lands, dry and cold and otherwise harsh, simply heal extremely slowly, or in some cases not at all.

"The types of environmental problems that occurred at NPL [Superfund] mine sites have a strong likelihood of appearing at active mining operations," said the EPA (Environmental Protection Agency) in a recent paper on mining. "The basic approaches to excavating ores and minerals and beneficiating them has not materially changed over time."

It's not, by a long shot, all ruination. "Glengarry is an open, festering wound," says Stu Coleman, an environmental specialist for the park. "If they can improve the site after they leave, we'll be better off." The large mining companies often reclaim old mining roads and abandoned mines, and a few do a good job of turning their own mine sites into productive land once the ore has been exhausted. And some companies—including Noranda at the New World Mine—are installing state-of-the-art environmental protection. However, the EPA says such technology "is the exception, not the rule."

One area where compromise has not been available is in the debate over the General Mining Law of 1872, signed into law by President Ulysses S. Grant and now substantially the same as it was then. While the era of the copper kings and cowboys on the open range has faded into the rosy glow of history, this is one remnant of the Old West that remains: a law that hands over, virtually free of charge, gold, silver, platinum and other metals to anyone who comes along and stakes a claim to it. That's how the site of the New World Mine, once public land, came to be. "People have a myth in mind, like the Treasure of the Sierra Madre," says Phil Hocker, director of the Mineral Policy Center. "The reality is we're strip-mining for gold, copper and other minerals, just like coal. You have to extract, break up and pulverize fifty tons of ore for an ounce of gold. It's changed, but the laws haven't caught up."

Staking a mineral claim under the law is a simple process. Lode claims are 1,500 by 600 feet. Each corner of the rectangle and the center of each long side is staked, these days with polyvinylchloride (PVC) pipe. On the corner designated as the location monument and marked with a flag, a rolled up copy of the deed—a one-page form with the date and area of the location, the name and address of the claimant and the name of the claim—is placed in the pipe. On some tracts of federal land, there are so many claims that PVC pipe has jokingly been dubbed the Nevada state tree.

It costs $10 to register a claim, and there is no limit on the number. The county where the claim is located also requires a $1 per acre fee. The only other requirement is that each year the claimant must certify that $100 worth of improvement—digging holes or whatever—was done on each claim. There is no charge to file that document with the federal government, but there is a $1.25 per claim fee to the county. After a property has proved its value, a claimant can apply for a patent, which means the title is transferred—for $250 for the first claim and $50 for each additional one—to the miner. What was federal property becomes private. Although there is a "prudent man" rule, which means that claims cannot be patented unless a prudent man would find the property worth mining, there is no way to police the frenzy of activity.

Claim jumping is a problem. "A lot of that still goes on here," Walter Phelps says. "Once every two or three months someone comes in and says, 'I was doing my claim work and so-and-so pulled a gun on me.' It's still the Wild West out there."

An estimated $4 billion worth of gold a year is taken off public lands. The public is also picking up most of the tab for the cleanup of many of the abandoned mine sites in the West, a bill that some estimates place as high as $20 billion to $50 billion. The price tag continues to increase each year as mines are started and abandoned. U.S. Senator Dale Bumpers, D.-Arkansas, an advocate of changing the law, calls it "a license to steal."

The simple law is so encompassing in its simplicity—"All valuable mineral deposits in lands belonging to the United States, both surveyed and unsurveyed, are hereby declared to be free and open to exploration and purchase, by citizens of the United States"—

that the Forest Service and the BLM often claim they can't say no to a project, no matter where it is or what kind of damage it would do to other resources.

The New World Mine is a good example. Federal agencies have done extremely well in overseeing possible impacts from the proposed mine, environmentalists say, but in the end they fear the agencies will have no choice under the mining law but to allow the mine to go ahead. It's not only the New World Mine they fear. There are thousands of mining claims in the Greater Yellowstone ecosystem, and the potential for more mines. "The law is based on the premise that there's nothing else on public lands we care about," says Hocker. "That's changed in the last century."

What galls many fiscal conservatives—many of whom also rail against the law—is the fact that the public's precious metals are being given away to foreign companies. Of the top twenty-five mining companies in the United States, sixteen are owned in whole or part by Australian, Canadian or British companies. Echo Bay Mining Company, for example, pays $2 million a year in royalties to the Canadian government for the right to mine gold in northern Canada. In Nevada, where it owns one of the largest mines in North America, it paid the U.S. Treasury nothing. The New World Mine nearby is a Canadian project.

A consortium of companies recently and legally applied to patent a platinum claim on public land next to a wilderness area in south-central Montana. The consortium asked that 1,714 acres of public land be transferred to its ownership for the $250 processing fee. A one-third interest in that property recently sold for $48 million. Hocker says the value of minerals owned by the taxpayer and now under application for patenting is, by the mining companies' own estimate, worth $93 billion.

There is also, according to the General Accounting Office, Congress's investigative arm, widespread abuse of the law. The GAO cited several examples in a 1989 report to Congress. Forty acres of federal land were patented for sand and gravel mining in 1983 for $100. A BLM appraiser said the land, located near residential communities, has a value of more than $400,000. In 1986, patent holders paid $42,500 for seventeen thousand oil shale patents. Several weeks later, they sold it to oil companies for $37 million. In Keystone, Colorado, a 160-acre claim, patented in 1983, cost the patentee $400. When GAO investigators visited, 44 acres, located near a ski area, were for sale for $11,000 an acre. "It's the law with no brain," says Hocker.

However, strong opposition to changes in the law has surfaced from several sources, including a group called People for the West! (always with an exclamation point), based in Pueblo, Colorado. Bankrolled by resource corporations and emphasizing patriotism, the group is made up largely of people who work in timber, ranching and mining on public lands. The organization has held boisterous, flag-waving rallies around the West to oppose changes in the law.

At a rally in Helena, Montana, hundreds of miners and their families, many sporting hats that read "1872—NOTHING ELSE WILL DO," listened to speakers denounce proposed changes in the law. A country band played music on a portable stage and a striped canvas tent offered lunch. "This law has served the public well," says John Willson, president of Pegasus Gold, a Canadian company which mines gold on public lands in the West. "It's a law that was wrought in the spirit of orderly free enterprise, and free enterprise is what the U.S. is all about."

At a time when jobs that allow a laborer to live a middle-class life are disappearing across the country, especially in the West, mining jobs are a godsend. Workers make anywhere from $10 to $15 or even $20 an hour, with benefits, the kind of money that allows people to raise a family comfortably. New jobs being created in tourism come nowhere close. "People are saying enough is enough," said Barbara Granell, an organizer of and executive director for People for the West!, who was dressed in a red, white and blue pantsuit at the rally. "Rural America is suffering. Changing this law is bad for the country, and it's bad for the West."

But critics say miners—as well as loggers and ranchers and farmers—operate in a false economy. There may not be any such thing as a free lunch, but there is such a thing as a lunch bill deferred. Taxpayers not only give the gold and silver and platinum to companies, but they pay for the cleanup, too. Meanwhile, other users of the public lands take a substantial hit as well. Resource extraction damages the natural environment and causes a decline in the number of fish, elk and other wildlife.

Noranda promises the Yellowstone ecosystem a "clean" mine, the likes of which has not yet been seen. Will that be the case? Will public and governmental oversight and good corporate citizenship make it work? Will possible future mines do the same? Or will Noranda, once it gets its operating permits, worry more about profit than pollution? Can the ecosystem have it all? High-paying mining jobs and corporate profits and gold for jewelry and investment as well as small, comfortable towns and the nearly pristine natural beauty of the Greater Yellowstone? Only time will tell.

3
Of Cowboys and Vapor Trails

IN THE CRIMSON LIGHT OF A COLD DECEMBER MORNING JUST after sunrise in 1985, a long, unlikely safari trudged single file through deep snow that crunched like Styrofoam beneath their feet. Leading the pack were two hunters in winter gear, each wearing neon orange plastic vests. Behind them walked several officials from the Montana Department of Fish, Wildlife and Parks and the U.S. Forest Service. Bringing up the rear were twenty or so broadcast and newspaper journalists, both local and national.

The quarry of the band were two shaggy-headed bison that quietly munched dry, dun-colored grass in a windblown Montana meadow, little columns of breath-steam rising from their nostrils. The hunters crept closer to the animals, which was really unnecessary, for having "escaped" from Yellowstone Park just a few hundred yards to the south, these bison were accustomed to throngs of people swarming around them, and coming close enough on occasion to touch them. From fifty to a hundred yards away, the first hunter took careful aim and squeezed the trigger. The rifle shot split the early-morning still, and the first bison, a big bull, dropped to his knees, struggled to stand for a minute and then rolled on his side, as the explosion continued to reverberate. A scarlet stain spread quickly in the snow. Unperturbed, the other bison continued eating until another rifle shot rang out.

Video cameras whirred, pens scribbled and still-camera shutters clicked as a horse-drawn sled pulled up and outfitters began eviscerating the massive brown beasts. Except for three bison quietly killed in 1953 here, these were the first buffalo shot since the unbridled slaughter of the immense herds that once carpeted the plains.

Buffalo hunting is not what it used to be. Pictures and stories of the hunt and interviews with the hunters alongside the hulking brown carcasses were bounced off satellites and sent to NBC, CNN, *The New York Times*, National Public Radio and numerous other press organs. As inhabitants of apartments in the concrete canyons of the East ate their dinner, they watched graphic video of all-but-tame Yellowstone bison—perhaps the very one they saw last year—dying at the hands of hunters. There was shocked and angry reaction, and letters and phone calls poured into the offices of the Montana Department of Fish, Wildlife and Parks and of Yellowstone Park.

One would be hard-pressed to come up with a more cogent symbol than a Yellowstone bison. The herds that wander the meadows and timbered hills of Yellowstone—at the time of the hunt some two thousand bison strong—are the last free-roaming herd in the United States. Fewer than two hundred are known to have been left standing in Yellowstone when the hide hunters were through killing millions of buffalo in 1884. Left standing because they happened to live in remote Yellowstone Park.

The bison in Yellowstone represent the white man's merciless carnage, and the other side of human nature as well, which drove them safely back from the buffalo jump of extinction. The remaining wild bison were nursed back to greater numbers by crossing them with domestic bison brought to the park. The U.S. Department of the Interior put the bison on its emblem, as did the National Park Service. Add to this the fact that watching the powerful, furry-headed bison in the park as they graze, roll in the dust, block traffic and gallop over the hills brings indescribable joy to millions of visitors, and you have one of the most symbolic animals in North America.

The first hunt took place in 1985. But despite the outcry, the hunt continued until 1990. At that time the Fund for Animals, an animal rights group based in Washington, D.C., produced public service announcements for television that featured bison dying in bloodied snow as a children's chorus sang "Give me a home where the buffalo roam."

It was too much for officials from the Montana Department of Fish, Wildlife and Parks, who feared an outcry by easterners could end sport hunting altogether. They ended the buffalo hunt. These days rangers and state game wardens do the dirty work. Quietly and only when there is no other recourse.

When the rifle smoke and controversy had settled, almost 700 bison filled freezers and decorated den walls.

One aspect of the buffalo shoot that never got much coverage in the press was the why of it. Why were the only wild bison in America shot as they set foot over the park's northern boundary, into areas they had historically occupied?

They were shot because cattlemen who graze their cattle in the Yellowstone ecosystem feared the bison might carry a disease that can cause domestic cows to abort their calves. Called brucellosis, the disease had infected cattle in Montana before. It was wiped out only at substantial cost. Montana's livestock industry was understandably concerned that brucellosis could make its way into the cattle herd.

Things, however, were not as simple as they sounded. That the bison had the disease was never proven. The bison tested showed only that they had been exposed to brucellosis, not that they had contracted it. Neither is there evidence that bison transmit brucellosis to cattle in the wild. And cattlemen and state officials seemed to ignore the fact that many of the tens of thousands of elk in the park, which come and go freely, also carry the disease.

What made some opponents of the hunt angry was that cutting down the park's bison was done because of a handful of cows that grazed on public land near park boundaries, that might be on the range, that could possibly mix with bison that might have the disease that may perhaps transmit it on to cattle. There was no consideration of an integrated approach to the problem. Moving cattle to accommodate the bison, for example, or buying out ranchers who grazed their animals in the places the bison wanted to call their own.

The bison hunt underscores the reality of the sacred cow, and the political power still vested in the western cattlemen. In spite of all the hard questions about how real a threat was posed by brucellosis and the fact that there were other possible remedies, the bison were dropped as America watched.

It is the way many ranchers have done business. If something gets in the way, shoot it, poison it or trap it. It is the Cowboy Way, and it has been handed down from generation to generation, an adaptation to a tough way of life and what it took, or what it was felt it took, to survive.

The Yellowstone bison hunt is a microcosm of the conflict between the Old West of the cattle rancher and the New West of parks and tourism and wildlife. There are people, like ranchers, who lease these lands they live near to graze cows and make a living. Even though the lands are owned by the public, those who live near them feel a sense of ownership. At the same time, Americans have a vested interest in the 600 million acres of public lands, nearly all of it in the West. Many people who live far from the West favor protection of the flora and fauna on the public land, and want to know that somewhere out there, nature is intact.

But there is change taking place on the range, some of the most dramatic change ever for an industry that has been around a long time.

The livestock industry landed in North America in 1519, when Hernando Cortés brought eleven stallions and five mares ashore at Veracruz, Mexico, to provide means for the conquest of the new land. The other half of the quotient landed a short time later, when Gregario de Villalobos brought a small herd of calves ashore on the Pánuco River, near Tampico, in central Mexico on the east coast.

Cattle numbers grew exponentially in the New World, and as they did, men were needed to tend to the far-flung herds of nearly wild animals. Spaniards felt menial tasks beneath them, so they hired Indians, blacks and others to ride the range and tend to the livestock. The first cowboy was a far cry from the Marlboro Man. Early Mexican cowpokes went barefoot, with jangling spurs strapped to their feet and floppy, wide-brimmed hats on their heads to keep the sun out of their eyes.

The first cattle came to what is now the United States in 1598, introduced by Juan de Oñate, a Spaniard and wealthy silver miner who traveled to the Rio Grande, with orders from the crown to colonize what is now the southwestern United States and turn the Pueblo Indians there into Christians. Oñate and some four hundred soldiers, some of whom brought their families, drove seven thousand head of bawling cattle into present-day New Mexico, where they founded the San Gabriel Mission, near San Juan. Ranching flourished for a while, here and in Arizona and California, primarily as a way for the far-flung missions to maintain a supply of fresh beef.

After Mexico received its independence in 1821, however, ranching all but died in the Southwest. The padres abandoned their missions, and ranching in the United States, for the most part, languished. It rose again in Texas, spurred by American settlers who came from the East. As the local market became glutted with cows, Texans took their calves on the road, eventually creating the long-distance cattle drive.

Texans drove calves to mining camps of the California gold rush and to the port city of New Orleans, where they were loaded onto freighters bound for the East. Texas cattle were driven to St. Louis. One of the most enterprising of the cattle drovers was Thomas Candy Ponting, an Englishman who ate dust behind a herd of 700 cattle all the way to Illinois, where he sold 550. Ponting was just getting warmed up—he took the rest of his beeves on to Cleveland, where he put them on a train and took them to New York City. After two thousand miles of looking at the rear ends of several hundred cows, Ponting turned a profit.

In 1858, a Delaware Indian named Fall Leaf found a few grains of gold, setting off a stampede of miners to Colorado, and eventually to Idaho, Montana and Nevada, among other places. Texas drovers turned their eyes to this new market to the far north. On August 29, 1860, a Texan named Oliver Loving drove a herd of a thousand cattle into Colorado, and the beef industry began to spread north.

The possibilities in this lush, high-plains grassland to the east of the Rocky Mountains, which stretched to distant horizons in every direction, seemed as limitless as the landscape itself. It was open range, free for the taking for the cattlemen and the cattle syndicates from Chicago, London and New York. There were, of course, a few barriers, but the smell of empire was a strong and heady aroma. "Once we get rid of the Indians and the buffalo," said Indian fighter General Nelson Miles, as he stood along the Yellowstone River in southwestern Montana and voiced a sentiment typical of the time, "cattle and sheep will fill this country."

Entrepreneurs—some who started with money, some who had none—began the grand, high-stakes game of piecing together huge tracts of land in the dry, sparsely settled West, sometimes within the law, sometimes outside of it. One of the largest is the King Ranch in Texas, a little spread patched together by Richard King, who came to Texas in the 1840s or 1850s. By the end of the century, he owned 1,270,000 acres of Texas earth, one of the world's largest privately owned tracts of land.

In 1889, seeds of fascination about Montana and a new way of life on the frontier were planted in the minds of Andrew McLary Chapman Howard and his brother Adonis, by their uncle General Oliver Otis Howard. The general had chased Chief Joseph and Nez Percé Indians through Yellowstone Park and then the Rosebud Valley of eastern Montana, and had fallen in love with the place.

The Howards packed up their belongings, left their home in Maine, and booked passage on a freighter to Panama, where they set out on foot across the isthmus until they reached the Pacific Ocean. They climbed on board another ship and sailed north to Oregon, where they purchased four thousand sheep and several hundred head of horses, rounded up a herd of cowboys and sheepherders and drove their stake more than a thousand tortuous miles across the deserts of Oregon and Idaho and over the cordillera to the Rosebud.

Only ten feet across, Rosebud Creek is nonetheless the giver of life in this broad, bone-dry valley, where come summer the grass crunches underfoot like shredded wheat. The Rosebud, named for a tangle of wild roses that grows on its banks, empties into the Yellowstone River (which originates in the park), a major artery in the state. One drainage to the east is the Little Bighorn River, the watercourse near which the famous boy general, George Custer, made his last stand.

The high plains of eastern Montana, a hundred miles or so to the east of the Yellowstone ecosystem, are far different from the scenery of western Montana. The rolling hills and plains are carpeted with blue bunch wheat, blue grama and needle-and-thread range grasses that make it the best cattle-fattening country in the West. The plains are broken by a surreal badlands topography—sandstone buttes, pillars and rimrocks that rise dramatically skyward and are covered with layers of prairie grass and pine trees.

A striking feature are the cliffs made of clinker, a clay baked to rock hardness by prehistoric underground coal fires. The soft red color runs like a theme through most of the Rosebud. Stirred by horses or cars or the hot, dry summer winds, red clinker dust collects on hair, clothing and cars. The roads are paved with crushed stone and look like red ribbons laid over the undulating hills. As a car zooms down the miles of dirt road, a huge rooster tail of dust rises up behind it, hangs in the air for a few minutes, and, long after the car is gone, slowly settles to earth again.

Encountered occasionally are natural coal outcroppings, thick, black indications that beneath most of the Rosebud lie rich veins of soft, low-sulfur coal, cleaner-burning than that which is found in the East. It is becoming more valuable as the nation attempts to clean up its air quality. It is, however, the bane of Patty Kluver's existence.

Nature is not the only thing at risk in the West. Whether it's logging or farming or ranching, the long American history of life on the land, of families separating a living directly from the earth, is diminishing.

It's apparent in the numbers. In 1950, there were more than 23,000 farms and ranches in New Mexico, for example. In 1990 there were 14,000. In Colorado there were 45,000 farms and ranches in 1950. Thirty years later there were 27,000. Numbers are similar throughout the West. Low cattle prices and high costs for machinery and feed are chronic problems. But those are old, familiar problems, the kind of thing ranchers are used to living with. Compounding the situation is a herd of new problems. The real world is closing in. Water is sucked out of the country and piped into thirsty, growing subdivisions. People from San Francisco, Chicago and Tokyo, where the price of land makes it untouchable, are coming to the American West to buy ranches where the cost of an acre is close to what they would pay for a square foot at home. Huge shovels tear up the prairie grasses to get at minerals beneath, or mines pollute the water ranchers depend on.

Ranchers in the Greater Yellowstone suffer many of the problems that other ranchers face. That might be expected on the scenic landscapes surrounding a famous park like Yellowstone, with millions of people visiting each year. Less obvious is that the decline of the cattle industry is happening everywhere, even in the heart of the all-but-unpeopled high plains, some of the finest cattle-raising country in the world.

Sharp cries ring out and a dozen frightened, wide-eyed calves trot out quickly from behind a tangled mass of wild rose bushes and cottonwood trees. Chased by a shouting man on horseback, the calves hustle toward a circle of green hay laid out in a snow-dusted meadow. Another rider surges through a small break in two sandstone cliffs. Moments later, five gangly calves charge mooing through the opening, in flight from another whooping figure on horseback. They are being driven to their feed in the snow.

Patty Kluver, her face lined like a map, sits in the cab of her pickup truck wearing a plaid winter coat and an odd baseball hat with devil's horns sewn on it and watches it all. She knows the routine. As a small girl she watched her father and grandfather drive cattle across the same ground. As a teenager she chased cows out of thickets. As a young wife she cowboyed beside her husband Elmer, whom everyone called Red.

Now in her sixties, Patty Kluver lets her sons and hired men handle the cattle. She is busy instead riding herd on the mining companies and bureaucrats she says seem bent on destroying her spread, the Wineglass Ranch, which covers more than 25,000 acres of Montana rangeland—slightly larger and a lot less crowded than the island of Manhattan.

She points to leafless ghost trees that are dead, she claims, from wastewater from two huge nearby coal-fired power plants at the town of Colstrip, wastewater that has spilled into her underground aquifer and poisoned it. Hay meadows irrigated by water from the aquifer are dead. The mining company says it is not to blame, but Patty Kluver doesn't buy it. "They're going to drive us out of business, if we let them," Patty says in her husky voice, made that way by a lifetime of yelling at cattle. "They're going to ruin this whole damn valley."

Poisoned water is not the only problem Kluver faces. Against her wishes, but within the law, the mining companies plan to tear up some of her cattle grass and take the coal beneath it. Burlington Northern Railroad owns the coal and has leased it to Western Energy, a subsidiary of Montana Power.

Railroads are one of the largest mineral-rights holders in this part of the country, a result of federal land giveaways during the opening of the West in the 1860s. As an incentive to develop a transcontinental line, Congress gave selected railroads every other section of land—a section is 640 acres, or one square mile—along their track right-of-way. At one time, the Burlington Northern owned 16 percent of the land in Montana, some 23,000 square miles. It later sold much of the surface rights to ranchers, like Patty Kluver's mother Genie, but retained the subsurface, or mineral, rights. Ranchers say when they bought only the surface rights they never envisioned the area becoming a regional energy center, for the only coal mined at the time was a small amount to fuel the locomotives.

Patty Kluver has fought the coal companies the way some ranchers went after rustlers. Coal exploration crews earned the right to come onto her property to survey the ground only after a legal battle that went to the Montana supreme court. At one point a survey helicopter from the coal company landed on the ranch and the occupants were greeted by several rifle shots that plowed into the ground nearby. Patty won't say who fired the shots; she just grins. "I'm not that handy with a gun," she says. "I just enjoy the *reputation* of being handy with a gun."

Constantly butting heads with company executives and lawyers has made Patty Kluver an angry, sometimes bitter, woman. She spends her days patrolling her land, checking for trouble spots and trespassers, and pouring her feelings into volumes of letters to the newspapers and state offices that monitor the environment. She blames Montana Power, politicians and bureaucrats for that "mess up the road." "They're killing everything around them and you can't get those bozos"—bureaucrats—"in Helena and Denver to do anything about it."

Kluver says she takes strength from the past and that her ancestors are the reason she clings so tenaciously to this piece of ground. "If they put up with some of the things they did," she says, "then so can I."

In 1892, after Andrew Howard had staked out his ground along the Rosebud, and it seemed the threat of Indian attack was tolerable, he sent for his wife, Martha, and three daughters, Belle and Mary and Alice, fourteen-year-old twins. Alice died about a year after arriving in Montana. Mary fell in love with the territory and with her father's hired hand Freeman Philbrick, another Maine native, whom she married at age sixteen.

The couple began life in a log cabin with gaps so large between some of the logs that snow drifted into the corners when the wind blew. Philbrick was shrewd and a hard worker and eventually built a sizable herd. His business was helped along by a couple of loopholes in the Homestead Act big enough to drive a buckboard and a team of horses through. Philbrick sat on the boards of two local banks. As other homesteaders, lured west by the promise of free and fecund farmland, went belly up in the harsh country, he bought the land. Much of it at cut rates. And like many of the cattle barons who came west during the time of the open range, Philbrick added to his holdings by claiming that federal land he had grazed for years was his by default. Through political influence, and force when necessary, he held onto the land. Law and law enforcement were a long way off.

Water was key to expansion. Following the custom of the time, Philbrick had his hired hands file Homestead Act claims on widely scattered plots of ground with springs on them. Then Philbrick bought the land. By controlling the water, he controlled the land in between by default, and eventually blocked up a total of around eighty thousand deeded acres, making him one of the largest individual landholders in the state of Montana. Some was repossessed during the Great Depression, but most of it is split among his heirs, including his granddaughter Patty Kluver.

Although the big ranchers did not own the open range, they sure behaved like they did. They often bitterly resented the intrusion of the homesteaders who came and strung fences throughout their grassy domain, even though it was legal. Some cattlemen fenced off public land to keep the public out, sometimes cutting people off from churches, schools and post offices. Homesteaders and farmers in turn retaliated by forming parties to go out under the cover of night and cut the fences.

Vigilantism was always a possibility in the West, with the closest law hours or days away, and even then it might be swayed by the desires of the powerful. One of the most famous examples of big business taking the law into its own hands occurred in Johnson County, Wyoming.

On April 9, 1892, a group of forty or so heavily armed ranchers, cattle detectives and gunmen rode to the KC Ranch, near present-day Kaycee, Wyoming. They had heard that two alleged rustlers were there. Others claim the big ranchers knew the men weren't rustlers at all, but small operators invading "their" turf—the public range. The two men were in a cabin, which the army encircled. One man came outside, and was cut down by ranchers. The other fellow was wounded, and then tried to escape, but was stopped by a swarm of bullets. Supposedly his body was found with a note attached: "Cattle Thieves Beware."

The "posse" rode off to continue its campaign. Eventually the real law caught up with the cattlemen and took them into custody. They might have been hanged had not the U.S. Cavalry arrived. In testimony to the power of the cattlemen, none were ever charged with a crime.

There was no drama like that in the life of Grandpa Philbrick, who peacefully went on to his higher reward. He passed on the spread to his daughter, Genie, who married Patty's father, Charles Dowlin. He died young, however, in 1933, and left his widow a ranch smothered in debt and two teenage girls to raise in the throes of a depression. The market for beef seemed bottomless, and a drought that went on for several years shriveled hay in the field. Then, like something from a biblical nightmare, a plague of grasshoppers and Mormon crickets descended and devoured most of the available vegetation. With no feed during the brutal winter of 1936–37, the widow Dowlin and her girls lost half of their livestock.

Like many ranchers, Genie Dowlin could not make her mortgage payments and her ranch was repossessed by the Federal Land Bank. But her property was intermingled with low-cost railroad leases, which she managed to maintain, because without those leases no one would buy her property. "What saved our hides," Patty recalls, "was tending a herd of buck sheep." Because ram sheep, or bucks, are ornery, ranchers want them around only during the rutting season. The rest of the year the Dowlin girls tended the bucks, eventually eight hundred animals, for $1 a month per head. The profit helped the Dowlins buy back their portion of Grandfather Philbrick's holding.

Shortly after Patty completed her first semester as an art student at Montana State University, her mother contracted tularemia, a tick-borne disease that inflames the lymph glands. Patty was forced to return home. Before she made it back to college, World War II broke out, and because of a shortage of cowboys, she found herself in demand as a cowhand.

Red Kluver started out life in the Army as a mule wrangler in New Guinea. He joined the Rangers there and spent the rest of his hitch in brutal, hand-to-hand combat in the Pacific Theater. Out of his company of 150 Rangers, only eight came back. Stateside, Red worked for a while at a dude ranch in upstate New York, tested bucking horses for a rodeo producer, and turned down an offer from Gloria Vanderbilt to be her farrier. Eventually he drifted back to Montana, to the place he was born—the Rosebud Valley. Soon after, he and Patty Dowlin were married.

Genie Dowlin didn't approve of the marriage, and Red and Patty "were kicked out of the family for a while." They moved to the Northern Cheyenne Indian Reservation, where they lived in a tent and became cattle herders. Several years later, they leased 2,500 acres near Ingomar, Montana, which they stocked with 104 head of cattle Patty Kluver still owned from the days she had ranched in partnership with her mother and sister. Living in a two-room tar-paper shack with no electricity and no running water, they managed to eke out a living and raise three sons and a daughter.

Time wore some of the hard edges off Genie Dowlin, and when she inherited another large ranch from her mother, she invited Red and Patty Kluver back to run their herd on the family land. They moved into a simple, cottonwood-tree-shaded home, miles from any neighbor, a home where Patty still lives.

On a June night in 1976, Red Kluver dropped to the floor in the kitchen of that home, clutching his chest. A heart attack, his second. He'd spent time in the hospital after the first one, hated it and came home much earlier than doctors wanted him to. He vowed not to go back. The boys carried him to the couch in the living room, where he passed away that night. "He didn't want to live as an invalid. He came home from the hospital to die," says Patty. "And that was his right. He loved this place. He had a way of contacting his Maker up in those hills." Red's buried in a small, local cemetery not far from the house. At the funeral someone sang "Don't Fence Me In." "It turns out his grave is blocking part of the road," Kluver says with a smile. "Mine will be too. He would have loved that. They're gonna have to go around us." Patty now lives with her son Kelly, while two other kids live in their own homes on the ranch.

Sitting at her kitchen table, Patty Kluver recalls the hardship of losing her husband. She remembers, a few years back, a grassfire on her ranch. Fortunately, neighbors arrived to fight the flames with hoses and wet gunnysacks. It was a godsend. Houses here are many miles apart, neighbors few and at times precious. They saved the outbuildings and kept the Kluvers in business. "What am I going to do," she asks now, "when my neighbor is a coal mine?"

Patty Kluver has been helped in her battle by environmentalists. A group formed in the 1970s called the Northern Plains Resource Council is a coalition of ranchers and environmentalists based in Billings, Montana, dedicated to preserving the family ranch. The Greater Yellowstone Coalition is also working on ways to keep working ranches alive, and to improve grazing techniques in the Yellowstone ecosystem.

These days, however, it is just as likely that ranchers and environmentalists will do battle against each other. That is the case in Yellowstone when it comes to wandering bison. Stockgrowers in Wyoming, Montana and Idaho have also successfully resisted efforts to reintroduce the wolf into the Yellowstone ecosystem, even though it is a native animal that was driven out by ranchers in the first part of this century.

The biggest clash between ranchers and environmentalists is over whether the cattlemen are being given too free a hand on when, where and how they run their cows. At issue are 268 million acres of land in eleven western states owned by the taxpayer, most of it leased for grazing by ranchers and managed by the federal Bureau of Land Management and the U.S. Forest Service. While ranchers lease federal grass to feed cattle and sheep, this sweeping expanse of public lands—about the size of New York, Pennsylvania, Ohio, Indiana, Illinois, Michigan, Wisconsin, Iowa and West Virginia combined—is open for other uses that include camping, hunting, hiking and wildlife watching. Some local and national environmental groups, backed with scientific studies, claim cattle have damaged these wide, open spaces of the West, and like mining, the damage has been subsidized by the American taxpayer.

While the battle over buffalo in Yellowstone has been high-profile because of the park's fame, there are plenty of battles in less well known places in the West. And many of the disputes are based on research done in the last few decades on what cow hooves do to the land.

One of the angriest skirmishes in the war is taking place these days in Catron County, New Mexico's largest county, 7,800 square miles of mountains and meadows abutting the Arizona border in the southwestern corner of the state. This is broad, sweeping country, where mountains are not crowded together, but spread out. Pine and juniper trees cover the hillsides. It is high desert, with just fourteen inches of rainfall a year. Rivers here would be creeks in the East. Mountain lions, black bears, coyotes, deer and elk prowl the canyons and mountains. Some 90 percent of this county is owned by the federal government, part of the Gila (pronounced *HEE-la*) National Forest.

In the middle of the county sits the town of Reserve. With a population of a thousand or so, it's the largest town in the county. The entire county has about 2,700 souls, with more than forty thousand head of cattle. Reserve is a quiet village that has grown up on either side of a two-lane highway. Pickup trucks are the vehicle of choice. Just out of town, San Francisco Creek and the Negrito River merge, small meandering streams lined with gnarly cottonwood trees.

Once a logging town, its only sawmill is now closed. The grocery store, the gas stations, the restaurants and the handful of other businesses now cater mostly to ranchers and especially tourists, who have come in and built summer homes. One of those businesses is Charlie's Supply, a hardware store in a large metal shed, just a half mile east of town. It is owned by rancher Charlie McCarty, and is located on the family ranch.

Wearing a long denim coat, a brown, battered cowboy hat and long, salt-and-pepper sideburns, Charlie says the ranch economy has changed. "Everyone still hanging on to a ranch has found a way to feed it with outside money," he says in a New Mexico drawl, as he waits on a customer. "A cow just don't make the money."

He walks outside, away from the crescent wrenches and nail pullers and points to a long, flat-topped mountain in the distance. "That's Eagle Peak, with the dab of snow on it," he says. "My place starts here and runs back to the top of that peak. It's a good day's ride from one end to the other, and to work it and find cattle takes about six weeks."

McCarty's grandfather, also a Charlie, was a Texas cowboy who drove cattle here in the 1880s, when this was still wild country. Bands of Apache Indians, led by Geronimo, raided the small settlements. In 1939 Charlie's father Owen took over the spread, and ran it until 1958, when he dropped dead of a heart attack while he was branding calves. McCarty's two boys and one girl were raised here, though all are away at college now. They won't be coming back to take over the ranch, he says.

Ranching is on the ropes, McCarty says, and now come the environmentalists. Federal agencies have saddled ranchers with regulations, reams of paper, acronyms, endless meetings. "They're coming after us with every gun they got," he says. "There's no end to the obstacles they put in the way of taking care of a place. They can't say 'grazing' without saying 'overgrazing.' "

Environmentalists claim the lumbering beeves cause widespread and serious damage. "To raise cattle you have to launch a full frontal assault on the environment," says Jim Fish, an engineer for Sandia National Laboratory and an avid hunter, who lives in Placitas, a suburb of Albuquerque. That assault is what led him to found the Public Lands Action Network, or PLAN, a tiny but active and boisterous group that works solely against livestock grazing on federal property, one of several such groups in the West. Dark-haired, bearded and wearing glasses, Fish is a quiet man. But when he talks about cattle, he gets riled. Cattlemen "have to destroy predators, get rid of competitors, put in artificial waterings, use herbicide to kill grass not suitable to cattle, and use pesticide to raise feed. We need an end to all public lands ranching," he says. "They screwed it up. Get them out." Fish calls the cowboys who graze at public expense "welfare ranchers."

Getting booted off public land would impact the cattle industry, largely because federal and private land are often intermingled. McCarty, for example, owns outright some two square miles of land, mostly along the river bottoms. He leases thirty-two sections of federal ground, some 20,000 acres, more than thirty square miles, and on that land he is permitted to run 199 cattle. The ratio of cattle to acres speaks of just how dry and rugged it is in the West. By contrast, cattle growers in Florida can raise a cow or two on a single acre. About 31,000 ranchers lease public land for grazing in the West.

The battle over cattle in Catron County was sparked by wildlife issues. A minnow called the spiked dace lives in these fragile streams and is endangered. No changes have been made to accommodate it, but because grazing damages streams, cattle numbers could be cut back. The Mexican spotted owl is a hot topic, a species listed as sensitive by the Forest Service. Logging near its nests was recently banned. Not long after, the local sawmill closed, throwing a hundred or so people out of work. Some locals blame the agency's insistence on protecting owl habitat. The Forest Service blames a lagging housing economy.

Ranchers also say the Forest Service allows too many elk on the range. Ranchers are not against elk, McCarty says, but feel their numbers have been allowed to grow too large. The animals knock down fences and eat grass ranchers are saving for their cows.

Ranchers got so steamed up they convinced the Catron County commissioners to pass three ordinances, which say that ranchers have more right to land they lease than do recreational users, that grazers are protected under the Civil Rights Act, and that the government cannot take any action—such as cutting back cattle—that would affect private property rights. If Forest Service agents go on leased land without permission, the ordinances say, they can be arrested.

Officials from the Office of General Counsel in Washington, D.C., a legal arm of the federal government, threatened county officials with legal action if they interfered with a federal land manager. The conflict is at a standoff—no one has been arrested, but the ordinances remain on the books.

Emotions are running high elsewhere. Radical environmentalists and vegetarians have been blamed for burning barns at a feedlot in Nevada. Barbed wire fences—including some of McCarty's—have been snipped. In Utah, someone—authorities suspect environmentalists—shot twenty-one cattle. In his book *Ecodefense,* radical environmentalist and "Earth First!" founder Dave Foreman describes in detail how to sabotage the cattle industry by cutting barbed wire fences, vandalizing water developments and slashing tires on pickup trucks.

Ranchers have also given in to anger. In southern Idaho, to the west of the Greater Yellowstone ecosystem, a rancher who leased public land grew angry when Forest Service ranger Don Oman insisted on cutting back on the number of cattle that grazing permittees were allowed to run on public land, because the cattle were damaging the land. "Either Oman is gone or he's going to have an accident," rancher Winslow Whitely told a reporter for *The New York Times*, which put the statement in a story that appeared on the front page. "Myself and every one of the permit holders would cut his throat if we could get him alone." Asked if he was making a specific threat on the life of a district ranger, Mr. Whitely said, "Yes, it's intentional. If they don't move him out of this district, we will." The threat, Oman says, was one of many.

Western ranchers vent their anger at the local forest rangers, but the change is much more deeply rooted. "There has been a change in the values of society," says Michael Gardiner, a forest ranger in Catron County. "There's still a lot of pointy-toed boots in state legislatures in the West," says Foreman, "but there's more Sierra Club members than there are ranchers."

Once known as "the forgotten lands," the public's acreage is being remembered. The real world is catching up. More and more people are coming to Catron County to hunt elk. Or to backpack and camp and swing in a hammock outside their summer cabin. They don't want cows in the campground or cowpies along the river. People want to see elk, deer and antelope, and because there is only so much plant-generated carbohydrates, or biomass, more cows means less wildlife. "What was aesthetically acceptable in the 1950s," says Pat Morrison, range management specialist on the Gila, "is not in the 1990s."

This is where ecology comes in and illustrates a gap between the way things have always been done and the way science says they should. Many studies have documented the radical change cattle visit on an ecosystem.

Creeks and rivers are critical to nearly all life in the dry country of the West. Based on a study in southeastern Wyoming, for example, the EPA estimated that 75 percent of all wildlife species depend on riparian, or streamside, areas. There are places in the Yellowstone ecosystem where cattle have so damaged rivers, especially parts of the Madison, that federal agencies are faced with the task of reclamation.

The problem is that thirsty cattle congregate along stream banks, where they denude the banks by eating and trampling aspen, willow trees and grasses. Without these strong-rooted, pliable plants to hold them together, banks break down and soils fall into the water. Streams widen, water flow slows, and the water temperature goes up. Warm water holds less oxygen than does cold, so fish die. Soil chokes the stream. Cattle waste pollutes the river.

The lack of vegetation along stream banks causes erosion problems, especially during storms and times of high runoff, as water runs without slowing into the streams and incises, or cuts, the stream channel deeper. When the water level in the stream drops, so does the level beneath the stream banks, which in a normal situation is at the same level as the river. That means that plants dependent on this natural subirrigation die from lack of moisture.

When the water table drops, streams that ran year-round, even during a drought, now dry up because the groundwater level is far below the streambed. Fish suffocate in waterless streams, and insect life, much of which lives in the stream and in the water, dies out. This kind of damage does not take long to happen. "Before about 1880," wrote J. J. Wagoner, in a history of the Arizona cattle industry, "the Gila River channel from Santa Cruz Junction to Yuma was narrow with firm banks bordered by cottonwood and willows, but by the early 1890s it occupied a sandy waste from one-quarter to one-half mile wide." The trapping and eventual decline of the beaver in the early days made matters worse, for the rodents slowed the flow and kept stream channels from washing out and caused water tables to rise. Not only does the rancher cause himself more problems, but he passes the problems—and costs—on to neighbors and to other users of the stream. And there are fewer otters and mink and kingfishers and other fisheaters because there is nothing left to eat.

Part of the problem here is a lack of comparison. Ranchers or agricultural professionals might think the stream has always looked like that, which means the damage could have been done a century ago and never corrected.

Cattle ranchers can also cause themselves problems by halting or slowing succession, the process by which nature moves to greater diversity. On heavily grazed land, nature can stall, and instead of many different habitat niches for many different species, there are just a few niches. There is nothing to compete with or prey on species like grasshoppers or prairie dogs, which thrive in the environment cattle create, and so their numbers take off and they become a nuisance.

Conservationists are also bitter about the U.S. Department of

Agriculture's Bureau of Animal Damage Control (ADC), which they've dubbed "All the Dead Critters." In 1990, ADC agents, by their own count, gunned down, trapped and poisoned 91,221 coyotes, 12,818 beavers, 8,349 skunks, 7,015 raccoons, 170 snapping turtles, 5 musk turtles, 6 wild turkeys, 255 mountain lions, 95 gray wolves and 247 black bears, among others, to protect crops and livestock. More than 600 pet dogs and 100 feral housecats were killed. In southern Arizona, at least 37 mountain lions were killed to protect one rancher's 135 cows. Hundreds of thousands of birds of many different kinds were killed.

Steve Johnson, a longtime antigrazing activist in Tucson, Arizona, calls the ADC a "dark little irony." "The American taxpayer owns this land, and he's paying the government to destroy its native wildlife—all so ranchers can lease it back from him and reap private profits."

The predator toll was evident at McCarty's ranch. Signs at the entrance to one of his pastures warned that poison traps had been set about by a county agent to kill coyotes, and two coyote carcasses lay in a pile of brush nearby.

There is, of course, a broad range of ways that ranchers treat the land and the things that inhabit it. "We respect life," says Patty Kluver. "We move our stock around before they graze a place out, and we don't shoot predators."

Where environmentalists have been most successful is in their attack on the economics of cattle grazing. They have targeted the fee ranchers pay to graze cattle on federal lands—at present, $1.91 to graze a cow and a calf for one month—what is called an animal unit month (AUM). The rate is a fourth or less of what ranchers who lease private land have to pay.

Cowboys argue that even though private leases are $8 to $12 per AUM, $1.91 per AUM is not really a subsidy. "You have to put in fences and water and do range improvement with your own money" on public land, says Pamela Neal, director of public lands for the National Cattlemen's Association, which is not the case with private land. "It's like renting an unfurnished apartment with no utilities versus a furnished apartment with all utilities provided. It's not comparable."

"Remember the old saying 'Let's burn 'em out' from the movies?" she says. "This is a 'let's price them off the land' move."

However, the "improvements" Neal referred to, such as fences and water development, negatively impact the land, from the environmentalists' perspective. And the fees come nowhere near paying for the cost of managing the land. In 1989, the Forest Service spent nearly $35 million to manage the range, but collected only $11 million or so in grazing fees.

There is more at stake in this part of the fight than just the cost of grazing. An underground market has grown up in the buying and selling of grazing permits. One rancher could sell a permit for a single AUM on the Gila, for example, to another rancher for as much as $2,500. The rancher can also borrow against the value, and often does. With two hundred AUMs, those permits could be worth $500,000. As cattle numbers are cut back, and the campaign against public lands ranching continues, the value of the permits has plummeted. "Cow units were sold for twenty-five hundred dollars a few years ago," McCarty said. "Now I'm lucky to get eight hundred dollars." Already as wobbly as a newborn calf, the economic legs of ranching are getting shakier. So far, though, ranchers have been able to beat back several attempts in Washington to raise fees.

Ranchers predict widespread doom for an already troubled industry if substantial changes are made in grazing on public lands. "It's fixing to be diminished considerably," says Bud Eppers, a New Mexico cattle grower. "Ranchers are fearful," says Karen Budd, a rancher and attorney in Cheyenne, Wyoming, who represents ranchers who hold grazing permits. "They say, 'If I'm so bad, how could I have survived for five generations?' "

"Some people would go out of business," agrees Dave Alberswerth, who works on range issues for the National Wildlife Federation, a Washington, D.C., environmental group. "But you'd have other people coming in who could pay this fee. It's time to put livestock on a pay-as-you-go basis. The taxpayers have been subsidizing the whole show."

It's not as if ranchers wear a black hat, or take pride in messing up the range. They are caught in the middle of a fundamental shift in society, a market quickly going global, and are ill-prepared to do business in a way other than the way their fathers and grandfathers did. It's what they know, and they resist change. It's the John Wayne mentality, the head-on, two-fisted approach to life. Early ranchers were part of the economic machine that annihilated the American Indians. They drove the wolf to extinction. Same with the bison. The grizzly bear. The issues were black and white. Good and bad. Us against them.

But the world is not so simple these days. Scientific advancements have changed the way the natural world is viewed. It's not the enemy anymore. We've made a 180-degree turn. For years it went without saying that ranchers were making things better, forcing the land to give up a living for them, their families, their community. Fat cattle on the land or a whining sawmill is a sign of progress, inroads against harsh, sometimes brutal country. Now ranchers are being told they have been making things worse, and they feel they are being pushed off the land so white-collar workers from Albuquerque or Tucson can come down and hunt on weekends. "All environmentalists do is fatten lawyers," McCarty says, sourly.

The cowboys aren't resigned to becoming ghostriders just yet. They represent a still-powerful political force on the national and state levels, and are fighting range cuts. This assault is not only a strike against cattle, but an attack on the whole cowboy myth, the image of cattlemen as rugged individualists who go one-on-one with the elements and make their own way in the world. No one believes more devoutly in the Cowboy Way than cattlemen. They hate being called welfare ranchers.

From Montana to New Mexico, Colorado to California, ranchers have circled their wagons and launched a full-scale counterassault. In Wyoming, ranchers closed their land to hunters if they were from Massachusetts, Georgia or Oklahoma, the home states of three congressmen—including Mike Synar, a Democrat, and himself a private lands rancher—pushing hard for increases in grazing fees. They issued a wanted poster with the three congressmen listed on it, and dubbed them the "Hole in the Head Gang." "Wanted for destruction of the West's social and economic structure and other acts against the peace and dignity of the western states," it reads.

Ranch houses aren't the only thing being boarded up on the range. As the ranches go, so do the towns that grew up to service them. Rock River, Wyoming, on a little-used two-lane highway in the south of the state, is one of many examples. Founded when the railroad came through in the 1880s, this once bustling high-plains town was one of the most important rail stops in Wyoming, shipping hundreds of cattle to market every day. But as the population of Rock River has dwindled, the hotels, haberdasheries, cafes and other businesses that once lined Main Street are gone, and the few that remain are boarded up and overgrown with weeds. Tumbleweeds often blow through the empty streets, driven by constant, fierce winds. The train whistle once was the cry of prosperity. Now it's an unpleasant reminder that the town of Rock River is fading into oblivion, as the trains roar by without stopping. At one time, the railroad decided the fate of small towns. Now it is the interstate, and the interstate is many miles away from Rock River.

During the energy boom of the 1970s, some 600 people lived in Rock River. Now there are perhaps 150. "They all left when the coal mines shut down," says Buzz Pittman, the soft-spoken owner of the Stockman's Bar and Cafe, Home of the Buzzburger and one of the handful of businesses still hanging on. "It'll be a ghost town if something doesn't come in here."

"The people who tend to migrate are the young and the well educated and highly motivated," says Paul Polzin, director of the Bureau of Business and Economic Research at the University of Montana in Missoula. "You get a perverse population distribution—the very old and the very young stay."

Rock River has a serious problem. A rambling, brand-new brick schoolhouse, built for three hundred students in the coal-fueled boom of the 1970s, now has about forty children and is one more reminder, says Pittman, of the decline of Rock River. "They closed the hardware store last year," he says, pushing back a brown, sweat-stained cowboy hat. "We even had a Dairy Queen until it burned down. And that," he says, pointing to a pasture full of cattle, "was the rodeo grounds. This was a thriving little town when I came here. Now look at it. There ain't going to be nothing left if things keep going the way they are." And so the spiraling down of the ranch economy continues. Fewer ranchers means less business on Main Street, which means fewer stores and jobs. Life on the ranch gets a little more lonely, and people leave for the city and some company.

It is not only the ranch and farm economy. Following the decline in uranium mining, for example, Jeffrey City, a town in the extreme southeastern corner of the Yellowstone ecosystem, is a shadow of its former self. For many years it wasn't a town, but a post office in a log cabin called Home on the Range. In the 1960s and 1970s, nuclear power plants and the need for nuclear weapons during the Cold War fueled a demand for uranium, which was mined nearby. Home on the Range became Jeffrey City and went through a period of atomic-powered growth. In 1970, there were 750 residents, and by 1977, 2,868. Then the price of uranium went through the floor. In 1990, there were 130 or so residents of Jeffrey City.

One of the reasons ranch towns are hurting is the difficulty young ranchers face in trying to get into the business. It takes major backing. New family ranches are as rare as two-headed calves. To put together an outfit, a rancher needs a five-hundred-cow breeding herd—the mother cows kept to raise calves sold to market. At $600 per cow, that's $300,000. He might need ten thousand acres at, say, $50 per acre. That's $500,000. For a pickup truck, tractor and other odds and ends, add another $150,000. Annual interest payments at 10 percent are $100,000. Yearly operating costs, such as those for fuel, feed and so on, are about $60,000. And of course there's no guarantee you'll make money. "What would you do with a million dollars?" one rancher says to another in a standard rancher joke. "Just keep ranching until it was used up," answers the other. The numbers explain why the average age of a rancher in Montana, for example, is fifty-one.

One of the great ironies of ranch country is that the cowboy is getting wiped out, in part by the very people who are moving in to drink in the myth of the cattlemen. The New West. The Cowboy Way is dying, riding quietly off into the sunset, while the myth, the cowboy's vapor trail, seems immortal. Museums and galleries brim with cowboy art; Ralph Lauren and others sell "authentic" denim jackets and other western duds at prices few real cowboys can afford; and real estate developers slice the range up into twenty- or forty-acre plots called "ranchettes." The Wild West has become the Mild West.

The trend has accelerated, especially in high-profile places like the Yellowstone ecosystem. Various captains of industry, professionals, and politicians (like former secretary of state James Baker and former secretary of the interior James Watt) all live in the GYE. A passel of actors and their families, including Michael Keaton, Mel Gibson, Harrison Ford, Whoopi Goldberg, Dennis Quaid and Meg Ryan, and Ted Turner and Jane Fonda, and a pantheon of other famous and not-so-famous musicians and artists have summer homes and ranches in the Greater Yellowstone. "They don't make land like that anymore," says NBC anchorman Tom Brokaw, who dropped anchor on the West Fork of the Boulder, just north of the park—in spite of and not because of the famous neighbors, he says. "Montana is special in the world. I come over a rise there and I feel like I'm in Tibet. I've always wanted a place I could really get away to."

Ted Turner, the cable television magnate from Atlanta, and his wife, Jane Fonda, own the 130,000-acre Flying D Ranch near Bozeman. Turner also sits on the board of the Greater Yellowstone Coalition. The man who has made his money selling commercials during old John Wayne and Randolph Scott movies has had his differences with the real McCoy. He sold off all the cows and introduced bison, claiming that as an indigenous species they do less damage to riparian areas. He also made the statement that "buffalo are better looking than cows. They don't have fat all over their butts." That statement, among others, did not go over well in ranch country, where part of the unwritten code is that you don't criticize a man's livestock. Republican U.S. senator Conrad Burns returned fire and claimed that Turner had ruined a good ranch with his bison, and shouldn't have been allowed to buy land in the state. "What he's doing just hurts the heart of a good stockman," he said. He later issued a halfhearted apology, saying he supported Turner's constitutional right to buy land wherever he wanted.

What happens when a herd of celebrities or corporate executives swarm into a valley is that land prices shoot up because the people buying aren't worried about paying their bills with profits from ranching. In places like Jackson Hole, Sante Fe and a host of other resort towns, many of the real ranchers are gone, victims of their own myth.

The power of the myth seems undiminished by the years. A Montana entrepreneur recently made a splash in New York selling "Montana Broke" jeans at $60 a pair. They were used dungarees worn by a real Montana cowboy, soiled by real Montana cows, on a real Montana ranch. The cowboy has certainly always been welcome on Madison Avenue. One of the most successful campaigns in the history of advertising was the western fantasy that peddled Marlboro cigarettes.

Several key components created the mythological cowboy. The

first was the stage on which the drama of the cowboy unfolded. The quiet, usually flat or rolling landscape of the East paled in comparison to the dramatic, glacier-etched mountains, dun-colored rimrocks, strangely shaped cactus, and surreal red round rocks of cowboy heaven. Immensely popular landscape painters like Albert Bierstadt, Thomas Moran and Thomas Hill, who bathed their landscapes in romantic, glowing light, set the stage for the cowboy.

The American cowboy was also born at a time of great national anguish over the Civil War. With its sophisticated weaponry and incredibly large number of casualties, the war was a terrible product of the Industrial Revolution, a glimpse into an ugly future. The cowboy was apart from that, physically and metaphorically, riding through the natural world of the West. A new chance to do it right. Redemption.

Michael Marsden, a professor of popular culture at Northern Michigan University, has another view of the cowboy's meaning. "The cowboy more than any other single character has distilled the two most valued American concepts—the heightened sense of individualism and absolute mobility," he says. "They are peculiar to the American character and they are exaggerated in the cowboy. The [mythological] cowboy is the ultimate individual with no specific roots, the free person who can come and go as he wishes and travel lightly." Add to that the qualities of being macho and noble, two attributes also respected by Americans. The cowboy was slow to anger, but had a strong notion of right and wrong and brooked no insult. If something challenged him, he beat it up, strung it up or shot it.

The mythical—as opposed to real—cowboy also cogently represents both an idealized connection between man and nature, and a struggle between the two. When the white man came to the West to do battle with the elements, the outcome was never certain, Marsden says, and either one could have emerged the victor. It was what he calls the "epic moment," played out again and again in the last home of the cowboy, the rodeo. "The rodeo is a careful balance between the wild and the tame," he says. "Rodeo riders want wildness in the stock. Cowboys don't want an easy draw, they want the toughest bull, they want to match themselves against nature. They are civilization, and there—in the bull—is nature. They want that epic moment, and it is re-created in the rodeo every time. That is the essence of the western story. It's that moment in time when the scales could tip either way. Either you're going to be gored by the bull or you're going to ride the bull for eight seconds."

The great paradox for the cowboy is that once the wilderness has been tamed, once he leads civilization to a new land, he can no longer live there. He is a bridge between wilderness and civilization, caught between those two worlds and saddled with the knowledge that he has helped destroy the very thing he loved. In that way he is a perfect symbol for our society. "The cowboy is ultimately lonely, free but melancholy," Marsden says. "That's what the story is all about—taming the wilderness and making it fit for human habitation. The cowboy likes to think he left it alone, but in his heart he knows he changed it. The cowboy is melancholy because he knows he's tampering with something. Like Shane, he has to ride on. He can't stay there, he can't enjoy the fruits of civilization."

This is where the horse comes in, an indispensable part of the myth. "You can't find one cowboy hero who mistreats nature, because animals are cowboys' link to the natural world," Marsden says. "That's why they ride. The horse is the great mediator between the wild and civilization. It's how the cowboy is linked to the wilderness."

William F. "Buffalo Bill" Cody first brought the cowboy in all his mythical glory to the East with his Wild West show. Dime novels continued the process. Owen Wister's *The Virginian* was the first. The writing was not that good, but the die of the hero cowboy was cast. Celluloid, with its unusual power to confer mythic status, would catapult the cowboy into his throne. Like the hat and boots, the chaps and big belt buckle, the myth of the hero, as old as history itself, was draped around the shoulders of the cowboy. Not the West as it was, said director John Ford of his westerns, but the West as it should have been.

Dan Muldoon is an easterner who found the lure of the myth irresistible. A native of Rochester, New York, he came west when he was seventeen and worked a variety of jobs before settling into a position as a cowboy with the Magness Land and Cattle Company. Now forty, Muldoon, who works in the high, mountain-ringed meadows of central Colorado, has been working as a cowboy for several years. He looks the part. He wears the requisite big hat, fringed leather chaps and a long, droopy mustache that hangs well past his chin. He was weaned on *Bonanza* and *The Rifleman* and held that view of the West when he first crossed the Mississippi. But the reality, he says, is nothing like that.

"Wild Bill Hickok wasn't a cowboy," says Muldoon. "I used to think that cowboys spent a lot of time in the Long Branch Saloon, getting into gunfights and all that sort of stuff. That doesn't really apply. If you want to be a cowboy, the first thing you have to have is your name on the payroll. You don't have to have a big hat and boots and a six-shooter. Louis L'Amour is the biggest bunch of bullshit there ever was."

Nonetheless, there is something to the Cowboy Way, he says, a true cowboy myth. There is the paycheck, of course. But there is also the psychic income. "This place just flipped all the switches," he says. "Good horses to ride in pretty country. There ain't nothing prettier than seeing the little calves in the spring out there in the tall grass. Working outside in all sorts of weather. I truly do like being pretty much by myself. You can sure do that up here. And I like the baling wire philosophy. Pretty much you got to get yourself out of whatever wreck you're in with baling wire. A lot of ingenuity and creativity in this line of work. And I like having all this wilderness out my back door."

Not everyone is so enamored of the Cowboy Way. In an era when the walls of the status quo are coming down all over the place, the cowboy myth has not escaped the iron ball of the revisionists. In her book *Legacy of Conquest*, a look at the European expansion into the West, University of Colorado at Boulder historian Patricia N. Limerick likens the cowboy and other white western hero figures to slave traders (because they subjugated a people). "The subject of slavery was the domain of serious scholars and the occasion for sober national reflection; the subject of conquest [of the West] was the domain of mass entertainment and the occasion for lighthearted national escapism. An element of regret for 'what we did to the Indians' entered the picture, but the dominant feature of conquest remained 'adventure.' Children happily played 'cowboys and Indians' but stopped short of 'masters and slaves.' "

"What's sad about the myth is that it is a social critique about our way of life, our industrial and postindustrial way of life, that gets aborted before it can [really examine] how we live and work," Limerick says. "[The critique] gets dissipated in the dreaming and yearning. The cowboy looks so good because our lives are so dreary, but it never gets any further, never becomes a real examination of our lives. Why are our lives so dreary? Do they have to be so dreary? They don't call it escapism for nothing."

Revisionism and reality notwithstanding, in some ways the cowboy myth is more powerful now than it ever has been. The baby boomers grew up playing cowboys and Indians, and watching *Gunsmoke*, *Bonanza*, *The Big Valley*, *Rawhide*, *Roy Rogers* and *The Lone Ranger*. In an urban society where people are hemmed in by concrete and asphalt, their jobs and bills due, where the air is thick and brown and any semblance of real nature is a long day's drive away, the attraction of an open range to ride across and an uncomplicated life-style free of tangled webs gives the myth all the more power. People who live in ranch country or a small town are real, with faces and names and a life—not just anonymous strangers. One of the last places the past still lives in a big way is on the family ranch. It is a subculture that has its own way of doing things, a history, a language, a philosophy. It is genuine, in many ways, while so much of America is not.

Some advocate a middle ground, somewhere between damaging the streams and prairies and buffalo on one hand, and ending a 125-year-old way of life on the western range on the other. This is what the Greater Yellowstone Coalition advocates—a balancing of needs in an integrated way that keeps both healthy.

Applied to the problem with the Yellowstone bison, it might work something like this. Some buffalo would be allowed to migrate onto public land outside of the park to the north and west. Nonlethal means would be employed—hazing and herding and traps to capture and test the animals for brucellosis—if they head for private land. If they test positive, they would be slaughtered. If they test negative, they would be quarantined. Grazing rights or even private land might be purchased from ranchers for the use of buffalo. And in the end, there might be some hunting. "It's not the knee-jerk shoot-them-at-the-border approach," says Jean Marie Souvigney, associate program director at the GYC. "It's a comprehensive look at managing wildlife in a developed valley." And as development continues in the West, along with the interest in wildlife, a careful, integrated approach to management is a concept that will be increasingly important, in Yellowstone and elsewhere, to keep things like the American ranch and the American bison from vanishing.

4
The Forest for the Trees

LYLE BEARD SPITS A TINY, DARK STREAM OF TOBACCO JUICE onto the ground and takes in the view around him. "They've pretty much wiped this country out," he says, pointing to a stump-studded meadow that a few years ago was a pine forest. "And they're proud of it, too, as if they were a farmer who had just finished plowing his fields."

In 1906, six brothers named Beard emigrated from Utah to a remote spot in Wyoming, just a stone's toss from the Idaho border, where they set up a sawmill in Leigh Canyon, in the southwest corner of the Greater Yellowstone ecosystem. On a patch of federally owned woods in the Targhee National Forest, the Beard boys set to work, cutting fir trees by pulling a huge handsaw back and forth and chopping with a hand-sharpened axe. They towed the timber down out of the woods with a team of yoked oxen, winter and summer, and dropped the logs at the mill. The saw, as tall as a man, with jagged teeth for ripping the logs, was run by a pounding steam engine, and the boiler for the engine was stoked with the slabs, or the long pieces of bark, that had been cut off the trees. When he was a boy, Lyle Beard kept the fire under the boiler burning. The Beard brothers cut much of the timber for the shops and homes in the Driggs and Tetonia area of eastern Idaho. No one got rich, but the Beards managed to scratch out a living, feeding and clothing six families.

At the head of Leigh Canyon, watching over the chugging sawmill and the rest of the little independent operation, was a timbered mountain that locals eventually came to call Beard Mountain.

Times have changed here. The steam engine was replaced by an engine from a World War II tank in 1952. The original Beard brothers passed on, but some of their offspring, including Lyle, continued to cut trees and saw them into two-by-fours. Tetonia, a town little more than a wide spot on Highway 33, a few miles north of the mill, has gotten smaller. Driggs, a few miles the other way, has gotten a little bigger. The price of land, homes and rent has grown exponentially in Jackson, Wyoming, twenty miles away over Teton Pass, so many people have found it more economical to move to Driggs.

Those aren't the changes, however, that rile Lyle Beard. On an October morning, a brilliant sun turns trembling aspen trees an electric yellow and Beard pours coffee into a cup in his ranch home, at the end of a long dirt road, miles from the highway. He is wearing a brown cowboy hat with sawdust on it, a denim coat and jeans, and worn-out western boots. A wad of snoose, or chewing tobacco that resembles coffee grounds, is jammed between his lip and teeth. His well-creased face and hands seem permanently tanned. A pair of silver spurs lies on the kitchen's linoleum floor.

Beard pulls out some faded black-and-white photos and shuffles through them. A picture of his dad, a steel-eyed sawyer who cut timber for the Army during World War I in Washington. Two men swinging axes at a tree six feet in diameter. Oxen pulling logs on a cart through a stream. The Beard brothers at work.

The big change came to this country, Lyle says, in the 1970s, when the U.S. Forest Service, which manages publicly owned timberland, allowed a logging company to clear-cut a patch of timber on federal land near his home that had been killed by insects. The cutting was meant as a salvage sale, so the dead timber could be harvested and sold before it went to waste. But the Forest Service never looked back at the kind of selective cutting of mature trees that the Beards had undertaken, Lyle says. Far less environmentally sound—but much more profitable—clear-cuts become standard operating procedure.

Unfortunately for Beard and the family-owned mills in the area, the size of the timber sales were massive, far beyond what the Beards or other small operators could raise the money to buy. So the logs went to Idaho Forest Industries (IFI), a large company based in Coeur d'Alene, Idaho, with a stud mill in St. Anthony, which cut only two-by-fours. Every time a sale came up, Beard says, it went to IFI.

Lyle Beard climbs into a four-wheel-drive pickup truck and rumbles up a logging road into Leigh Canyon, toward Beard Mountain. "This is where we did a lot of our cutting," he says, pointing through the windshield. The one-mile-by-three-mile stretch of woods that the Beards carefully maintained is gone now. Vanished. Only stumps remain.

Farther back in the woods, near the Wyoming line, Beard jounces over a rough new road cut by the Forest Service for sales of timber even farther back into the woods along the South Fork of Leigh Creek. He brings the pickup to rest in yet another man-made clearing. A few years back, he says, it was a forest. The new meadow is broken by jagged piles of what loggers call slash. The piles are ten, twelve, even fourteen feet high.

It's bad enough, he says, as he spits another stream of tobacco juice on the ground, that the Forest Service sells only large-scale clear-cuts, including one behind his house, and drives him out of the sawmill business. And it's bad enough that all this cutting is being done to keep alive a mill that will probably soon be out of business because there is very little merchantable timber left to cut here on the Targhee. "If it hadn't been for clear-cutting," he says, "timber would have been here forever. It hurts to see the trucks go by with timber from your backyard and know you can't have any."

What really chaps Lyle Beard's hide, however, more than anything else, are these giant slash piles, ready for burning as waste by the Forest Service, piles that are filled with logs six to ten inches in diameter, some of them ten or twelve feet long. Many were longer but were broken when they were bulldozed into piles. Idaho Forest Industries takes only very select trees for studs. Most of the rest—a considerable amount—goes up in smoke out here in the fields. "Each one of these piles could heat three or four homes for a winter," he says, as he looks out over a collection of fifty or sixty slash piles, just a single clear-cut's worth, and then spits a stream of tobacco juice on the ground. "Two of these piles have enough house logs to build a cabin. There used to be a hundred different families that cut firewood or post and pole and eked out a living here. Now there's ten or maybe fifteen."

Though he still runs the mill a month or so out of the year, cutting what timber he can get, Lyle Beard has mostly moved on to other things. So have his five sons. Like many westerners, Beard pieces together a living off the land. He burns wood for heat and hunts for meat. He builds cabins for summer people who have bought land near here. He guides hunters, though in other parts of the state, for he says many of the deer and elk have left this country, driven out of their habitat by the logging.

The Targhee National Forest in the southeast part of the ecosystem is, in fact, one of the most criticized national forests in the United States. From the air it is obvious most of the predominantly lodgepole pine forest has been clear-cut. And it is a simple task to see where the park boundary is. The rolling hills of the Targhee look like a forest of clear-cuts with islands of trees, and a network of roads that looks like a terminal case of varicose veins. The forests within the park are intact, a rolling green blanket that stops abruptly at the edge of the Targhee. Hunting season for elk on the Targhee once lasted for forty-five days. With new timber roads allowing increased access, and fewer places for the elk to hide, the season dropped to five days, and with so much hunting compressed into so short a time, the woods are filled with hunters. Locals call it the "Five-Day War."

Idaho Forest Industries has been cutting timber in the Northwest since the turn of the century. It's a "small" timber company with some five hundred workers that does an important job, says executive vice-president Jim English, who works at company headquarters in Coeur d'Alene. That job would be providing wood for homes and manufacturing. English is proud of the fact that the employees at IFI make a living wage, averaging $35,000 a year, with another $15,000 in benefits.

Idaho Forest Industries, says English, cut trees down and made them into two-by-fours at the St. Anthony mill with as little waste as possible. "To say that small operators are more efficient is simply not true. I don't know how anyone could have been more efficient."

Environmentalists and people like Lyle Beard, English says, have blown the problem way out of proportion, convincing people that the forests of the Yellowstone ecosystem and the West are being destroyed, when that is far from the case. "Clear-cutting had to be done on the Targhee in order to stop the spread of disease" from an insect called the pine beetle. It's like a surgical procedure, removing sick and dead trees, in order to save the healthy ones. Without such cutting, he says, fires like the ones that burned in Yellowstone in 1988 would have destroyed much of the timber on the Targhee. "Rather than let it burn up, we took it and used it."

The debate over logging on the public lands in the West is the fiercest resource debate of all. To many westerners, the saddest, most unreasonable chapter of all in the saga of developing the resources of the West is the logging that has taken place in the last century or so, especially the past three decades. On every level, they say, it defies common sense. They call it indiscriminate. Rapacious. Biologically unsound. But mostly they say it is damn ugly. Some of these clear-cuts are so big they are visible from satellite photographs.

The companies and the people who work for them say it is business. Communities depend on logging for jobs and economies. The housing industry in the United States depends on a steady supply of timber. Companies depend on profits. But they are squirming. More and more people who live in cities, removed from nature, want it preserved. Environmentalists say the companies know that, and are trying to cut as much timber as they can before they are stopped. One of those who opposes the logging is Robert Redford. The actor has a home in Utah. "It's indiscriminate, savage lumbering," he says. "They know the jig is almost up. They are screaming to the finish line and raping the forests."

One of the reasons people have become so incensed with the cutting is that it is not taking place on privately owned tree farms, but on the 191 million acres of Forest Service land owned by the public. The Forest Service works for the taxpayer, managing the timber for sale to private companies. But under the National Forest Management Act, the Forest Service is charged with managing the forests under a principle called multiple use. Timber cutting is supposed to be done in a way that also provides protection for fisheries, for recreation, for grazing and a host of other uses.

In the opinion of many, including many dissenting professionals within the Forest Service, the cutting of taxpayer-owned timber now being allowed is so far removed from sound timber-management practices of sustained yield that they call it timber mining—that is, it will only yield one crop. On top of that, streams are being choked with silt and wildlife habitat is being destroyed. And the future of logging and milling in the West is dubious, they say, because the resource is being squandered.

Studies indicate that forests are not being replaced in many places, especially in the Rocky Mountain West. Trees planted by the Forest Service have a high mortality rate in the cold dry climate where many of the forests are. And there have been few studies of how well the replanting works.

The story of timber cutting in the West is not just a battle between environmentalists and timber companies. It is a battle between small operators like Lyle Beard, who make a living cutting trees in a way that will sustain the forests and their economic future, and the big companies like IFI, Louisiana Pacific and Plum Creek, which have leveled the forests of the West in a way that is profitable for large companies headquartered in some faraway city, but which, in many cases, has devastated local economies and environments for decades to come.

The reason the forests are so overcut, environmentalists claim, is that the levels of timber harvest, which are set by Congress, are established for political instead of biological reasons. The Forest Service also has a financial stake in cutting more timber: it gets to keep gross timber receipts for its budget, a kind of profit that fuels the bureaucracy. Until World War II, the national forests cut about one billion board feet a year; that level is now eleven billion per year.

It is not only the destruction of forests that angers critics, but the fact that the destruction is so uneconomical for timber companies that the federal government has to subsidize much of it. Part of the problem is that private owners claimed much of the good timber in the last century, and the forests left to the government were of poor quality. These forests are so unprofitable for timber companies that the Forest Service pays for the preparation of the sales and for the expensive roads into a sale site. By almost everyone's measure except the Forest Service's and the corporations', timber cutting on public land is a massive subsidy to timber companies.

Environmentalists sail under the issue of economics as a flag of convenience at every opportunity, for that argument is most compelling. Economists for Congress and groups like The Wilderness Society estimate that taxpayers are charged about $200 million a year to sell their forests. That does not take into account the damage done to other values. In 1990, the Forest Service estimates that of its 122 forests, 65 lost money. Independent estimates place the number of money-losing forests at 108. One ex-forester and Congressional Research Service economist estimates that in the last decade the subsidy to timber companies amounted to $5.6 billion. It costs taxpayers $20 million to sell timber in the Greater Yellowstone alone. "Why not just give the money to the millworkers and loggers directly?" says an angry Michael Scott, head of the Northern Rockies Office of The Wilderness Society, in Bozeman, Montana. "Why should the taxpayers subsidize the destruction of the ecosystem?"

Most of the money for timber sales is spent on road building, a transportation network that allows access to the timber. The national forests are crisscrossed with an estimated 340,000 miles of dirt roads built to accommodate logging trucks, eight times the length of the interstate highway system. A hundred thousand miles of new road will be built in the next half century. Primary logging roads cost the Forest Service $45,000 a mile to build; secondary ones about $15,000 a mile. On the five national forests in the Greater Yellowstone, it's estimated there are 12,000 miles of logging roads, with 13,000 new miles to be scraped into the earth in the next fifty years, according to Forest Service plans. That would be equivalent to eight cross-country drives across the U.S.

The Forest Service was greatly embarrassed when, during the conference about the Earth's environment in Rio in 1992, a conference that focused on global warming and destruction of the Earth's forests, *The New York Times* ran side-by-side photos of the Amazon rain forest and those of the Pacific Northwest taken by the National Aeronautics and Space Administration. It was a stark contrast; compared to the old-growth forests in the Northwest, the Amazon looks relatively intact. "These pictures, taken from 700 miles above the Earth, show a pattern of clear-cutting throughout the entire rain forest of the Northwest that is so extensive the land looks perforated by a giant blast of buckshot," the *Times* said. It estimated that 90 percent of the U.S. rain forest has been cut, while only 10 percent of the Amazon has been logged.

The chorus for change grows louder all the time. A former Forest Service employee named Jeff Debonis has formed a group called the Association of Forest Service Employees for Environmental Ethics, which puts out a publication called *The Inner Voice.* The group claims one thousand Forest Service employees and ex-employees as members. This group believes that environmental quality has been sacrificed on the altar of profit.

These rebels say the problem starts with Congress, which sets unrealistically high limits on the Forest Service to "get the cut out." One of the rebels, in fact, turned out in 1991 to be John Mumma, a regional forester in charge of 25 million acres in fifteen national forests (including three of the four forests in the Montana portion of the Yellowstone ecosystem). At one point in tears, he told a congressional subcommittee that Congress had mandated the cutting of timber beyond any reasonable levels, and was actually forcing the U.S. Forest Service to break the National Forest Management Act, the Endangered Species Act and other federal environmental laws—doing serious damage to the nation's forests. "I am here today with a heavy heart—a heart that's in shock at what's happening in the national forests of this country."

No amount of anger, appeals or indignation seems to stop the timber juggernaut. The Forest Service, Congress and the timber companies keep right on cutting. John Mumma was forced to resign.

Controversy and corruption seem to have always hovered above the timber in the national forests. Until 1891, in fact, the national forests were a free-for-all. The term *wide-open West* referred to more than the landscape. The woods were full of theft and the kind of waste that comes with a frontier gold rush. In one 1897 federal law, a "land lieu" clause was written in to allow anyone who wanted to donate forested land to a national preserve to claim an equal amount of land somewhere else. The Northern Pacific Railroad gave up 540,000 acres (of the 57 million acres of mineral and timberland given it by the government as incentive to build the railroad) in exchange for much more valuable land.

In time, what was worthless becomes priceless, one of the West's great themes: the half a million undesirable acres in Washington became Mount Rainier National Park. It has happened time and time again. The most notable example is, of course, Yellowstone.

One of the most famous forest scandals took place in 1903. A dishonest real estate man, Stephen A. Douglas Puter, worked the woods with a then-common "dummy entryman" scam. Like the Anaconda Company had done, he hired a homesteader to file claims on 160 acres of timberland and then bought the land from the homesteader and logged it. But he took it a fatal step further: he concocted fictional homesteaders and filed claims under their names. Caught in the act, Puter testified against U.S. Senator John H. Mitchell, a Republican from Oregon, who he claimed had taken bribes from himself and other lumbermen to approve spurious claims. The distinguished senator was convicted and sentenced to six months in prison. (Before he was imprisoned, the senator died, at the hands of an inept dentist.)

President Benjamin Harrison had begun to try to protect some of the public's timberlands, with the creation of the national forest reserves in 1891. But reform comes slowly, especially on the frontier, miles from the seat of power in Washington, D.C. Things began to change in 1898 when President William McKinley hired Gifford Pinchot to tend to the nation's forests.

Pinchot, the godfather of the U.S. Forest Service, was the consummate professional, and is credited with bringing that attitude to the forests. He was a distinguished-looking gent, with gray temples and an enormous, droopy mustache. Not a preservationist in the mold of John Muir, who favored protecting forests intact, he instead favored sustainable use of the forests, orderly exploitation of the resource, and tree farms—a set of concepts learned in European forestry schools. He became a golden boy in the conservation-minded White House of Theodore Roosevelt (even occasionally wrestling with the commander in chief), and consolidated his power. His influence during Roosevelt's reign was so great he almost single-handedly brought the notion of selective cutting to the American forests.

Earlier, in 1891, Pinchot had taken a job managing the North Carolina estate of railroad magnate George W. Vanderbilt, and it was here that the ideas of selective cutting were incubated in America. He selectively cut mature trees for timber. Seedlings were protected. The economic returns were maximized and the timber crop perpetuated itself. The forest floor was kept clean of litter to reduce the chance of fire. It was a neat forest. A functional forest.

In 1897, one of President Grover Cleveland's final acts as president was to transfer 21 million acres of public land available for timber cutting into thirteen forest reserves—off-limits to the saw and axe. (The first national forest, in fact, was in the Yellowstone ecosystem—the Shoshone, to the south and east of the park.) The western lumbermen, used to having their way with the woods, cried foul. Pinchot, realizing the federal government was alienating the lumber barons, fought and won the right for the timber companies to cut the trees as long as it was according to Pinchot's rules. By 1913, there were 187 million acres of national forests; 4 million have been added since.

Pinchot became the embodiment of the new idea of timber husbandry, spearheading an effort to get a forestry school at Yale, founding the Society of American Foresters, and lobbying for and winning the transfer of forests to the Department of Agriculture, under the administration of the newly created United States Forest Service—a fitting place for Pinchot's crop of trees. "All the resources of the Forest Reserves must be brought about in a thoroughly prompt and business-like manner, under such restrictions only as will ensure the permanence of these resources," he said. The functional, theoretically perpetual, forest was officially born. Now, biologists say, Pinchot's idea of sustainable cutting—even though it has some drawbacks—has been thrown out the window in favor of clear-cutting, which is far more devastating.

New knowledge of ecological systems has also altered the notion of what a sustainable forest should be. Rather than cutting all the trees or keeping a neat forest or putting out all fires, ecologists these days advocate that nature have a freer hand. In the long term it is better for the forest and can head off larger problems further down the road. If fire had been allowed to burn periodically in Yellowstone for the past century, for example, instead of a policy of complete suppression, the fires of 1988 might have been less severe.

The biggest threat to Pinchot's vision of orderly exploitation of the forest—after the human element had been reined in—was wildfire. Therefore a fundamental mission of the Forest Service was its dedication to the protection of forests from fires. Fires have always been a threat, and in a dry year can consume hundreds of thousands of acres in a couple of days.

The forest fires in the West are the stuff of legend, none more so than those of the summer of 1910, one of the most dramatic fire seasons in recorded history in the West. Although by 1905 the Forest Service had begun to think about fire fighting, five years later there was little infrastructure in place.

June was the beginning of a bone-dry summer. Dry winds sucked the life out of the woods. Streams dried up. Duff on the forest floor was desiccated and crunched underfoot. Fires, sparked by dry lightning storms, began to flare up. The Forest Service began to pick up fire fighters wherever it could find them—lumberjacks, miners, homesteaders, members of the "Wobblies" or the radical union International Workers of the World. Work was offered to people in bars and flophouses.

The work was arduous and the conditions tough. The men lived in fire camps—canvas tents in the backwoods—with saws, shovels, axes, food and other provisions. Their job then—as it is today—was to cut a three- or four-foot-wide line around the fire, a line that was clear of sticks, moss, leaves and humus, to deprive the fire of fuel. The perimeter was patrolled, and as embers were blown over the line, crews extinguished the spot fires.

By early August, three thousand small fires and ninety large ones were brought under control, and the Forest Service was lulled into believing in the effectiveness of this nascent art of fighting wildfire.

Then the winds came.

On August 10, with the humidity low, the wood in the forest drier than kiln-dried lumber, unmerciful gusts blew in. Fires grew exponentially in Washington, Oregon, Idaho and Montana. Even Minnesota. Fire lines were extended. Fire fighters looked to the sky for rain. President William Taft ordered in ten companies from the U.S. Army. Mining and logging camps were shut down and the crews sent out to man the lines. By the third week in August, some ten thousand fire fighters were building fire lines in Idaho and Montana. When wildfires reach a certain point, however, the number of fire fighters is meaningless.

The rough-and-tumble mining town of Wallace, in northern Idaho, with about 3,400 people, bore the brunt of the fire's fury. It began with wind-borne pieces of burning bark flying through the air and landing on homes, according to one account, as if an unseen enemy was softening up the town with mortar shells. Winds howled. People moved their furniture out of their homes and into open areas like the town's ball field. Citizens kept busy wetting their homes and businesses.

On August 20, however, winds screamed in from the north at one hundred miles an hour, making a mockery of fire-fighting efforts. A semicircle in the forest, 160 miles long and 30 to 50 miles wide, was engulfed by flames. By four in the afternoon the sun was blotted out by clouds. A baseball game in Hamilton, Montana, was called for darkness. Glowing coals dropped from the sky, and ash floated down like snowflakes.

Through walls of flame, the Northern Pacific Railroad sent in rescue trains to haul people and a few of their belongings to refuges in Spokane and Missoula. Troops rode along to clear the track of burning logs. That night those who remained in Wallace—including prisoners, who had been released—gathered fearfully in the ballpark. The sky glowed an eerie orange. The all-consuming fire sounded like a freight train. The maelstrom hit Wallace from the east, and before it was through, it had consumed a hundred buildings—a third of the town. Two townspeople were killed.

As the fire passed, refugees from burned-out homes outside of town wandered into the city. Fire fighters who survived came into town, bringing with them horrible stories. On Big Creek (in Idaho), thirty men were brought down by the fire. On Setzer Creek twenty-nine died, including one who committed suicide before the flames hit. On the West Fork of Big Creek, eighteen men died.

One of the heroes of the summer of fire was a forty-two-year-old ranger on the Wallace district, Edward Pulaski. Trapped by the blowup, Pulaski knew the woods and led his forty-two men and two horses quickly to the tunnel of the War Eagle Gold Mine. They took refuge in the cool, damp depths and held wet blankets against the mine mouth as the flames roared. Stope timbers inside the mine caught fire. With heat and smoke and gas in the tunnel, it became difficult, then almost impossible, to breathe. Consumed with claustrophobia and fear, one of Pulaski's men tried to flee. Pulaski pulled out his revolver and threatened to shoot him if he left and ordered his men to lie on the ground while he put out the fire on the mine timbers. Soaking a blanket in a trickle of a stream, he held it over the mouth of the cave until, overcome by the smoke and heat, he collapsed.

When the fire had passed, five of the forty-two fire fighters had suffocated and lay dead on the floor of the cave. The horses were badly injured and had to be shot. The lives of the thirty-seven who survived were credited to Pulaski's clearheaded actions.

On Tuesday, August 23, a blessed drizzle ended the unchecked advance of the fire. A week later, heavy rains fell, and the great fire season of 1910 had come to an end. Seventy-eight fire fighters had died, and were buried where they lay. Seven civilians perished. More than three million acres of timberland had burned, and the charred, smoking trees and blackened ground rolled on for miles. It was the Forest Service's first big barbecue.

World War II would be another watershed era in the Forest Service's fire-fighting efforts. In 1942, General Jimmy Doolittle led an immensely destructive air raid on Tokyo. The Japanese wanted to respond, but the Battle of Midway had deprived them of staging areas for a raid on the continental United States. The Japanese had discovered the jet stream, however, and they launched an attack with what was called the *fu-go* weapon—fire balloons. A paper balloon, thirty-three feet in diameter, was armed with an antipersonnel bomb and two incendiary bombs. Fires in the woods could cause tremendous problems, the Japanese knew, especially with many of the able-bodied men in the war. Some nine thousand were offered up to the eastbound jet stream. Perhaps a thousand or so reached the continental United States, but did not cause the kind of widespread chaos the Japanese had hoped for, though 285 incidents were reported. At one landing in Oregon, six civilians were killed.

The war created a wind that blew the Forest Service's antifire efforts into a major campaign. It was patriotic to protect the woods from conflagrations, the Forest Service said. In 1945, the wartime propaganda machine felt it needed an animal to spread the antiwildfire message. Professional advertisers, working for the war effort, tossed around the idea of using Bambi as the Forest Service's symbol. But there were licensing problems. Finally the idea of a bear was settled on. With a ranger's hat, pants and a shovel, the baritone-voiced Smokey the Bear was sent marching out to warn citizens of the perils of fire.

In 1950, after a fire in the Lincoln National Forest in New Mexico, an orphan bear cub was being nursed back to health by a state game officer. Forest Service officials in Washington seized the moment and flew the bear cub back to a new home at the National Zoo in Washington, where the bear became one of America's most famous symbols. It was a public relations coup, and Smokey got so many letters he was given his own zip code. After more than twenty-five years of public service, the cub that became Smokey the Bear passed on to that verdant forest in the sky in 1977.

Smokey was a general in the campaign against fire, a campaign the Forest Service approached steeled with the mental and physical mobilization of those entering a great military battle. It adopted a "ten A.M." policy, which stated simply that all fires were to be out by that time the next morning. It built fire towers on mountaintops so fires could be spotted early and "ground pounders," or hiking fire fighters, could be sent to a fire as quickly as possible. Technology began to improve the weapons against fire. Airplanes dramatically changed things, especially in 1940, when the first "floaters," or smoke jumpers, were flown in with their equipment and parachuted to a blaze. A fire-resistant material called Nomex was developed, and the clothing of fire fighters is now made from it. Lightweight aluminum fire shelters enable a fire fighter surrounded by fire to cover himself or herself and survive. Computer programs predict how quickly and which way a fire will spread. Remote sensors scattered throughout the forests detect lightning strikes, determine which of the four kinds of lightning has struck, and then report the whereabouts electronically to Forest Service headquarters. Hundreds of remote weather stations feed hourly information on wind speed and direction, temperature, humidity and precipitation back to Forest Service weather officials.

However, the mission of Smokey's army has changed in the past couple of decades. As the knowledge of the environment increases, the Forest Service's two basic missions, timber and fire protection, have gone and are going through a biological audit. Ironically, it is apparent that while Smokey was protecting the woods from fire so that trees could be harvested for timber, experts say the logging has been doing more biological damage than the fires.

The big shift in fire fighting came when the Forest Service, the Bureau of Land Management and the Park Service moved away from the ten A.M. policy on every square acre of the land they manage. As the science of ecology progressed, it dawned on researchers that as prevalent as fire is, it might be important to ecosystems, especially in the West.

In 1963, the *Leopold Report* was published, a watershed document that changed the thinking of many federal officials and called for a reconstituting of natural systems. Gradually, the federal agencies began a program of allowing some lightning-caused fires to burn in parks and wild areas. Though it has been called the "let burn" policy, federal officials say the name is misleading. A host of factors go into the determination of whether and where to let a fire burn—landscape, proximity of homes or towns, dryness of fuels, weather and so on.

That was the thinking behind the National Park Service policy, adopted in 1972, that allowed lightning-caused fires to burn, a policy that was one factor in the dramatic fires that swept Yellowstone in 1988.

Few natural disasters match the ferocity of the fires that swept the Yellowstone ecosystem in 1988. They were caused by a combination of factors: several years of record drought, followed by unusual summer storm patterns, including frequent thunderstorms without moisture and unusually high winds.

The first fire started on June 23, 1988. By September more than fifty fires had started, eventually becoming eight major blazes burning around the Yellowstone ecosystem. A complex of fires the size of those that consumed much of the park makes its own rules. Fires grow so hot they suck in vast amounts of oxygen to fuel themselves and create hurricane-force winds. As pieces of bark catch on fire, they are blown by the winds and can float far off into other parts of the forest to start fires there. Or downed stands of lodgepole pine, a mile or more in front of a fire, simply and inexplicably explode.

Coupled with severe drought conditions, the fires behaved in ways that seasoned fire professionals had never seen. They spread at the rate of two miles an hour or more. Rivers are often a barrier to flames, but the fires of 1988, whipped by seventy-mile-an-hour winds through bone-dry fuel, frequently jumped rivers and creeks, including the Grand Canyon of the Yellowstone. On one hot, dry day in August, 165,000 acres of Yellowstone burned, a record in fire-fighting history. That day is called Black Saturday. Even with ten thousand fire fighters in the park, including several thousand Army troops, fire-fighting efforts were all but ineffectual.

For months the park was locked in an incredible drama as the fires roared toward buildings and towns, both inside and outside the park. In early September, one thousand residents of Mammoth Hot Springs, where the park headquarters is located, were evacuated as flames roared toward the town. Farther north, flames from the Fan Fire blew toward the Royal Teton Ranch, owned by a sect called the Church Universal and Triumphant. As the fire neared, hundreds of members trooped to a meadow to chant away the flames. When the wind turned, the group declared victory. Idaho farmers donated sprinkler systems to surround towns and wet down fuels. Fire fighters, meanwhile, sprayed foam on buildings and wrapped telephone poles in fire-resistant foil, conceding the fire whatever else it wanted.

One of the most dramatic fires started on July 22, when a cigarette butt thrown on the ground just east of the park on the Targhee National Forest ignited the North Fork fire. Saliva tests later helped investigators trace the butt to a man named Leland Owens, who was cutting firewood at the time. He and three other woodcutters later pleaded guilty to starting the fire.

The fire swept eastward into the park and eventually headed for the Old Faithful area, which in addition to the geyser has a complex of buildings, including tourist cabins, a store, a restaurant, a gas station and a massive, eighty-five-year-old historic log hotel. At first the fire was predicted to burn to the east, safely away from the complex. Slurry bombers flew over the approaching edge of the fire to drop cherry-red retardant, in hopes of keeping it away from the hotel.

On September 7, the day the fire hit, smoke billowed in the midday sky, making the day darker and darker, and drastically reducing visibility. Fire fighters sprayed a whipped-cream-like foam on cabins. Tourists were evacuated, but hotel employees, mostly college students, stayed. They sat on top of a bus and watched for a while, cheering at dramatic bursts of flame, as the fire burned not to the east, but directly toward the historic structure. They were soon ordered to evacuate.

As the fire surrounded the Old Faithful complex, fire fighters and journalists gathered in the giant asphalt parking lot behind the hotel, which, because of a lack of fuel for the fire, was deemed the safest place to be.

Soon one-hundred-foot walls of flame bellowed through the

crowns of trees, burned to the edge of the parking lot and screamed through nineteen unfoamed cabins to the south. The noise was punctuated by the explosion of fire extinguishers. A crew of fire fighters came running out of the woods; they had almost been overtaken by the fire. In the parking lot, the heat was oppressive and inescapable, and people in it covered their mouths with bandannas to try to filter out some of the choking smoke. Glowing embers and pieces of bark rained down. The constant and ominous roar continued unabated. Television satellite trucks, meanwhile, continued to beam images back to stations in other parts of the country.

Just as the fire burned to the edge of the parking lot, a deluge system on the roof of the Old Faithful Inn—installed the previous year—was activated, and water came rushing across the wooden roof from a series of pipes at the top. It saved the inn, for the fire jumped clear over it and began burning in the woods on the other side of the complex. As the fire moved on and the road opened, those people that remained assembled a convoy and drove to the town of West Yellowstone, just outside the park.

On September 10, a cold front dropped into Yellowstone. Within a few days the fire would be stopped, not by the $120 million spent in Yellowstone, but by a few days of rain and snow. Detailed post-fire assessments showed 1.4 million acres had burned in the Greater Yellowstone.

Biologically speaking, in many ways the fires were a plus for the park. In more humid environments the cycling of nitrogen, potassium, calcium and other minerals through the ecosystem happens primarily by decay. A tree falls to the ground, rots and is processed by insects and microbes, and natural fertilizers leach into the soil and are taken up again by the plants.

In the arid West, however, decay is replaced by fire. The litter on the forest floor and the dead trees contain minerals and nutrients, energy needed by growing flora and fauna. Fire reduces the litter to ash, which gives up its nutrients and is taken up by trees and other plants. Witness the rolling meadows of vibrant wildflowers and green grass, green almost to the point of glowing, that erupted in Yellowstone after the fires there. Officials in Yellowstone say the trout have gotten noticeably bigger after the fires because of the fertilizer unlocked by the fires and cycling through the system.

The native species of the West are, in fact, the result of episodic fires and would not exist without flames. Lodgepole pines, for example, have serotinous cones, which open up and release their seeds only when subjected to intense heat. California's sequoia trees have developed thick bark, winners because of it in a fire-prone environment. Fire also stops seral succession. In many places in the West, grassland evolves to shrubs on to aspen to lodgepole pine to spruce and fir. At the final stages, the variety of plant species declines. With less food, animal species decline. A fire interrupts the move toward biological diminution, opening a forest up and increasing the diversity of species. Aboriginal Americans used fire as a tool to increase forage for deer, elk and bison, so to improve hunting.

Periodic small fires also clean out branches and dead grass and other downed litter on the forest floor. By extinguishing all fires, the Forest Service and other federal agencies were inadvertently inviting real trouble. When fuel builds up, the fires burn much hotter. Fires that burn hot can cause ecological damage by sterilizing the soil or frying it into something resembling bisque pottery.

Fires may dramatically change an area like the Greater Yellowstone—a reshuffling of the ecological deck, though there are exceptions. An analogy can be drawn with human beings. If a human being is healthy, and catches cold, he or she will be sick for a while and then get better. However, if a human is in a weakened condition, with four or five serious problems, a cold could be fatal. In other words, if humans continue to undermine natural systems, a big fire could be the coup de grace that causes widespread extinctions of everything from grizzly bears to insects.

Timber-cutting practices allowed by the Forest Service have also undergone a similar kind of ecological audit. Clean-sweep clear-cutting, the leveling of twenty to forty acres or more of trees and the burning of most waste, from a standpoint of keeping the forests healthy, diverse and sustainable, has been found to be egregiously lacking. Even the conservative Pinchot premise of keeping the forest producing year after year has largely been discarded. In fact, logging the way it is practiced on every national forest in the West sterilizes the woods. Yet the politics of logging have not yet caught up with the ecology.

As the European settlers followed the call of Manifest Destiny westward, the great forests crashed to the earth before them. Now it's estimated that just 5 percent of the aboriginal forests that existed before the coming of the Europeans remains. Some of those remnants grow in Washington, Oregon, northern California and parts of the Rocky Mountain West. Out of the original twenty million acres of Pacific coast ancient forest (which is especially grand and lush because of rainfall that reaches 140 inches or more a year), perhaps two million acres remain. The shining, timbered hills that once seemed without end, that embodied the notion of the limitless frontier, are all but gone.

In the meantime, recent research results have shown that forests that are replanted in the wake of logging are nowhere near as rich in biological diversity as the old growth. Once an ancient forest has been brought to the ground and carted off, it is gone, and with it myriad species. In fact, scientists who study biodiversity say that in recent years it has become clear that the diversity of species in the nation's old-growth forests rivals that of the tropical rain forests, and they have called for an end to the loss of this irreplaceable diversity.

The concept of biodiversity, the study of the wealth of species that are choreographed into a delicate web of life in a forest that has evolved over thousands of years, is only beginning to be understood. While some research on this concept is being done in the park and on the national forests of the Greater Yellowstone, it has been studied most extensively in the cloud-shrouded rain forests of the Pacific coast.

The floor of the ancient, redolent forest along the glacier-fed, turquoise Hoh River is bathed in an emerald half-light as the sun filters through the dense green canopy. Sitka spruce, red cedar, hemlock, and Douglas fir trees, centuries or perhaps a millennium old, soar straight up into the sky, and sword-shaped ferns grow around their bases. Soggy, rotting trunks lay on the ground. Green moss carpets these logs and the soil and hangs like long strands of hair from every branch, absorbing sound and giving the forest an extremely quiet, hushed feeling. The calling of a bird sounds like the cry of a child. These forests are far different from the thick stands of lodgepole pines of the Targhee.

From a high point where the forest opens up, the green quilt of trees that covers the mountainsides of Olympic National Park appears endless. It's an illusion, however, for just outside park boundaries there are clear-cuts everywhere, on hillsides, ridge tops, steep mountain slopes and along the highway. Entire mountains have been stripped. In some clearings, trees have begun to grow and reclaim the land, while in more recent clear-cuts, blackened stumps and slash pines have been left to rot, and new trees have not been planted. The land looks devastated, even to the people who manage the land. In an attempt to explain, they've placed large signs in these clear-cuts that bear the message—some say epitaph—"Managed Forest."

This kind of logging is not the exception, it is the rule. Nearly all of the forests of western Washington, save a few areas like Olympic National Park, are a mosaic of large clear-cuts and small islands and strips of forest.

Along a dirt road deep in the 1.7-million-acre Mount Baker National Forest that lies to the east of Seattle, lumberjacks in hard hats with huge, snarling chainsaws have cut down trees that would take six people holding hands to encircle. For the first time in hundreds of years, sunlight floods the forest floor. Engines whine and roar, and the sweet pungent smell of pine pitch and the sour smell of diesel fumes mingle in the air. Finished here, the sawyers have moved on to another stand. Meanwhile, in the middle of trees they dropped, a tall yellow tower called a spar pole stands, anchored to the ground with taut lines the size of bridge cables, and a large engine beneath it. A metal cable is attached in a loop through two pulleys, one to the spar pole, the other to a tree up at the top of a slope, a system that works much like an old-fashioned clothesline.

At the top pulley, only their white helmets visible above the fallen trees and branches, loggers called choker setters wrap cables around two logs. A signal is given, and the ancient giants, stripped of their branches, are skidded down the slope, the ends smashing through branches on the ground, splintering them and plowing the damp earth. At the end of the ride, a machine called a yarder, with a giant metal claw, picks up the trees like Lincoln Logs and stacks them in a neat pile. From there they'll be loaded onto logging trucks and taken to a sawmill. The result is another cleared patch of land some forty acres in size. Nearby, another forty-acre patch of land is being cleared.

If it were up to them, the loggers and lumber companies would have continued this way until the ancient trees ran out in an estimated fifteen to twenty years. There is a wrinkle in those plans, however, in the form of a bird called the northern spotted owl.

Forest Service wildlife biologist Sonny Paz purses his lips and lets out a call. "*Whoo—who-who—whooo.*" It is the call of the spotted owl, a bird that is reprising in the Pacific Northwest the role the snail darter played in Tennessee. There is no answer to Paz's call, but this is winter and the birds are not active in cold temperatures.

Bird locators such as Paz generally work in the evening, in the spring when the birds are mating. Wearing headlamps, they walk through the forest calling and waiting for a response. If they find a bird, the next step is to find the nest. The biologist takes a mouse and waves it at the owl. Then the mouse is set on a branch, where it is seized by the owl. The bird is followed to the concealed nest, and the young, if any, are counted.

If a nesting site is found, 1,500 to 4,000 acres around the nest site will be placed off-limits to logging to protect the site and the surrounding forest, which the owl depends on for flying squirrels and other food sources.

Paz says he admires the spotted owl, and as he walks down a path through a grove of old trees, he considers himself fortunate to work with the bird. "They like to roost on the ground in the summer, when it's hot," says Paz, a short, thickset man with dark hair. "And if you're quiet, you can come right up to them and actually stroke them." The owl is found only in these temperate forests.

The owl is the focus of a debate over whether the forests should continue to be cut for timber, which would probably wipe the species—and many others—out, or whether the owl, which is dependent on the habitat of ancient forests, should have its habitat protected. An estimated 2,500 pairs remain in northern California, Washington and Oregon. Biologists and others are concerned for the owl. But it is not an owl that stands between the loggers and their trees, a point many have missed. The owl is an indicator species, a proverbial canary in the coal mine. A mycorrhizal fungus grows on the roots of old-growth trees. This kind of fungus encourages the growth of root hairs that allow the trees to fix, or process, nitrogen and other nutrients. Small mammals spread the fungus around so that it falls on the young trees and attaches to the roots. If the spotted owl declines, it may be an indication that there are not enough squirrels and chipmunks—two of the owl's preys—which may mean the trees aren't getting enough fungus to allow them to fix nitrogen, which may mean a serious decline in the overall health of the forest. Other species might well be lost.

After several court challenges, the Forest Service and Bureau of Land Management were ordered to protect the remaining owl habitat, at the expense of those who cut timber for a living, loggers and companies alike. But the debate is far from over.

Rage among those who make their living removing the woods is thermonuclear. The town of Forks, Washington, is spread out along a two-lane highway on the Olympic Peninsula, to the west of Seattle. The peninsula is wet and warm, and is habitat for some of the largest trees on the planet. Huge and numerous holes have been eaten into the blanket of trees around the town. This is home for about 3,400 people and is, in Forest Service jargon, a timber-dependent community. A dyed-in-the-wool logging town, Forks comprises the kind of people environmentalists refer to as "timber beasts."

These towns that grew up rooted in the timber industry are proud of their heritage as logging communities. Tiny museums and historical societies up and down the coast are crammed with old saws and other equipment used to drop trees in the old days. And almost every town has an old black-and-white photo of a gang of loggers, filled to the eyes with purpose, standing around a giant tree with a huge saw-cut in it, just before it drops. Often there is a logger lying in the cut, or several loggers, to show just how big the trees used to be. Most of those trees are gone.

Jerry Leppell was a logger. Stocky, with dark blond hair and a mustache, Leppell owns a saw shop in Forks now, selling chainsaws and accessories. A wall poster for a brand of chainsaws at his shop pictures a leggy young blond woman in cutoff shorts with a hard hat and the caption "We Came. We Sawed. We Conquered." "A lot of people aren't working. People are sitting around, or thinking about going north," he says. "There's work in Alaska. A lot of them are walking away from their house" because they can't meet the payments, he says.

Leppell says the remaining Pacific old growth should take about fifteen years to log. That fifteen years is critical, he says, for that is how long much of the second growth will take to become large enough to log. He is angry that the state, to get around the log shortage, has begun to offer trees for sale that aren't yet mature. "Those are trees my daughter should be cutting," he says.

But there is more than just a job at stake for the loggers. There's a way of life that many loggers in the Northwest feel sets them apart from the suit-and-computer crowd and which they don't want to give up. It is a work characterized by independence. Hard, tough work. Honest work, many loggers say. And fun. "Falling an old-growth tree," Leppell says in all earnestness, "is like having sex. It's thrilling. When the tree comes down and all the limbs and bark start flying, see if you don't get a thrill. You just have to do it once to understand it. People should be jealous who are behind a desk."

And it pays well. At a time when most new jobs being created are service jobs—Motel 6s and Burger Kings, jobs that pay $4 or $5 or $6 an hour—logging, like mining, pays $15 or $20, for people with a minimal education. It's not just loggers losing jobs. Jim English says IFI was forced to close its Medford, Oregon, mill and terminate the high-paying jobs because of the spotted owl.

Loggers have organized themselves to fight against the protection of any more land, both among themselves and with groups like People for the West!, which have been especially active in the Greater Yellowstone. Leppell and Colin King, an injured logger, started the American Loggers Solidarity Movement, which is part of Communities for a Great Northwest, based in Libby, Montana. The group, largely sponsored by the timber industry, is trying to mobilize loggers to fight back in the arena of public opinion, especially in the press. The group estimates that tens of thousands of jobs will be lost because of protection of the spotted owl.

The effort has resulted in some successes. Sporting yellow ribbons, logging truck convoys rolled through Seattle in a peaceful protest. Truckers drove twenty-one loads of donated West Coast lumber to North Carolina for victims of Hurricane Hugo. Houses throughout the West sport signs that read "This family supported by timber dollars." Threatening a boycott, a few years ago loggers convinced Stroh's to pull its beer commercials from an Audubon special on ancient forests on WTBS. The show aired anyway.

More angry sentiments have sprung up as well. Bumper stickers read "Save a Logger. Kill an Owl." One log sailing down the highway on the back of a logging truck had a slogan spray painted on it: "Spotted Owl Motor Home." In Oregon, a Forest Service ranger found a spotted owl that someone had mutilated and hung from a noose. Owners of restaurants in logging towns offered such menu items as "fried spotted owl" and "spotted owl fricassee." In downtown Forks, Leppell and King erected a wooden cross with five wooden cutout owls sitting on top of it and a cluster of flowers on a mock grave at the bottom. A large white sign with red lettering reads "Here lies [*sic*] our children's hopes for the future." "If a grown man can do it in the back of a Volkswagen," asked one logger, "why does an owl need fifteen hundred acres?"

The notion that the ecosystems, the whole planet, is in trouble seems remote, even unimportant to people whose retirement, whose future and whose children's future seem to be melting away.

This kind of sentiment can be found in almost any state in the West where logging is part of the economy. In the Greater Yellowstone, loggers and ranchers are angry about protection of the grizzly bear and the possible reintroduction of the wolf. In New Mexico, they are angry about protection for the gyrfalcon and Mexican spotted owl. In Idaho, economies may have to change to protect salmon.

Peter Morrison sits at a computer at the offices of The Wilderness Society. The keyboard clicks as the sun sets over downtown Seattle. On the wall behind him hangs a poster, with a photograph of a particularly brutal-looking clear-cut. "Pardon me thou bleeding piece of earth," the caption reads, quoting bard Shakespeare, "that I am meek and gentle with these butchers."

Morrison hits a key on a computer, and a map of the Olympic National Forest around Olympic National Park appears in green on the screen. This is the forest prior to 1962, and it is largely green. When he hits another button, however, an overlay appears, showing clear-cuts since then. There appears to be more area clear-cut than there are intact forests. Another button and the logging roads appear on the land, a tangled network of black lines.

No one really knows how much old growth is left, and even precisely how it is defined. The Wilderness Society has extensively mapped the state and estimates that about two million acres remain. The Forest Service, using a different classification, estimates it is more than five million acres.

While the little islands of green between the clear-cuts on Morrison's computer graphics are an effort by the Forest Service and timber industry to preserve some shreds of old-growth habitat, recent research shows that the strategy has not worked, conservationists say. The woods are dying.

Jerry Forest Franklin is a Blodell Professor of Forest Ecosystems at the University of Washington in Seattle. He is also the son of a sawmill operator. In his early sixties, Franklin, with wire-rim spectacles, thinning gray hair and a mustache, is an avuncular-looking man. He is considered one of the most knowledgeable forest ecosystem specialists in the country. Franklin's research, and that of his colleagues, is changing the way people look at forests and has cast serious doubts on the present-day management of America's trees. In fact, the growth of knowledge about forest ecosystems on the sixteen-thousand-acre Andrews Experimental Forest in Oregon has been so startlingly rapid that it illustrates how precious little humans understand about the functioning of natural processes.

Franklin says the reason the spotted owl is losing ground in spite of efforts to save portions of old growth is something called "fragmentation," or the turning of a forest into a large Swiss-cheese-like mosaic of cut and uncut areas. "It makes the forest so small," Franklin said, "it really doesn't function as a forest anymore."

Something called the "edge effect" takes place. At the edge of the islands of forest left behind by loggers, the trees are exposed to the wind and sun, which have a drying effect, changing the habitat. Because trees regulate heat, temperatures inside the island drop. Winds blow down the trees around the edge, and species that dwell near the edge find their habitat has changed dramatically. Cut off from the rest of the gene pool or suddenly exposed to predators, they often die out. Many islands of trees are so small they are virtually all edge, and the rate of extinction soars.

Clear-cuts pose even greater ecological problems. The trees are simply stripped away, and the waste is piled and burned. New trees are planted, and in the rainy Northwest they grow relatively quickly. But an in-depth study that began on the Andrews Experimental Forest in 1970 has recently yielded results showing that these second-generation tree plantations are biological deserts compared to old-growth forests, with a tenth the number of species. When the forests are cut again, they lose their vitality and productivity. Yet these kind of plantation forests are what is being planted as the original forests are leveled. It takes more—far more—than trees to make a forest.

Recent Andrews Forest research hints at the role that mites, spiders and centipedes, which live on and beneath the forest floor, play in the long-term health of forest. The diversity of these unseen species is so great—3,400 at one study site—that scientists say it rivals the diversity of species in the tropical rain forests. The species process branches, moss and other organic debris into smaller and smaller pieces, freeing the nutrients and allowing them to be taken up by the plants.

The problem with clear-cuts is this. When a forest is logged, the woody debris that once littered the forest floor is gone. This material contains the insect populations and organic material—called a biological legacy—that would begin again a rich, diverse new forest. The newly planted trees, meanwhile, are evenly spaced, and all grow taller together. In an old-growth forest, the trees are a great variety of sizes, types and ages—a multilayered canopy, which provides habitat for a variety of plants, insects and fungus. Snags, or dead trees, for example, provide homes for insects and for cavity nesters such as woodpeckers. "Foresters felt [planting trees] represented good stewardship," says Franklin, who has worked extensively on the Andrews Forest. "We simply didn't have any appreciation for the complexity and importance of these ecosystems." Chaos, in other words, means health to the ecosystem. Pinchot's clean forest works if the goal is only to cut lumber over the long term, but is detrimental to many other values. Clear-cutting trees beyond their capacity for regrowth is even more radical, for not only is the health of the forest destroyed, but so is the ability of the land to sustain logging over the long term. What is needed, scientists say, is a Pinchot approach that sustains not only trees, but insects, birds and mammals along with recreation, research and other opportunities for humans.

Ecosystem science, Franklin says, is in the embryonic stage. The irony is that as scientists begin to understand the complexity and importance of intact forest ecosystems, the intact forests are on the verge of disappearing.

Nowhere is the "you don't know what you've got till it's gone" principle more graphically illustrated than in the case of the Pacific yew tree. A derivative of the bark of this tree, which grows only beneath the canopy of the ancient rain forest along the coast, has proven successful in treating some types of cancer. But the cutting of old growth and the collection of yew bark for cancer research have placed the tree's survival in jeopardy.

The yew thrives in the high-humidity conditions beneath taller hemlock and fir trees, and its needles are broad to take advantage of the dim light that filters down. When the old-growth overstory is cut, the yews get "sunburned" and stop reproducing. Some die. The yew was also a weed tree to loggers, something that blocked their cutting of more valuable trees. Just a few years ago it was piled and burned as waste.

Weyerhaeuser, a giant lumber company based in Tacoma, Washington, is studying the feasibility of raising yew-tree bark commercially to make taxol for research and eventually treatment. However, yew trees are among the slowest-growing plants in the forest because taxol, which slows cell division in cancer patients, also affects the tree's rate of growth. Synthesizing the molecule has proven difficult and may be years away. The only source of taxol now is wild yew trees. A pest a few years ago, the yew is now priceless.

Clear-cutting has also been killing streams, which create the Northwest's multimillion-dollar fishery, and sustain animal life of all kinds. A stream is more than a channel of water running across the ground. It has a life of its own, but a life that depends in great measure on the forest around it. Leaves, needles, cones, twigs and other organic material tumble into the stream. Large boles, or tree trunks, crash into the stream, pooling and slowing water, allowing tiny woodland creatures to do their job. Downed trees are vital to diversity, for they create plunge pools and myriad other niches. They are baffles, keeping streams from speeding and channeling and eroding. They provide cover for fish and other species. Water, as it flows over a log, acquires dissolved oxygen, vital to fish. Litter is the primary source of energy for the life in the streams. Wood gives up nitrogen, a critical source element for growth.

In the smallest, or first-order, stream—you can step across it—types of insects called shredders, grazers and collectors process the organic material that has fallen into the water. Predators feed on those insects and other invertebrates. As the stream gets larger and larger, the creatures get larger and different, but the process of breakdown continues.

As the stream becomes third- or fourth-order, things change. The canopy over the stream has a gap in it. Light falls on the water, and algae blooms. Cutthroat trout, tailed frogs and the Pacific giant salamander are found here, feeding on the organic matter delivered by the tributaries. Moss covers boulders and logs. Each stream processes wood and other litter and in turn provides a ready-made food source for the others below. Finally, these streams flow into the great rivers. Insects of all kinds pour from the streams into the rivers. Fish wait at the mouth of the tributaries, feeding voraciously. And the rivers feed into the ocean, carrying dinner and breakfast and lunch for salmon and a host of other fish. Whales feed on the salmon. It all begins with twigs and bark and other raw material falling into a stream that a child could jump across.

An intact forest serves human society in other ways. Each fall, warm Pacific rainstorms—called the Hawaiian Express—sweep ashore in the northwestern United States. These rains tend to arrive after some snow cover has accumulated. In an old-growth forest, the snow is spread out in the treetops and slowly melts, to drip to the ground and be absorbed, and held in place by the roots. With hundreds of thousands of mountain acres devoid of trees, as well as homes and asphalt and concrete covering thousands more acres, this gradual absorption does not take place. When a rain falls on snow on a clear-cut, the snow and water rush to the streams and onto the lowlands. With rivers overflowing their banks and water rushing down streets and parking lots, flooding becomes a nightmare. Some three thousand people in the Seattle area were left homeless in a flood in 1991 that caused $150 million worth of damage. Clear-cuts are partly to blame.

In 1992, the Pacific Fishery Management Council placed the most restrictions ever on the salmon fishing industry in the Pacific Ocean off of California, Washington and Oregon, for a lack of salmon. While in 1982 fishermen caught 1.2 million chinook, the top commercial salmon, in 1992 that number was 268,000. Contributors to the decline of fish, biologists say, include dams and home developments along the rivers. And logging. When ground is denuded, the soil washes into rivers, clogs them, and suffocates salmon spawning. "It's years and years of habitat disintegration and destruction," says Jack Coon, salmon staff officer for the Pacific Fishery Management Council.

The cost of the shutdown to the economy of coastal towns that depend on fishing was pegged at $75 million for a single year. A restoration of the fisheries may cost as much as $1 billion. But in rivers such as Hood Canal and the Klamath, salmon populations may be too low to ever recover. A century ago, sixteen million salmon returned from the ocean to spawn in the Columbia River. Now a million or so return. One of the saddest stories is the Snake River sockeye salmon, a subspecies. (There are other sockeye in other rivers.) In 1991, a lone female and a few males made the nine-hundred-mile run from the Pacific to their ancestral home at Redfish Lake in central Idaho. In 1992, a single male made the trip. They have been caught and are being bred in captivity.

The situation has pitted angry fishermen against loggers, whom they blame for the decline of their livelihood. In 1982 in Oregon, 3,269 fishing boats landed salmon, mostly chinook and coho. In 1991, there were 1,217 boats fishing. In Washington during the decade, the number dropped from 2,253 to 811, and in California, from 4,013 to 1,763. In essence, the income being made by the logging industry is being paid for by fishermen and people who must pay for flood damage, for a loss of forests and other things.

More false economics, environmentalists say. These and other costs of logging are simply not figured into the economic assessment when trees are sold.

It's difficult to imagine two sides being further apart. It's not only economic: The debate at its heart is a religious one. To cut the forests, environmentalists imply, is a sin. "It's a legacy that belongs to all Americans just as much as the timber towns," says Jean Durning, The Wilderness Society representative in Seattle. "These forests have been evolving since the last ice age. They are the most magnificent forests anywhere, a biological legacy. They are forests that deserve the name green cathedral."

Contrast that with the view of the timber companies and loggers. They refer to old growth as "decadent" and "overmature." Not to log these stands, they say, is to waste them, to leave the wood on the ground to rot. A different kind of sin.

A group that has done the most to turn the debate over the environment into a religious one is a peculiar Western phenomenon called Earth First! (always with an exclamation point). Earth First!ers believe in Deep Ecology, the notion that a cosmic force is manifest in nature. They are environmental vigilantes who view themselves as a warrior society arrayed against the forces destroying the planet. Earth First!ers have gained notoriety for their monkey-wrenching, or the disabling of equipment they view as destructive. Radical environmentalists have sabotaged bulldozers, Caterpillar tractors and other logging equipment. They have pounded metal spikes into trees so that lumber companies will not cut them and send them to sawmills where the spikes, when hit by a saw blade, will explode. They are also involved in acts of civil disobedience, especially when it comes to logging. Silver-helmeted loggers have come to work and started bulldozer and chainsaws, only to find the way blocked by protesters, their arms linked, their voices raised in song, perhaps "Burn That Dozer" sung to the tune of "Hold That Tiger." Other Earth First!ers have camped out on platforms in old-growth trees about to be dropped.

One of the most dramatic stories concerns the Medicine Tree. Protection of ancient trees is an Earth First! priority. Some one hundred residents of Garberville, a small town in northern California, wanted to stop the logging of an ancient grove of redwoods on land owned by Georgia Pacific. The site is considered sacred by the Sinkyone Indians, and was adjacent to a state park. One of the trees, estimated to be three thousand years old, is known as the Medicine Tree. From the grove, says eco-activist Mike Roselle, you can hear the ocean surf pounding and sea lions barking. "Nobody in their right mind, except a hardened logger, could cut those trees down," Roselle said. "How could anyone look at those trees and say, 'Oh boy, hot tub material'?"

A local environmental group tried to get a temporary restraining order to stop the logging, based on a California law that governs forestry practices on private land, but was told by the judge that a TRO could not be levied until logging actually commenced.

Roselle, a veteran of the antiwar movement, held a week-long training session in direct-action techniques for locals. Meanwhile, an illegal, twenty-four-hour camp was set up on Georgia Pacific land in case the lumber company quietly commenced logging. When loggers began revving up their chainsaws, environmentalists on watch got the word back to Garberville. The owner of a movie theater on Main Street put up a message on the marquee: "GP IS CUTTING TREES!"

Loggers felled a few trees during the first day. But that night a hundred or so people, Roselle said, caravanned to the grove. They camped at an archaeological site near the Medicine Tree, a tree so large it took seven people holding hands to circle it. When the loggers showed up for work in the morning, they were surprised by a determined band of "tree huggers." With TV cameras watching as protesters blocked their path and circled the Medicine Tree, the loggers didn't go to work. Meanwhile, lawyers for the local environmental group frantically tried to get a TRO.

The next day, however, the timber company was prepared. Numerous sheriff's deputies and company security people showed up with two buses. And as the protesters, wearing bright colors and balloons and blowing airhorns so they would be seen, dashed among the cathedral of green to slow the loggers down, they were hauled off to jail. As the police would take away one group of protesters, a handful of others would rush in. The logging was slowed, and finally, the restraining order came through.

But the venue of the case was changed to another jurisdiction, so the injunction was void. While a new injunction was sought, Georgia Pacific resumed logging. The next morning, loggers were determined to cut the trees—Earth First!ers or not. Trees crashed as protesters darted among the giants. One woman suffered a fractured collarbone when a falling redwood hit another, smaller tree and the latter pinned her to the ground. People were arrested. Roselle and another protester moved to block the loggers from the Medicine Tree. Roselle was taken away by the authorities as the other protester tried to stand between a chainsaw and the tree. An angry logger swung at him with an axe—and missed. Chainsaws began tearing deeply into the tree, sawdust and chips showering the ground. Then, in a modern-day version of the nick-of-time cavalry and its welcome bugle call, the sheriff arrived with a bullhorn. The restraining order had come through. "Anyone who continues cutting this tree will be arrested," he shouted.

The protesters replaced the pieces of the Medicine Tree with an asphalt salve used for sawn limbs, and Indians performed a healing ceremony for the tree. The 7,100-acre grove was purchased in 1987 by the California Trust for Public Lands for addition to the Sinkyone Wilderness State Park. The Medicine Tree, says Roselle proudly, is still standing.

Many of the public forests of the West, however, have not shared that fate. They have been cut down and carted away. As the logs have left, so in many cases have the forests, the wildlife, the jobs and, in the opinion of many, the future.

Indeed, at the end of 1992, Idaho Forest Industries closed the mill at St. Anthony for good, claiming environmentalists had appealed so many sales, locking them up for months in administrative processes, that there was not enough timber left on the Targhee to sustain it. English said that IFI had wanted environmentalists to back off on their opposition. "We had meetings with environmentalists to try and keep the mill open, to keep one shift going," says English. "I think we could have come to some agreement, but not with someone as difficult to negotiate with as Louisa Willcox. There is no negotiation with Louisa. I would categorize it as impossible."

Environmentalists blame overcutting. The diseased stands were all cut, and to begin cutting healthy trees on a forest that has been so ravaged, they say, would be biological ruin. Whatever the case, the 105 jobs the mill provided at one time are gone. "Clear-cutting has been a disaster," says Lyle Beard. "If it weren't for that, the timber would have been here forever."

5
Water Flows Uphill

THE HENRY'S FORK IS A WIDE. FERTILE STRETCH OF MEANDERing river in Idaho, which flows from the base of the Island Park Dam, in the southwest part of the Yellowstone ecosystem. On a deep black night with a new moon, and snowflakes swirling, an airboat, the kind with a giant fan on the back, skims along the river, occasionally over ice and snow, in search of trumpeter swans.

The front of the craft has brilliant aircraft landing lights attached, and once the swans are spotted, the boat, lights blazing in the swirling snow, zooms up to them. With luck, the birds are hypnotized by the spectacle. "The snow and the lights create a kaleidoscopic effect," says Ruth Shea, a trumpeter swan biologist who works with the U.S. Fish and Wildlife Service. "It confuses them and they are easy to catch." The gentle, big birds—they can weigh more than twenty-five pounds and have a wingspan of seven feet—are picked up by wildlife experts on the boat. The swans offer no resistance. The biologists tuck the head of the bird under its wing, and it is placed in a box for a trip to a new home.

Though the swans have lived on the Henry's Fork for generations, swan experts have come to the conclusion that life on this river—which is a wildlife refuge—is no longer safe for many of the birds.

* * *

The Henry's Fork population of trumpeters—so called for their brassy, two-tone warbling call—are a remnant population of a species that was once widely distributed throughout most of North America. Slaughtered commercially for their feathers, which were used to decorate hats, and for their quills, which became ink pens, by the turn of the twentieth century the birds were thought to be extinct. In 1919, however, a handful of trumpeters were spotted in Yellowstone National Park, where they had taken refuge. Later, a small, separate population of swans was discovered in Alaska.

Adult trumpeters pass their knowledge of where to feed and migrate on to their young. But during the years the swans were hunted, those that were migrating out of the Yellowstone ecosystem to less harsh climates were being killed, leaving behind only those swans who wouldn't, or didn't know how to, migrate. This behavior saved them. A few years ago, ironically, that same behavior almost wiped them out.

In the summer, the trumpeters spend their time in numerous places in and around the ecosystem, on potholes and lakes. Come winter they all flock to the Henry's Fork in Idaho. The river flows across the Island Park Caldera, which is to the west of Yellowstone, and is smaller than and separate from the Yellowstone Caldera. This Idaho caldera has created geothermal features, and warm springs bubble up and flow into the river. As winter comes down on the Yellowstone plateau, the birds gather around the warm springs and eat the vegetation that grows abundantly in the warm flows.

In 1988, on the heels of a summer of drought, a brutal cold front swept through the area. The swans might have survived the blast of Arctic air. However, the federal Bureau of Reclamation, which manages the water behind the Island Park Dam, decided to send only a minimal amount of water down the Henry's Fork, so there would be water in the reservoir for potato farmers and power generation come summer.

As temperatures plummeted and the wind howled in from the north, sending the windchill factor down to somewhere near one hundred degrees below zero, biologists feared the worst for the trumpeter swans. Ruth Shea and others came to the river to find, to their horror, that it had frozen, save for four little pools kept open by the warm springs. In these pools four hundred to five hundred swans were huddled against the cold. The ice and the riverbank, meanwhile, were littered with the bodies of a hundred dead swans.

There was simply not enough flow to keep the river from freezing up. The ice cut the swans off from the aquatic vegetation they eat and they starved to death in the cold.

Volunteers swung into action. A grain storer and his friends loaded up his truck on a Sunday and drove it to the Henry's Fork for the remaining swans. A few days later, the farmers and Idaho Power gave the federal government permission to release some of their allotted water to open the river back up to save the rest of the swans.

For the long term, however, it was decided that the climate on the Henry's Fork is simply too harsh, so most of the swans must be moved elsewhere. There are only some 2,500 swans in this Rocky Mountain flock (the Alaska population has 13,000), and another freeze-out could decimate the population. That's why waterfowl biologists have moved hundreds of trumpeters—to a wildlife refuge in Oregon, to the Snake River in western Idaho, to the Green River in Wyoming. Even actor Harrison Ford has a pair living on a pond on his ranch near Jackson. With any luck, they will forget all about the Henry's Fork, Shea says, and there will not be seven hundred but less than four hundred trumpeters living on the Henry's Fork, the number she thinks the vegetation can support.

Water—or the paucity of it—is the West's greatest theme.

The crux of the problem is that in the deserts and semideserts of the West—most of the region gets nine to fifteen inches a year—there are far more people who want to do many more things than the amount of precious water will allow. It's a simple statement that has and continues to flood the West with contention and confrontation. The plots, subplots and sub-subplots about western water are as labyrinthine as the connections of pipes, reservoirs, ditches and streams that have been cobbled together in the West to send water rolling across the landscape. A major theme for water these days, though, is the three-cornered battle between the cities and natural systems and agriculturalists over who will get the West's limited supply of water.

Orville Tomky strides into a cafe on Highway 96—Main Street in Olney Springs, Colorado—called Ding's, and Ding herself comes out from the back to say hello. Tomky, tall and rangy and bearing a passing resemblance to Walter Brennan, takes off his straw hat, eases into a booth and sets his big, weathered hands on a worn Formica-topped table. A sign on the wall says KWITCHERBELYAKIN. Tomky pays no heed. As several farmers in bib overalls sit around drinking iced tea and talking rain, Tomky talks about a different kind of water: the kind that used to flow to Crowley County in southeastern Colorado in great abundance, but that now has been reduced to a trickle, as irrigation water gets diverted to other uses. "When I first came here to Olney Springs in 1951, there was a grain elevator, a hardware store, two cafes, three grocery stores, one bar and two filling stations," he says, nodding out the window to a graveyard-quiet collection of closed buildings. "Now there's a cafe and a convenience store." He sips his iced tea and adds, in a loud voice: "They've raped this county, is what they've done."

Doug Kemper walks from the coffee machine on the fourth floor of the Aurora, Colorado, municipal building and sits down at his desk, which is positioned in front of a window that overlooks part of the urban sprawl that is Aurora: a shopping mall, with a huge new brick Montgomery Ward's on one end, a parking lot swarming with cars, a Pizza Hut, a Wendy's, beyond it more roads, more cars and more buildings that continue in an urban jumble off to the horizon. In the far distance, rain called virga hangs from the bottom of huge, fluffy white clouds, rain that will evaporate before it reaches the ground, water promised but not delivered. "The projection," says the red-bearded, red-headed Kemper, manager of water resources for the city of Aurora, "is that Aurora will grow to 500,000. It is now about 222,000. We need the water."

They are huge voracious flowers or weeds—depending on your point of view—that sprawl across the arid landscape, and the West's great cities require copious amounts of water to continue their growth. Rivers near these cities have been drained, dammed and driven to extinction to keep things green and growing, and aquifers—giant underground rock cavities—have been emptied of their water. Ostensibly these aquifers fill up again, or recharge, when it rains, but some are being drained faster than they fill and so are being emptied. Some contain fossil groundwater—water that filled caverns thousands of years ago. Sealed by geologic forces, they are currently being mined for their water. A one-shot deal, the water will be used for showers and lawns or farming and drinking and then be gone forever, along with any options for other uses in the future.

Growth is the unbending credo of these cities, because new subdivisions and businesses fuel their economies, and a growing economy, by this way of thinking, is a healthy economy. People moving to town means more people bringing more businesses, and more people who have jobs means more people paying taxes and buying homes and refrigerators and stereos and cars. As a consequence, there is a great deal more money to be made channeling farm or ranch water to urban areas where houses, shopping malls, office buildings and factories are put up, than there is to be made flooding soil to grow crops.

The rule governing much of the West's water, however, is something called prior appropriation—"first in time, first in line." Those who claimed the water first, back in the 1800s or the early part of this century, have title to use that amount every year, as they would property. If their allotment of water is all that is in the stream, downstream users are out of luck. It's a contrast to riparian rights in the East, where those with stream or lake rights cannot do things that would decrease their neighbor's flow.

Prior appropriation was created by the miners who needed great quantities of water for their activities, though now all users play by the rule. What is done with the water does not matter, as long as—according to the law of most states—it is put to beneficial use. That is, it is removed from the stream and used to make money. And so the concept of water ranching or water farming is flourishing—buying the land solely for the water rights, retiring the land and taking the water elsewhere.

The West is thought of as a giant cattle ranch, but farming is important as well. Dryland farmers grow wheat in Montana, and irrigators grow potatoes in Idaho, peppers in New Mexico, cotton, sorghum and citrus in Arizona, rice and almonds in California. Many ranchers grow alfalfa, so they can cut and put up hay to see their cattle through the winter. But the decision is being made, by dint of the marketplace, that farming is not that important anymore, at least not when it comes to the growth of urban areas. Nowhere is it written that the water needs to be used for farming.

A milestone in federal water policy came in late 1992 when Congress passed the Omnibus Water Act, which officially took the agricultural emphasis out of water policy. It mandates that cities get water that had been reserved for agriculture, raises the rates charged farmers and requires that some water used in the past for farming be left in the rivers for maintenance of the ecosystem. One of the places these changes are happening fastest is in Colorado.

The Arkansas River roars down out of the Colorado Rockies, near the mining town of Leadville and the continental divide, the kind of river seen on a calendar: through canyons lined with boulders and tall pines. A turbulent mountain river at first, it settles down and flows calmly through the prairie, much of the year the color of chocolate milk. Some 1,500 miles long, it eventually empties into the Missouri.

The soil along the Arkansas River in eastern Colorado is good, rich, thick soil that produces especially fine melons, sweet, succulent and flavorful. Like the melons, the towns here—Rocky Ford, Swink, Olney Springs, Sugar City, Ordway and La Junta—were nourished by the richness of the soil. But this part of the world, known as the Melon Valley, gets only a little more than ten inches of moisture a year. The soil needs water from a river.

Some of the water used on the ground here comes from Twin Lakes Reservoir, two hundred miles away in the mountains. The water is released from the reservoir into the Arkansas when the farmers want it, and three days later, at noon, when it is figured the water has reached the farms near Ordway, the head gate of the Colorado Canal is opened to allow the water to flow in. From the fifty-mile-long canal, which was dug in the 1870s, the water spills into smaller ditches and even smaller concrete troughs that run like arteries through the fields that people like Orville and his wife Loretta own. The water floods over the side of the ditches and inundates the fields, seeping down into the soil, embracing the seed and coaxing out life, until finally tiny green shoots burst through the soil. Tropists, searching for the sun.

Orville and Loretta Tomky, when newly wed, bought the beginnings of their farm here in the Arkansas River valley in 1951. It's rolling land, none of the mountains that Colorado is famous for, but land that rolls gently on. Huge Chinese elms frequently dot the countryside, many of them planted by the first settlers. Orville, from Brush, Colorado, was fresh from the service when he moved here. He had served in the U.S. Army's 10th Mountain Division in

Italy, the infantry on skis, searching the ground for land mines in front of tanks, packing mules and working as a demolitionist. The Tomkys started with eighty acres. Then, by adding a little here, a little there, they increased the parcel to the point where Orville, his son and his son-in-law now farm eight hundred acres together. Mostly alfalfa, tomatoes, corn and famous Rocky Ford melons, including the Rocky Sweet, developed here, a cross between a cantaloupe and a honeydew.

The population of Crowley County peaked with the 1920 census —6,383 souls. It has been downhill ever since. Drought in the thirties and again in the fifties forced people out. The sugar beet industry took a pounding at the hands of foreign imports in the 1950s, and the sugar beet mill at Sugar City was boarded up in the 1960s. The real body blow to the region began in 1968, says Orville, when the Crowley County Land and Development Company, or CLADCO, showed up in Crowley County, checkbook in hand, and offered farmers $328 an acre-foot for their land and water—the going price was then about $200—for about 28,000 acres' worth. The farmer could live in his homestead, but the land and water belonged to CLADCO.

CLADCO officials said they were going to raise lettuce and Christmas trees, but they didn't get very far. In 1975 they sold 28,000 acres of land and 55 percent of the water that went with it to Bill Foxley and the Foxley Cattle Company out of Omaha, Nebraska. The Foxley Cattle Company hired locals, some of them landless farmers, and started plowing. It tore down many of the houses that had been abandoned on that land. But it did something else that Orville Tomky will never forgive Bill Foxley for—it separated the water from the farmland. Foxley sold 28,000 acre-feet of water (an acre-foot can cover an acre of land to the depth of one foot, or a football field to the depth of ten inches) to the growing towns on Colorado's east slope: Aurora, Colorado Springs, Pueblo and Pueblo West. Eventually the cities bought up 90 percent of the Colorado Canal water, the major artery to the fields of Crowley County. In one fell swoop, three fifths of the irrigated land in the county was mothballed, rendered useless to farmers without its annual blessing from Mother Arkansas, giver of life. Crowley County's economic condition went from serious to grave.

There is constant reminder of the loss of water. Part of the deal was that the land would be revegetated. While some of the purchasers, like the city of Aurora, have lived up to that agreement, others, like the city of Colorado Springs, have not. Land covered with spotted knapweed, tansy mustard and other weeds rolls on for miles in Crowley County. "We're surrounded by one goddamn weed patch after another," Orville Tomky says. From them, seeds blow onto his property and cost him in increased use of herbicide. Tomky is also afraid his water will dry up should a very dry August come. When there are dozens of farmers taking water from the canal, each loses a little—it soaks into the unlined canal. But when there are only a handful of farmers, there are fewer to share the loss.

This movement of water from the country to the city in the West is nothing new. The great archetype is the Owens River of California, which drains the White and Sierra mountains and was dried up in the early twentieth century. The Paiute Indians, using a technology learned from the Spanish, were the first to divert water from the Owens River and use it for farming. White settlers came along in the 1860s and coveted the Indians' land. Indians were accused of rustling cattle, tensions rose, and someone murdered a white woman and child. White citizens formed a militia and killed 150 Paiutes, 100 of which they drove into Owens Lake and drowned. The white folks had the land and irrigation know-how, borrowed from the departed Paiutes. It was a rich valley and farming took off.

Perpetrating a series of legal subterfuges and ruses, an official from the U.S. Reclamation Service, Joseph Lippincott, secretly moonlighting for the city of Los Angeles, scouted the Owens Valley to identify the best sources of water. Then the City of Angels proceeded to buy water rights. It drained the river, lake and valley dry, of both water and inhabitants.

It's a repetitious pattern, as the cities continue to grow and the rural areas decline. In Arizona in 1989, the state legislature passed a law that required new subdivisions to have a hundred-year supply of water: it mandated conservation laws and also allowed water ranching. Developers went on a hunt all over the state. The city of Phoenix went to remote La Paz County, a sparsely populated farming area near Arizona's western border, and bought a ranch, laying claim to 14 percent of the fossil aquifer's water, to be pumped back to Phoenix through the Central Arizona Project. After a huge outcry by rural areas, and after they hired former Arizona governor Bruce

Babbitt (who had urged the passing of the law to begin with) to lobby for their interests in the legislature, the law allowing water ranching was repealed (though the sales that had taken place stand). There's been a lull ever since, but no one thinks the fight is over. "It's like a war," says La Paz County commissioner Gene Fisher. "Did we come out of it unscathed? No. We took hits on it. But it's over for now."

The city of Las Vegas (Spanish for "The Meadows") was eager to keep its green felt meadows green and its reputation as the fastest-growing city in the United States intact. So water officials laid claim to a huge unappropriated underground reservoir beneath twenty-six sparsely populated ranching valleys in three rural counties to the north. They scaled their proposal down after a huge public outcry. The only reason they filed on it in the first place, says Patricia Mulroy, general manager of the Las Vegas Valley Water District, is because they heard California was going to claim it. "Without it, there would have been a moratorium on building in Las Vegas by the year 2000." And in Colorado, a private company filed for rights on a huge rechargeable aquifer in the San Luis Valley, just north of the New Mexico border.

Locals in all three locales are up in arms, and fear their future will disappear along with their water as it gurgles down the pipeline to Denver, Las Vegas or Phoenix. "If they take your water," says Nita Bowman, a county commissioner in Arizona's La Paz County, "it takes away your right to grow."

California is the thirstiest of all, a burgeoning giant that makes everyone else nervous. Thirty million lived there in 1990. Fifty million may live there by 2010. With a great deal of political power and money, California is scouting Idaho, Oregon, Washington and other neighbors as sources for water to be piped in so California can continue its growth. Some of the water will be taken away from California agriculture, thanks to the passage of the Omnibus Water Act.

Crowley County, Colorado, now has a population of three thousand—it lost eight hundred people between 1980 and 1990. That three thousand includes nine hundred prisoners at a medium-security prison recently built there. As the spigot has been slowly closed, the land has reverted to weeds or rangeland, draining the county of its tax base. When farmland is producing melons or tomatoes, the farmer pays the county $5.84 an acre each year. For rangeland, that payment drops to 25 cents a year. The dwindling tax base is breaking the county's back, says Orville Tomky. "When Aurora pulls out, I predict we won't have enough money to run the county, and we'll go bankrupt," he says. Until Foxley sold out in 1968, there was about 56,000 acres of irrigated land in Crowley County, a county that covers about 360,000 acres. In 1992, there were about 10,000 acres in the county still being irrigated. When Aurora takes its 8,000 acre-feet of water, it leaves 2,000 acres still in irrigation. Orville Tomky and his family own 800 of those.

Orville Tomky's world is divided into two kinds of people in Crowley County—those who sold their water, and those, like himself, who didn't. Those who sold their water sold their county down the drain, betrayed their neighbors. "It's a moral issue," he says. "Do you have a right to sell out your neighbors? Your town? Your county?"

A sad aspect of the affair, says Loretta Tomky, are farmers who still live on their land but have no water. They sold out at age forty or forty-five, and now are lost. "They're farmers," she says. "That's what they do. Now they can't farm." Orville got into a shouting match with neighbors who sold out and who then tried to use water that belongs to the Tomkys so they could farm again. These are people he has known for forty years.

As the water goes, so goes the county, spiraling further and further down toward what many fear is ghost town status. The farmers retired on their land or left the county, so there are fewer farmers buying feed and seed and tractor parts. And clothes and cars, and even dinner at Ding's. The main streets in the little towns show it. They are almost museums of the 1950s, with locally owned clothing stores that sell "Dad and Lad" clothing or cafes that still make their pies fresh daily. Many businesses are simply closed, as people drive to the Walmart in La Junta.

The talk here is full of used-to-bes. Used to be that there were four schools in Crowley County, now there's one. Used to be that there were dozens of farmers who sold melons and tomatoes and corn at stands along Highway 50. Now there's just a couple. Used to be that farms were passed on to the kids. Now there's nothing to pass on. "It breaks up families," says Loretta Tomky. "People who used to farm with their kids don't anymore. The kids move to town to take a job." She shrugs.

To Loretta and Orville, watching their county dry up conjures up feelings of powerlessness and frustration and sadness, always a sadness, similar perhaps to watching virga. "What can you do?" Loretta says, with a shrug. "You know what they say. Water flows uphill to money."

Doug Kemper says he sympathizes with the people in Crowley County but says the cities along the east slope of the Colorado Rockies need water to grow, to stay vital. "The value of water to municipalities is three times what it is to agricultural areas," he says. It is time, he says, to make hard decisions. "We have a free market system. Resources get reallocated. It's got to be dealt with as if it were a real estate transaction. It's a changing world. Agriculture has changed. The area around Denver has changed."

"The cities had a future," says Ken Weber, a Colorado University anthropology professor who studied the decline of Crowley County. "The farmers had the water and they didn't have a future."

Aurora is not alone in its need. It is part of the Denver megalopolis, cities like Thornton, Englewood, Westminster and Arvada, which together have a population of 1.8 million. Water has become especially important since the demise of Two Forks.

The Two Forks Dam was a 1982 proposal by Denver and eight other towns to place a dam on the South Platte River to create a huge reservoir, about fifteen thousand acre-feet of water for Aurora alone. It used to be that the Bureau of Reclamation would build such facilities, but an era of massive federal subsidy, the era of the "water buffaloes," ended in 1979, when the Carter administration said it was ending all funding for new dams.

The city of Aurora figures that it needs about one acre-foot per five people per year, and there are about three people per tap, or per home. Before the idea of a new dam came up, Aurora went over the divide. The east slope of the Rockies has for decades often gone to the much more lightly populated west slope, and much of Aurora's water comes from there. There are several giant tunnels that bring water through the mountains and into the city. Aurora filed a claim on the Taylor River, a tributary to the Colorado, thirteen thousand acre-feet. "One big hit," Kemper says, "for all our water needs." Officials claimed what they say was unappropriated water on the west side of the divide. Local ranchers were hopping mad. Worried about being turned into a water ranch, they went to court to fend off the unwelcome advance. That was in 1986. In 1991, already into legal fees for $2 million and with a raft of litigation left to go, Aurora pulled out. A dry hole. Water battles often come down to staying power in water courts: a matter of who has the deepest pockets.

The Two Forks proposal was next and looked extremely promising. The coalition sunk $40 million into the project, $6 million from Aurora alone. In 1990, however, the Environmental Protection Agency decided the dam would cause too much environmental damage and vetoed the project. Another dry hole. An expensive dry hole. The scramble by the municipalities to find enough water to float them into the future was on.

Finally, says Kemper, "we went back to our roots—agricultural transfers." Aurora had gained independence from Denver's water monopoly in the 1950s when it bought the rights to thirty thousand acres of high-altitude ranch country. This time it looked to the east. In Crowley County in 1987, Aurora bought 8,100 acre-feet at $3,000 an acre-foot. (An acre-foot is paid for once—if a farmer has one hundred acres of water rights and gets $3,000 per acre, he would get a one time payment of $300,000.) Those who sell out have the first hundred feet of their irrigation ditches filled in.

Aurora does not waste water, Kemper says. "We have one of the most stringent conservation programs in the country," he says. "Sonic leak detectors, permits for people to have lawns, education on water conservation in kindergarten through twelfth grade, and wastewater use." Water in Aurora costs the user about $1.70 per thousand gallons, and the per capita use is about 160 gallons per day.

What about the growth? Doesn't anyone complain that Aurora's growth from 220,000 to 500,000 people might adversely affect the quality of life in the suburb? "No," says Kemper. "Just the opposite. People argue that if we don't grow, the quality of life will decline." Without growth, he says, the economy stagnates.

Aurora is still looking for eighty thousand acre-feet of water, but it says that rural areas have nothing to fear, that Aurora and other cities will get water by making things more efficient and picking up a little bit here and there. In fact, says Kemper, the notion of cities raiding farm towns for water is overblown. "The demise of Two Forks was not a cue ball into Denver that sent a rack of people scrambling all over the map for water," Kemper says.

"That," Orville Tomky says, is a "load of shit." "You want to dry up this part of the state and send everybody to Denver?" he says, as he tools his pickup truck down a dirt road near Olney Springs, speaking in a tone that indicates he couldn't think of anything sillier. "There's enough damn urban sprawl. There's traffic and crime and gangs there and everything else. You want to live like that? I don't. If that's progress, hell."

Tomky cannot loosen his grip on anger, especially toward CLADCO, and Foxley, which he says started it all. "If I was as old then as I am now and had my family raised," Tomky says as his pickup jounces past weed patches. "I'd have gone out on night patrol and shot three of them. Maybe they would have caught me, or maybe not." He says it in a way that is neither kidding nor boasting. Water is that important here.

The Denver area, meanwhile, sits on a huge ace in the hole. Beneath the greater metropolitan area is a 300-million-acre-foot fossil aquifer, half of it recoverable. There are a few wells that penetrate the pool of clean cold water, and pull water to the surface to use, but mostly it's being held in reserve. "The aquifer is being managed for a hundred-year life," Kemper says. "We're keeping it available for droughts."

Serious drought is no stranger to the West, and there are predictions the desert will return to reclaim the cities that occupy the thin margin of an arid environment. It has happened before. With the Anasazi. Tree ring analysis shows that an unbroken drought lasted between 1276 and 1299. It's believed that an extended drought struck the Southwest, desiccating the once great agricultural society that spread through the canyons and crevices of the Colorado plateau, a society that was at the peak of its efflorescence. The Anasazi could have stored two or three years of corn, beans or other crops, in large round jars called ollas, or in rock shelters, but after that they were finished. As snow and rainfall decreased, the water table lowered and the elaborate system of check dams and gravity-fed irrigation canals was useless. Deer and other game declined in numbers. Natural foods, like wild berries or pinyon nuts, would wither in the unremitting heat.

The Ancient Ones may have been the victim of their own success, having attained a population level which had incremental negative impacts on the environment and which could not be sustained. Trees were stripped from the land for roof supports for the Anasazi's elaborate structures—one alone at Chaco used five thousand trees—and for firewood. During the twelfth century, as many as a hundred thousand trees may have been cut. Farm fields denuded still more land. When rain did fall, it may have washed away unprotected topsoil and caused further cutting of deep arroyos along streams, again further lowering the water table. The number of Anasazi shrunk considerably, and the people retreated from their once magnificent cities to the Rio Grande valley in New Mexico. Even the frog with the turquoise eyes, their rain fetish, could not bring the rain.

Does the probable fate of the Anasazi hold a lesson for contemporary cities? Historian and writer Wallace Stegner thought so, as do many others, since cities continue to grow and consume water as if a day of reckoning will never come. Water is the weak link in the great unbroken chain of growth, he said, and a twenty-five-year drought will dry the cities up. "Five years of drought have not slowed down the growth," Stegner wrote in an introduction to a book of essays. "But ten years would, and fifteen would stop it cold, and twenty would send people reeling back not only from Los Angeles, but from San Diego, Albuquerque, Denver, Phoenix, Tucson, every artificial urban enclave."

From a social perspective it's unfortunate that western farmers are finding themselves on the losing end of the water wars. The environment, however, may come out the winner. According to the Environmental Protection Agency, farming and ranching in the West constitute one of the region's worst polluters. When a field is flooded to grow alfalfa for cows, for example, several things happen to the environment. Fertilizers wash into streams and percolate into underground aquifers. These farm chemicals cause algal blooms and change ecosystems. Some native plant species are adapted to nutrient-poor conditions, and when these species get hit with nitrogen or phosphorus, the soil becomes too rich for them, and other, exotic species invade. Likewise, herbicides and pesticides are carried into the groundwater and streams.

Yet another problem is erosion. A third of the topsoil that was on the land when the white man came is gone, stripped off by wind and water. Much of it chokes rivers and streams.

The three national wildlife refuges in the Greater Yellowstone—Red Rocks in Montana, Gray's Lake in Idaho and the Elk Refuge near Jackson, Wyoming—have escaped serious problems from agriculture, but some other refuges have been so polluted by runoff from irrigation, so contaminated by salts and heavy metals (which occur naturally in the soil and are concentrated by farming), pesticides and herbicides, that they are toxic to the wildlife they were meant to protect.

Pollution of the environment is not the only problem with irrigation and farming. These activities are often carried out through massive federal subsidies to the industry, subsidies that are often contradictory. In a thorough series on water in Colorado in 1992, *Denver Post* environmental writer Mark Obmascik revealed that Colorado's farmers get a total of $47 million a year in federally subsidized water to grow crops. They also get another $200 million in Conservation Reserve Program payments to reduce the number of crops they grow. "The Bureau of Reclamation encourages 10,710 Colorado farms to grow more food by supplying them with cut-rate irrigation water from sixteen federal water projects," Obmascik wrote. "These government dams and canals deliver a staggering 340 billion gallons a year—more water than the city of Denver uses in eight years. State farmers pay an average of fourteen cents on the dollar for this taxpayer-subsidized water." Throughout the West, the federal government subsidizes farmers with more than half a billion dollars' worth of irrigation water each year.

In 1992, large city utilities from Denver, Las Vegas, Phoenix and elsewhere formed a Western Urban Water Coalition to lobby for more water for cities and to "oppose uneconomic and inefficient water uses." Which means agriculture. In Colorado, 92 percent of the state's water goes to farm fields; yet just 2 percent of the jobs are in rural areas. The Denver metropolitan area uses 6 percent of the state's water but has 63 percent of the state's jobs. The ratio is similar in all western states.

What is taking place, essentially, is a transfer of subsidies. The developers of the sprawling western cities are shouldering out the farmers and taking over the expensive, federally built dams in the West. And they have managed to convince Congress of the need for more subsidies. A $5 billion concrete-lined ditch called the Central Arizona Project, which slices several hundred miles east from the Colorado River through the Sonoran Desert, is a good example. Originally intended for agriculture, the water will now be used by Phoenix and Tucson.

Historically, dams have played a major role in the West, sponsored at first by the Bureau of Reclamation, an agency created to build dams that would "capture the peaks" or store the spring floods, and then release that water a little at a time. Many of the dams, especially the big ones like Hoover in Nevada and Glen Canyon in Arizona, and the Grand Coulee on the Columbia, sent water through tremendous spinning turbines, taming its wild run to do the electrical bidding of Phoenix and Las Vegas and Seattle and Portland and the like. Smaller dams were built on rivers and streams around the West to store water for agricultural uses.

The water buffalo mentality was so pervasive that, according to Yellowstone research coordinator John Varley, at one time or other every river that flows out of Yellowstone Park has been proposed for a dam. Dams were the linchpin of taming and making productive the "Great American Desert." But the old view is Old West and dams are no longer seen as goodness and light, witness the demise of Two Forks.

The hidden costs of building and maintaining dams are surfacing. Few instances are as illuminating as the situation on the Columbia River, the largest river in the West, which runs 1,243 miles from its headwaters in British Columbia to its Pacific Ocean outlet in Oregon. The Columbia has serious problems, the old Death of a Thousand Cuts scenario. A billion gallons of waste pour into the river every day, from agriculture and municipal sewage. Logging washes sediment into the river, and is a serious problem. But it is the dams, 130 of them, including the Grand Coulee, one of the world's largest, that have dealt the death blow to the salmon populations that once filled the river and its tributaries. The river is no longer a river, but a managed stretch of lakes behind dams. Spawning salmon, leaving the Pacific Ocean to search out the tributaries that smell of home and procreation, can, with the help of fish ladders, get up the river. But the young salmon cannot get back to the ocean. Fifteen percent of the salmon of each perilous run to the sea is claimed by dams. In some cases there is a 90 percent mortality rare. As a result, three species in this river system are listed as endangered.

Salmon protected as an endangered species pose a problem, and will cause a reshuffling of priorities as water is taken away from one user, such as the shipping industry, or the power companies that use the water to generate power, and used to flush salmon over the dam and back to the sea. Hundreds of millions of dollars are at stake. This is the kind of thing that has led some, like those of the anti-environmental Wise Use Movement, to attempt to weaken or even repeal the Endangered Species Act.

Dams, oddly enough, have also created some of the best fishing in the West. When a dam is plugged into a river, the flood flows are stanched, and the torrential spring flows that wiped out fish habitats are gone. Instead, the tailwater below the dam often flows steadily, like a spring-fed creek. The Henry's Fork, where the swans live, is one of the finest trout streams in the country.

In the changing aquatic West, farmers and ranchers are most nervous of all, for they are coming under increasing scrutiny. The cities have grown so large, even in sparsely populated states like Nevada, Montana and Wyoming, that rural areas have seen their political power drained along with their water. The cities can and often do control the state legislatures. But people in the cities don't always want the water for drinking and lawn watering: these days the powers that be want the water left in the streams for something called "in-stream flow." Rather than having a river sucked dry for growing alfalfa or to fill a city reservoir, the people of the cities want some water left in the stream to keep fish and aquatic systems healthy. There's a strong constituency for the environment now that wasn't there thirty or forty years ago. To many farmers and ranchers, whose whole view of the water world is "beneficial use," leaving water in the stream to "go to waste" makes no sense at all. It's a classic New West–Old West battle.

On a log bridge with a plank platform that spans the purling, cobble-studded Gardiner River, John Varley, the park's research coordinator, points to a small dark pool gathered behind a large, round-headed boulder. A few minutes later, a pair of fish lips break the surface to sip in a small-winged insect. "Brown trout," Varley says.

Varley, with salt-and-pepper hair and beard, glasses and wearing a scotch cap, came to this park as a fisheries biologist in 1972. "It was said as far back as the 1930s," he says, "you don't have to kill every fish you catch." But it wasn't until 1973 that a "catch-and-release" policy was implemented here in Yellowstone. Anglers could catch fish and creel some, but only a few. The rest had to be returned to the rivers and lakes so they could make babies and populations could carry on naturally, without stocking.

The idea was heresy. However, despite the fact that fishermen stormed public meetings and called for the heads of park officials, the policy was adopted. And it has been a success, spreading to other rivers and streams throughout the West.

It was a major shift in thinking, away from that of the Old West: "When I was a boy it was different," says Varley. "It was kill everything so your creel was full and shoot the mergansers and osprey because they eat fish too." No longer was the management goal to allow fishermen to haul as many fish as possible out of a river "for free" to stock the freezer. (Never mind that the fisherman was paying for the fish indirectly through license fees—a curious kind of financial myopia.) The New Western philosophy holds that fishing is an "experience"' and a sport. The natural order of things is also important. It recognized that humans could overpower nature and were indeed doing so. Rules had to be set up to stave off destruction.

The Yellowstone region is a likely birthplace for such policy, the mother of many waters and home of the world's finest trout fishing. As mentioned earlier, three of the West's great rivers get started here: the Yellowstone, the Missouri, and the Snake. Additionally, smaller rivers, such as the Lewis, the Bechler, the Gibbon, the Gardiner, the Firehole and the Lamar, flow out of the park. There are 2,500 miles of waterways in Yellowstone, and each waterway gets its start in the same manner—a small dark trickle of water washing down a cliff face, the product of melting snow or a small spring that bubbles to the surface somewhere. The trickles gather together to become a small creek, the creeks become streams and the streams become small rivers and then adolescent rivers and occasionally a full-grown river that screams down canyons and off the plateau.

Where there's cold—thirty to fifty degrees—water and a respectable insect community, there are trout, and the Yellowstone ecosystem is trout heaven—brown trout, rainbow trout and cutthroat trout. When it comes to cutthroats, there is a particular payoff with the catch-and-release policy. Cutthroats are famous for being dumb and easy to catch; a trait that appeals to many tourists. The average cutthroat trout in the Yellowstone River lives seven years and, thanks to catch and release, is caught nine times each year, over a five-year catchable life, which means the average fish provides a fisherperson pleasure forty-five times. "It would cost about forty-eight dollars to raise that fish in a hatchery," Varley says. "It's too valuable to kill."

In the north of the ecosystem in the Bighole River of Montana, is the Arctic grayling, a beautiful fish with a large, purplish dorsal fin. Once abundant as far east as Michigan, sedimentation from grazing, logging and farming, and competition from exotic species, have driven the fish to near extinction in the lower forty-eight states. It is now found only in the upper Bighole, some streams in Yellowstone and a handful of other places.

The most unusual river in the Yellowstone ecosystem is the Firehole, a glassy river that flows out of the high country, a typical rock-strewn ribbon of gray-green water, until it picks up hot water that burbles in from geothermal springs. The heat and chemicals enrich the water, and the stream is superabundant with plants and insects. But backward runs the Firehole. When most rivers are locked in ice, steam hovers over the free-flowing Firehole and things keep growing. Rainbow and brown trout grow a remarkable inch per month for nine months, and then stop growing in July and August because the stream is too hot—ninety degrees. That's when the fish in other streams have their growth spurt. While rainbow trout usually spawn in May and June, the Firehole trout spawn at Christmastime.

There is a trade-off for such rapid growth. Trout in Yellowstone Lake can live to be eleven years old, while a fish in the Firehole that lives three years is an old fish. "Maybe it's the Chinese heartbeat theory," muses Varley. "You're only allowed so many ticks of the heart, whether you use them in three years or eleven years."

In recent years, fly-fishing in the Rocky Mountain West, the tying of artificial insects over an iron hook and casting in hopes of fooling a fish, has achieved cult status. It's a big part of the New West and a part of the reason rivers are seen these days as more than a way to water crops. There is something fundamental about it, a returning to nature for people. For all the refinement about it—extremely expensive clothing and equipment, $300- or $350-a-day fees for a guide, food and a bunk, and air fares to remote locations where the fishing has not been destroyed—fly-fishing is a return to a world seen through a predator's eyes. A good fly-fisherman becomes a part of the river, like an otter or a heron, thinking about likely banks for a trout to hide under, worrying about the angle of approach so as not to be spotted, and causing the fly to behave in a natural way that entices the fish. Attention narrows down to the point where there is only the fish and the fisherman.

Those fly-fishermen with the means are buying their own trout stream. Corporate executives, Ted Turner and Jane Fonda, Tom Brokaw, Charles Schwab, even rocker Huey Lewis are among those buying up ranches with a trout stream winding through it.

If you can't afford a ranch and stream, you might have one installed in your living room. Steve Fisher, the owner of a Missoula, Montana, business, Indoor Trout Streams, hopes to put babbling trout streams, complete with hatching insects and live trout to eat them, in the living rooms of America. "I've always wanted to have a trout," the wiry, goateed biologist says, explaining how the business came about. "After a while it gets to the point where the trout recognize you when you come into the room."

Part of the appeal is the ability to create one kind of trout stream one day, and several weeks later to change it to something different. Perhaps taking out the brown trout and putting in rainbow trout to match a new sofa.

Like aquariums, Fisher's trout streams are built in large Plexiglas tanks. They measure five feet to thirty feet long, eighteen to twenty-four inches wide and two feet deep, and are filled with river cobbles from the size of footballs to the size of golf balls. Water is pumped onto the surface of the tank at one end to create a realistic stream riffle. Some clumps of dirt with plants hang on the side of the tank and create terrestrial habitat for insects. Beneath the tank, in a hand-rubbed oak cabinet, sits a filter for cleaning the water, and a chiller, or refrigerator unit, that keeps the water between fifty-five and sixty degrees. Special fluorescent tubes mimic daylight. The tank must be at least thirty feet long to enable the insects to reproduce.

To put his trout through their paces, Fisher grabs a coffee can and disappears into the weeds outside his shop. A few minutes later he returns with a coffee can full of grasshoppers. "This is the most fun part of the deal," he says with relish, as he drops the bouncing hoppers into the water. Within seconds the insects disappear into the mouths of the five voracious, lightning-fast cutthroat trout. The only indication that there were ever hoppers in the water are a few spindly legs sticking out of the fishes' mouths. "It's great," said Fisher. "It's like you're God changing their little world around."

"Every fish is an individual," Fisher says. "I have one and all he wants to do is sit upside down between two rocks. They do that kind of stuff. They're weird animals. But I can't talk him into doing something different."

What does a personalized trout stream sell for? A basic, no-frills, one-hundred-gallon trout stream is about $5,000, while a deluxe, thirty-foot-long model would run into the tens of thousands.

But indoor streams will never replace those in the out-of-doors. The Yellowstone-style natural management of streams and rivers is a growing trend these days, especially as people find out—as they did on the Columbia River—that end runs around Mother Nature are expensive. The state of Montana is a leader in natural fishery management, having had an interesting experience with "put-and-take" management. In the early 1970s, Montana fishery biologists stopped stocking nearly all of Montana's fifteen thousand miles of cold-water rivers and streams—a move which had the most profound change in the state's fish population since 1865, when the territorial legislature outlawed the practice of fishing with dynamite.

Fishing is not just a diversion in Montana or other western states. It is big business. In Montana alone, it brings an estimated $105 million a year.

The roundabout journey back to nature started in the early 1900s, when the state built six hatcheries. Wading into streams with large nets during the spawn, fishery managers captured rainbow and brown trout, which are nonnative but had driven out native fish and established thriving wild populations. Slippery, squirming fish were milked for their eggs, their eggs carried back to the hatchery and incubated. The fingerlings were brought back to the river.

In 1958 Montana went to a different genetic strain of rainbow trout, a hybrid that reproduced in the hatchery. This new type of fish eliminated the expense and hassle of trapping fish. Before long, hatchery tank trucks were backing up to Montana's rivers and steams and dumping in millions of what are known as "catchables" —seven- to ten-inch hybrid rainbow trout. The Madison River alone, the state's premier fishery, was receiving an infusion of rainbows at the rate of a hundred thousand a year. In 1959, more than eighteen million fish were being raised and stocked.

It wasn't until the development of electrofishing that state officials realized the damage stocking was visiting on the fishery. (Electrofishing consists of placing two battery-powered electrical rods in the water—one negative, one positive. The fish are attracted to the current, are netted, counted, measured, weighed and marked. Then they swim away.)

Biologists discovered that "catchable" rainbows were ill-equipped for life in the wild, and not really catchable at all. Four weeks after being dumped into a stream, 70 percent of the domestic rainbows had died off, and 95 percent disappeared within three months. A creel census showed that fishermen were catching 40 percent of the catchables at best; in most instances it was far less—15 percent.

There was even worse news. In 1967, biologists were studying the effect of low spring water flows caused by a dam on two sections of the Madison River, which is in the northern part of the Greater Yellowstone. For some odd reason, increased water flows increased fish numbers on one study section, but not on the other. The only difference between the two sections was that where the fish numbers did not increase was a stretch being stocked with fish. The section where the number of fish increased was not being stocked. It didn't make sense.

To find out if stocking was somehow having a detrimental impact on numbers, stocking was discontinued on a test stretch of river. Over the first three years, the population of wild fish—now reproducing naturally—soared from 7,000 to 12,000 fish. The population of trout in another study section, where catchables continued to be introduced, dropped from 1,600 to 1,400 during the same period. In a third test, stocking on a spring creek near the Madison River was stopped. Here the brown trout population doubled, and incredibly, the rainbow population increased tenfold. Not only that: the size of the fish also increased.

Fish biologists were incredulous, and searched for an explanation. What they surmise was happening is this: Catchables, raised in crowded concrete raceways in unnatural hatchery conditions, couldn't cope in the wild. There are no predators in the hatchery, so no survival skills are developed. All that matters is eating. In the river, the dumb-as-a-rock hybrids gave no thought to cover or energy expenditure and they were paying for it with their life—gobbled up by osprey, otters and other predators. "It's like sending your dog out to live in the mountains," says Dick Vincent, who conducted studies on the Madison and is still a fishery biologist in Bozeman. "He knows how to eat, but that's not enough to survive." At the same time, the rainbows were invading the territory of the wild trout pell-mell, eating them out of house and home and driving down their survival rate.

It was irony on a grand scale. Montana was paying a great deal of money—$10 million the last big year of the hatcheries—to introduce trout into Montana's rivers and streams for fishermen, and in effect destroying the fishing. It was Old West. You want more fish, you put them in the water, never mind nature.

The Montana Fish and Game Department—which later became the Montana Department of Fish, Wildlife and Parks—proposed an end to stocking. Like the Yellowstone officials, they didn't anticipate the fight of their life. It simply made sense to fishermen that a truck full of trout spilling in upriver meant more fish to catch downriver. A number of meetings were held around the state to introduce the new policy—and in the end, wild fish prevailed. In 1972, the Montana Fish and Game Commission made it illegal to stock fish in rivers and streams. Angry resistance from fishermen, says Dick Vincent, remains the most trying part of his long career as a fisheries biologist. "The argument was that tourists and dumb fishermen wouldn't come to Montana," Vincent recalls.

The proof has been in the catching. As the products of wild fisheries began to show up on the end of a line, fishermen warmed to the idea. There's no doubt that while the challenge of catching a wild fish is greater, so are fish numbers. "Part of the experience is challenging a wild animal in its environment," says Vincent. "It's like hunting an elk versus hunting a cow. The same thing is true for fish."

Wild trout also mean more large trout. Because so few hatchery fish were surviving in the wild, they seldom got beyond the seven- to ten-inch size. That's not the case anymore. Catching an eighteen- to twenty-inch fish is common in Montana, which because of the cost of building hatcheries, feeding and trucking, would each cost hundreds of dollars to raise in captivity.

The key to maintaining a wild fish population is managing fishermen, not fish. That has been accomplished by reducing the limit from ten to five fish per day. And on some rivers, there are limits on size and species. That means catch-and-release fishing is anathema to people who keep several pounds of fish in the freezer. The movement to make rivers off-limits to bait fishing and to allow only fly-fishing has led to cries of elitism. To some, catching a fish and releasing it is something like shooting a deer and nursing it back to health.

The real test of whether fishing regulations can allow trout in a heavily fished river to sustain themselves is on the Madison. So far it appears to be working, though not everyone may be pleased with the necessary regulations. Forty miles of the Madison is catch-and-release fishing only. None may be creeled. The other ten miles, where the cover for fish is better and they are harder to catch, is a reduced limit. One rainbow or five brown trout can be kept, for a total of no more than five. A shocking census is done twice a year, and regulations are adjusted accordingly.

Natural management of fish can work only where habitat has been protected, and that has been the case in Montana. Not through any scheme to protect the fishing—at least at first—but largely because Montana is a lightly populated state and streamside development has not reached crisis levels.

In the same way that certain latitude, soil and other natural attributes of a locality produce fine grapes for wine, Montana—and much of the West—is blessed with the right conditions for large and numerous trout. Mountains are natural reservoirs that hold moisture until late June, which keeps rivers cool. And nutrients in the soil spawn large numbers of the right kinds of insects.

But most important is keeping water in the streams, and that is often very difficult. During the last several years, Montana, Idaho and other western states have suffered through severe droughts. Farmers and ranchers continued to irrigate their alfalfa fields through parched summers—despite pleas from state officials—and miles of some of the state's finest trout habitat have evaporated. Because wild trout are genetically suited to their stream of origin, it is difficult to stock these dead streams with wild fish. It may take as many as ten years before these streams recover and are able to support the fisheries they once did.

Most wildlife benefits from a natural river. Trumpeter swans thrive when a river flows naturally. And fish, too, of course. "When we went to natural fish management, our fishery was on the verge of collapse," he says. "The creeks at Yellowstone Lake were averaging thirty-eight hundred fish. The last ten years, they are averaging fifty thousand." More fish means more of those things that eat fish. More osprey, more kingfishers, more bald eagles, more otters. Even more grizzly bears.

6
Where the Wild Things Were

IN THE SPRING OF 1989, A SOW GRIZZLY AND HER TWO CUBS ambled down from hibernation to the tourist complex of Lake, on the north shore of Yellowstone Lake. A huge body of water in the southern half of the park, Yellowstone Lake is home to a large population of cutthroat trout. As the ice melts and the spring sun begins to warm the Yellowstone Plateau, these cutthroat trout swarm up the tiny meandering creeks—creeks like Cub, Columbine and Chipmunk—that flow into the lake, where the females lay their roe in the gravel on the stream bottom and the males wriggle over them and deposit clouds of sperm.

As the fish play out the ancient rhythms of their biological imperatives and swarm into these tiny streams—some not much wider than a grizzly—bears from around the park give in to their urges as well. These streams are vital to the Yellowstone grizzly. Bears spend most of their time and energy running down and unearthing groundhogs, churning up alpine meadows for tiny, onion-like glacier lily roots, or wandering the landscape looking for dead elk. Here are concentrations of fish, of valuable protein, all in one place. It is a critical food to bears because the return on their investment is so great, and it comes at a time when the bear needs it most, as it attempts to gain back its strength after a winter-long sleep. It is all the more important because the isolated grizzly bear population in Yellowstone is threatened and such food sources are critical to each bear, especially females, which are key to reproduction and the viability of the whole population.

Unfortunately, this grizzly—known to officials as Grizzly Bear Number 134—was habituated; that is, she showed no fear of humans. She did what bears do—walked up the streams, picking fish up in her paws to eat them, teaching her cubs to do the same. She didn't threaten or attack people who were staying at the historic hotel or in nearby cabins, but park officials felt the potential was there.

To complicate matters, in 1989 one of her cubs had been injured and had its spinal cord damaged, probably in an attack by a coyote or another bear. It dragged its legs, and when it could not keep up it would cry and yelp for its mother; 134 would return to its side and act defensively. Officials had once trapped and relocated her, many miles away, to wilderness in the southeast corner of the park. Within days she was back at the rich food source. Deterrents were tried, and she was shot with a "bear thumper," rubber bullets fired from a gun. She stubbornly remained. The fish were too many to give up.

At the end of the first week of April, in 1990, the bear and her remaining cub (the crippled one had died) came back to the fish and the development at Lake. It was 134's last visit. She was trapped and shipped off to a research facility out of the park—lost to the population—and the cub was sent to another part of the Yellowstone ecosystem.

Environmentalists were outraged. Here was a grizzly bear, doing what bears do, trying to survive, and it was shipped out of the park because for a few weeks in the spring people were at Lake Lodge. Politics, conservationists said, had won out once again over biology. Instead of moving the bear, the hotel should have been closed for two weeks to accommodate the bears.

The grizzly bear is one of the most threatened species of wildlife in the Greater Yellowstone, and the Yellowstone region is one of the two last refuges for relatively healthy populations of grizzlies left in the lower forty-eight states. There are two hundred or so here and eight hundred or so in the northern continental divide ecosystem, in and around Glacier National Park in northern Montana. Both populations are protected under the Endangered Species Act.

There are also very small, isolated populations of bears in the Cabinet Mountains in northwestern Montana and the Selkirk Mountains of northern Idaho and northeastern Washington. There are an unknown number—probably no more than a handful—in North Cascades National Park in Washington and the Selway-Bitterroot Wilderness Area, which is on the Montana-Idaho border. There are much larger populations in Canada and Alaska, but for the most part they are isolated from the populations in the lower forty-eight states.

These islands of bears are what remain of the hundreds of thousands of grizzlies that once lived on the continent. The remaining populations are like tiny slivers of ice left over after a massive ice age, for grizzlies once swam in the Pacific Ocean, hunted gophers on the prairie as far east as what is now Minnesota, and wandered the mountains of Mexico.

Fierce, beautiful, wide-ranging and unable to compromise, the grizzly bear is a symbol for the park and the battle being waged to keep it wild.

As charismatic as the grizzly bear is, however, there is a movement among conservationists and scientists to swing the spotlight away from animals with popular appeal, like the wolf, or bear or mountain lion, to recognize instead the myriad and intricately related life-forms—from microbes to fungus to insects to mammals—that make up an ecosystem. Research in the past few decades has shown just how dependent an ecosystem is on each part. Tiny microbial soil dwellers, like bacteria and fungi, decompose logs, grass and other organics into minerals that growing plants can use. Since plants make up 70 percent of the bear's diet, the damage or demise of tiny microbes because of acid rain could place the bear in jeopardy. And so the goal of a sustainable ecosystem is not just to protect the grizzly bear habitat or wolf habitat, but to keep as much of the ecosystem intact as possible, to preserve biodiversity. "No one knows how it all works," says the GYC's Ed Lewis. "If you pull a thread here, you have impacts you didn't anticipate. That's why you can't manage based on political boundaries. You have to look at ecological realities."

Biodiversity is diminishing, experts say, at an alarming rate. In and around Yellowstone, the bald eagle, the whooping crane, the Kendall Warm Springs dace (a fish), the bog bearberry, the yellow spring beauty and the peregrine falcon are endangered, while three dozen other species are of concern, including the lynx, the wolverine, the mountain plover and the Arctic grayling—either in the park or in the Greater Yellowstone.

The biodiversity of the Rocky Mountain West is more intact than in any other part of the country, outside of Alaska. (By default rather than by design; it's simply more remote.) But there have been plenty of losses. The Las Vegas leopard frog has vanished. Arizona's Monkey Spring pupfish is gone. Nevada's Grass Valley speckled dace. Arizona's thick-billed parrot. Arizona's Merriam's elk. Arizona's Chihuahuan pronghorn antelope. And ocelot. Idaho's wood frog. Idaho's kit fox and the smooth green snake. New Mexico's fritillary butterfly. Wyoming's eskimo curlew. Utah's fisher. Colorado's small-flower beardtongue. Montana's black-footed ferret. Among many others.

Some species—deer for example—adapt fairly well to places where there are people. But there are other species, like the grizzly or desert tortoise or mountain lions or myriad others, that can't bend around the activities of humans. Where people come into wildlife habitat and a conflict develops, wildlife invariably loses out. Very few human activities in the West are designed on ecological principles. Individuals like 134 lose out, but more critically, when large areas of land are taken over for human use, whole species or populations lose out. Unless species are extremely rare—as with the grizzly—the loss of individuals is unimportant. The real threat to wildlife is the loss of habitat, pure and simple. Wildlife and wildland are inextricably linked.

What has happened to wildlife in Yellowstone is what has happened to wildlife throughout the West. Boundaries drawn up years ago don't mesh with ecological reality. For more than a century, roads were built, towns and cities grew, rivers were diverted, swamps drained, timber cut, minerals mined, and cattle grazed, and often all of these things took place in the same valley. No one knew at the time that wildlands were being fragmented, divided up so that populations of bears and wolves and mountain lions and other species were cut off from each other, from their habitat and from their food sources.

* * *

Yellowstone is the focus these days for another raging wildlife debate—this one over an animal that probably doesn't even exist in the park anymore. Environmentalists, park officials and others want to reintroduce the wolf—actually bring wolves in, in trucks or planes, to establish a new population. Absent from the park for half a century, some people want the wolf home, one of the very few missing pieces of the complement of park biota. But ranchers and the resource industries don't want an endangered species—especially one that eats sheep and cattle—brought back if they can help it. "We need the wolf back," said former Montana Republican congressman Ron Marlenee, "like we need another drought."

The natural movement of wolves from healthy populations in Canada and south through the northern Rockies may soon render the question of whether to bring wolves back to Yellowstone moot. It has in the ecosystem around Glacier National Park.

A small Cessna drones through a spacious, blue-domed sky, flying along the western edge of the snow-mottled peaks of Glacier National Park. The silvery snake of the North Fork of the Flathead River braids below. Diane Boyd, dressed in a heavy flannel shirt and well-aged jeans stained with diesel fuel and woodstove ash, puts on headphones and flicks on a radio receiver. Immediately, she picks up a pinging through a field of static, the sound of a radio collar some of the wolves wear. Her eyes scan the blanket of trees broken by meadows on the ground below and suddenly she shouts, "There they are!" The pitch of the engine changes as the pilot sends the aircraft into a sharp dive. As the plane flies tight, stomach-churning circles just above the treetops, Boyd counts eleven wolves, some of them silver, the others black as midnight, all of them oblivious to the mechanical bird above them. The animals look like big, big dogs, with full winter coats and a sleekness that speaks of their life in the wild. When the canine census is over, the plane pulls out of its circling pattern and heads back to the Moose City airport.

The wolves are at Diane Boyd's door, where the Rocky Mountains come into the United States in Montana, and the thirty-seven-year-old biologist wouldn't have it any other way. This country is rugged and unrestrained, full of beauty and cruelty in full measure —as full as it gets in the Lower Forty-eight. It teems with grizzlies, cougars, mountain goats and bighorn sheep. Muscular, branch-antlered elk bugle in the meadow behind Boyd's log home, and green, red and white northern lights occasionally scream overhead, through a sky where the stars look like glowing glass beads stitched to a midnight fabric.

The thirty or so wolves that hunt and howl near the North Fork of the Flathead are the vanguard of what appears to be a wholesale return of wolves to the western United States, a half century after they were hunted, trapped, dynamited and poisoned out of existence by ranchers and federal trappers. Boyd is on the scientific front lines of that comeback, living in a cabin with neither power nor running water.

Using the scientific information she's collected, she also struggles against deeply embedded Little Red Riding Hood–style myths about wolves. The wolf, Boyd says, is far different from what people think. "I'd love for people to learn about the real wolf," she says. "So wolves will be allowed to exist." No easy task. There are some ranchers, hunters and others who possess a bottomless hatred for the wolf, and see it only as a competitor. Though wolves are protected by federal law, they meet their demise by foul play throughout the state of Montana on a regular basis. Wolf haters even have a motto: Shoot, shovel and shut up. Whether the wolf survives in the Lower Forty-eight will be a measure of just how wild the West still is. There is so much potential conflict with humans that wolves are collared and followed, moved, trapped and sometimes shot. And there are problems as their habitat gets carved up by loggers, oil well drillers and subdividers.

Boyd works for a small study called the Wolf Ecology Project, which is based at the University of Montana in Missoula. Her job is to paint a detailed ecological portrait of the animals so decisions can be made on how land should be managed to protect them, since they are an endangered species. She collars them with a cigarette-pack-sized radio transmitter and then, from above or on the ground, tracks the nomadic animals as they move, hunt, kill, eat, mate, set out on their own and form new packs.

One of the biggest parts of Boyd's job is wolf trapping. When a new pack evolves, or new wolves move into the area from Canada, she and her dog Max, a gangly, shaggy-haired product of the pound, look for wolf sign—a dead elk or moose, wolves' hairy scat or their distinctive urine. Once she finds a likely spot, Boyd takes out one of her heavy, black, iron-jawed traps. They are the same fearsome instrument trappers used to rid the West of the wolf years ago, with one difference: the jaws are offset so they don't fully close. While the wolf is held, the risk of injury is minimized.

She digs a small hole, pries the jaws of the trap apart and sets the trap in the depression. A dab of a pungent scent—made from cut-up pieces of muscles, glands and other animal parts that Boyd ferments in a jar in the sun for a year—is placed behind the trap. When an animal steps on the trigger, the jaws snap shut. On a typical trapline, Boyd sets between twenty and thirty traps over many miles, along forested trails and other places where wolves travel. Once the traps are set, she hikes or rides a motorbike every morning to check the trapline.

The real work begins after a wolf is captured. Talking softly to the animal, she moves around it with a four-foot jab stick, and sticks the animal in the rump with a sedative-filled hypodermic. A few minutes later, the wolf is asleep. She moves in and presses a stick against the wolf's whiskered muzzle to check its bite reflex and make sure it's not still partially awake.

Boyd quickly goes to work. The animal's rectal temperature is taken. The animal's body temperature needs maintenance, or it could die. If it's low, Boyd covers the animal up with her goose-down jacket. If it's too warm, the animal is placed partially in a creek or continually doused with water. A bandanna is wrapped over its eyes to keep out the sun.

Boyd fastens a sling to a portable scale and weighs the animal. A fiberglass collar is fastened on, paws are checked for injuries, a blood sample is taken, and the wolf is given penicillin in case it was injured. Testicles and mammaries are measured. Antiseptic ointment is dabbed in the animal's eyes in case it injured them after it was trapped. When the half-hour routine is finished, she stands back to make sure the animal successfully shakes off the anesthetic.

The life of a radio-collared wolf is no longer secret. Boyd drives the rutted, teeth-jarring dirt road that runs along the North Fork

Road with an antenna affixed to the truck or hikes the trails of Glacier and environs with a portable receiver and antenna or flies above them. All the time listening to the beeps. If a pack of wolves stays in one place for a while, Boyd assumes it is feeding on a dead animal, and when the wolves leave she hikes or skis to the kill site. The dead creature—an elk or moose or a deer—is sexed and a tooth is pulled for its age.

Boyd has made some interesting observations. From the plane, she watched a grizzly bear with his paws around an elk carcass. Six wolves had surrounded the bear and were hounding it, she says, "like kids torturing the neighbor." One wolf moved in close to the bear, and the bear took off after it. The other wolves dove into the carcass. "He'd be running and you could almost see a light come on over the bear's head," she said. "Ding! He'd reel around and head back and the wolves would scatter like ravens. Then they would do it again."

Under a nickel gray sky, with the tips of Glacier's magisterial peaks in the grip of low-lying clouds, Boyd hikes into a remote mountain meadow. Thanks to the pinging receiver, she knows there are wolves behind a rise, less than a half mile away. Steady beeps indicate they are not moving. Boyd cups her hands around her mouth and sends a long, low, lugubrious howl off into an absolute silence. She listens, waiting for the breeze to bring back the wolves' answer. Howling is a common way of locating wolves. No answer returns. She howls again. And again an answer is refused. She shrugs. Sometimes wolves howl. Sometimes they don't.

Boyd takes great pains to point out that her life is nothing like the movie *Gorillas in the Mist*, in which biologist Dian Fossey befriended a group of mountain gorillas in Rwanda. "People have a romanticized vision of us living like wolves, skiing with them and watching them," she says. "We do not. We stay removed from them to minimize contact. Wolves that are not afraid of people are dead wolves."

There is good reason to worry. The thirty wolves in and near Glacier face daily the possibility of extinction. Last year a whole pack was wiped out, probably by humans.

For some reason the wolf, more than any other animal, is the object of unbounded, irrational fear. Maybe it's such stories as "The Three Little Pigs" and "Little Red Riding Hood." To the Navajo, the word *mai-coh* meant both witch and wolf. Even the

French have a saying "*Elle a vou le loup*": "She has seen the wolf." A term for lost virginity.

White settlers who pushed West in the 1860s and 1870s killed wolves as a matter of course, partly because of the threat to cattle and sheep. But there was also a fear, a deep-seated irrational hatred. The method was simple. They shot bison and laced the carcasses with strychnine. The killing was done by "wolfers," who earned $2.50 per pelt, sometimes making $3,000 a season. Later the killing got even more efficient. A bounty was levied on the wolf, and in four decades more than eighty thousand wolves were slaughtered in Montana alone. Wolves were shot and poisoned and their tiny offspring dynamited in their dens.

By the 1880s, the vast herds of bison on the plains were gone, and cattle and sheep took their place. For a while, living was easy, as cattlemen simply turned their herds out onto the oceans of grass. But the brutal winter of 1886–87 wiped out 95 percent of some herds and forced ranchers to retrench. Fences went up, feed was planted, and the cost of operating increased. Deprived of bison, the wolf turned to cattle and sheep. With the ranchers' margin of profit thinned considerably by the blizzard and new costs, the wolf was hunted with a vengeance.

Some lone wolves defied traps and dodged bullets and strychnine to become legends—The White Wolf of the Judith, Snow-drift and Old Three Toes. One livestock-killing wolf was described by a newspaper reporter as "not merely a wolf, but a monstrosity of nature—half wolf and half mountain lion—possessing the cruelty of both and the craftiness of Satan himself." By the 1930s, however, the wolves were gone from the West. Nevertheless they remained in Canada, and after wolf hunting ended in the 1970s there, wolves began moving south into old territory, like a curtain coming down. They recently formed the first western U.S. packs in a half century. (There is a large population of gray wolves in northern Minnesota and in Wisconsin that were never extirpated.) There are verified new populations of wolves in northern Idaho, Montana and the state of Washington. Protected as an endangered species, it looks as if a wholesale return of the wolf to much of the West is on the agenda. Officials in New Mexico and Arizona are meanwhile studying the reintroduction of Mexican wolves into the Southwest.

* * *

Boyd doesn't worry about wolves. In the corner of her cabin sits her arsenal, a shotgun and a .30-.30 rifle. The shotgun is for protection. One day she drove to a small lake in Canada to check a site where wolves had been radio-located. She clambered out of the truck and Boyd pumped four slugs into a shotgun. "In case there's a grizzly bear on the kill," she explains, matter-of-factly. Grizzly bears, which grow as large as five hundred or six hundred pounds here, are the only thing besides human beings Boyd worries about. She has surprised wolves on a kill, she says, and felt no threat. None. "It's wild," she says. "The wolves are scattering and barking and hollering. All I have for defense is a ski pole, looking at ten wolves that have been filling their bellies with raw meat. I thought, Gee, why don't they take humans? We'd be easy, easy prey. But it's not a concern."

Boyd lives on deer, elk and moose meat, which she shoots and butchers herself. She knows the idea of hunting doesn't go over well in the city, for she came here opposed to hunting herself. However, the North Fork is a different world. There is life and death all around, she says; it is nature's constant. A dead elk along the river means life for a litter of wolf pups a half mile away. "You guys go out and have your pork and beef slaughtered for you," she says. "Those animals don't lead a pleasant life. I shoot my own meat. I butcher it myself. The animals I kill have lived all their life in the wild, have never been fed drugs, and there's a ten-second delay between being alive and being dead." In fact, Boyd met her boyfriend when he shot a coyote she had collared and she picked up the signal coming from his house.

Boyd says she has no problems with the wolves on the North Fork being hunted occasionally. In nature, individual animals come and go all the time. Boyd's strong, unsentimental love and concern is for an entire species. The real battle in the preservation of things wild is over habitat and public policy. And that is based on good science.

Work is hard on the North Fork. Days are long. Worth it, Boyd says, to reach her goal: finding a place for the wolf, a refuge where it can exist without being wiped out again. Her hope is that the information she is gathering will explode the myths, and teach people about the real wolf, for people alone have the power to destroy it. Wolves don't attack humans. They don't wipe out game populations. And she believes there are effective ways to control wolves that occasionally kill cattle. "Wolves are much less of a threat to people than other things out there, especially other humans," she says. "If people knew more about wolves, there would be a lot less polarity, a lot less hostility. There is room for the wolf."

There is nothing, Boyd says, quite like looking at a wolf face-to-face. "You get this big black animal with yellow eyes that turns and stares at you," she says. "Their eyes are like little coals or two little balls of fire looking back." Her voice cracks, and a mist clouds her eyes. "They have this magnificent predator essence about them. They are wildness personified. It's pretty intense."

"The wolf is a magnificent animal, there is no doubt about that," says Troy Mader. The problem with the wolf, says Mader, who heads a group out of Gillette, Wyoming, called Abundant Wildlife of North America, which is a leading opponent to wolf reintroduction, is that the wolf is protected as an endangered species and can't be controlled by ranchers and farmers. "Most of the people in this country don't have to live on the land and compete with a natural enemy. What this country is doing [by protecting wolves] is stepping back into history. So the ranchers, farmers and outfitters see the wolf as an enemy again. If they would delist the wolf and allow it to be controlled, there would be less hostility. There wouldn't be many wolves, but there would be some in the wilderness and high country."

Things are bound to get more acrimonious, for the Endangered Species Act calls for reintroduction of endangered species back into their former ranges, where they have been gone for many years, and in the future, grizzly bears and wolves may be brought back to other western states.

While the controversy over predators grows in the West, so too does the notion of people as predators. While Yellowstone and other national parks are off-limits to hunting, it is allowed almost everywhere else. Hunting is one of the great moral debates, and of course it plays out dramatically in the West, where hunting is a sport, an avocation, even a way of life. Come October, newspapers in small towns around the West are filled with ads for ammunition and hunting clothes. The glow of safety orange fills the woods and cafes and motels, while hunters' cars and trucks take on a macabre look, as gutted elk or deer are strapped to the hood or roof.

It is a time of bonding for father and son, even mother and daughter, as hunting in the fall is a ritual that signifies a coming of age. Moral or immoral, the ancient role of humans as predator emerges again.

Difference of opinion on this issue points out the difference between the largely rural, land-based culture of the West, where in many places wildlife—elk, deer, even a bear or bison—are common, and the urban East, where people seldom see much more than a pigeon or squirrel.

Given the reality of the altered environment, biologists say without hunters to make up for the loss of other predators, prey species like deer and elk would run rampant. They point to a boom in the population of deer in the East, and the nuisance they've become as they eat crops and shrubs, wander in front of cars and take over yards. Death is one of nature's great themes. Deer are slaughtered by cougars every day; is it any more evil to have a hunter do it?

Yes it is, in the minds of some. "When I was a boy I bought a BB gun at Sears, Roebuck," says Cleveland Amory, leader of the Fund for Animals, an aggressive animal rights group that has taken on hunting issues in almost every western state, believing that hunting is barbaric and morally wrong. "I shot at a bird and hit the goddamned thing. As it flopped around I screamed for my father. He said, 'You shot it, you kill it.' I did it and I never forgot it. I've been antihunting ever since."

Amory says all hunters are his enemy, although "when a person goes one-on-one with a deer to put venison on the table, well, he's the least of my enemies." Amory continues to push for laws against hunting of all kinds, to rally public support against it, and to try to disrupt hunts with direct action such as noisemaking during bear hunts or running in front of hunters at a buffalo hunt. "I don't think I will live to see the end of hunting," says Amory, sixty-six, "but it's declining, steadily going down. More and more people will see things our way."

Hunters are worried, for the laws come from urban areas, and the population centers are where much antihunting sentiment resides. The growing antagonism against fur, for example, resulted in the bottom dropping out of the market for fox, coyote and other wild pelts and has forced some people to abandon trapping as uneconomical. Lion hunts in California and a grizzly bear hunt and a bison hunt in Montana were ended by animal rights activists. Hunters and hunting groups, meanwhile, claim that sportsmen are paying for on-the-ground conservation, both through license fees and through groups like Ducks Unlimited and the Rocky Mountain Elk Foundation. "Who will buy habitat if there's no hunting and fishing?" asks Ron Aasheim, of the Montana Department of Fish, Wildlife and Parks. "We spend $16,300 a day on wildlife conservation."

There are two kinds of hunters. There are those who hunt for meat, a kind of subsistence hunting, the hunters that Amory said were the least of his enemies. And there are those that hunt for the sport or the trophy. The latter are the ones that animal rights activists like Amory and others have targeted. Even people who hunt deer and elk and other animals often draw the line at trophy hunting. There seems to be—and even some hunters say so—something morally repugnant about people who kill grizzly bears, mountain goats, cougars or elk solely for the thrill or to hang the head in the den.

Nonetheless, trophy hunting is booming. Elk are one of the most prized species. There are game farms where people can come to legally shoot penned elk, or the owners can make it semiwild. On the White Mountain Apache Reservation in Arizona, Apache guides take fifty-four hunters each fall into the pine forests and meadows for a six-day-long elk hunt. The price: $10,000. The elk are so well protected and so carefully managed that the place is full of trophy-sized animals and a likely place for trophy bull elk to come from. There are so many elk that it's not a question of shooting one, but a question of which one. The success rate is higher than 95 percent, and would be 100 percent if hunters always took a bull. "Hunters are showed ten to fifteen bulls every morning, and it's up to the hunter to shoot them or not," says Sylvia Tessay, who works on booking hunts for the tribe.

Another, more unusual, kind of sport hunting in the West is varmint hunting. The International Varmint Association in Coeur d'Alene, Idaho—which publishes a magazine called *International Varmint Hunter*—claims 2,300 card-carrying members, whose sport of choice is lining up a rifle on a ground squirrel or a coyote. Those species are often poisoned, the hunter says, so why not allow someone to have fun and get rid of them? People actually make hunting trips and pay a guide to come and hunt varmints for three or four days.

As the opportunity to hunt diminishes in other parts of the country, because of urbanization and environmental problems, some hunters are willing to pay high prices to come west and experience things wild. Leased hunting is a growing phenomenon. As long as the cattle were left standing when the smoke cleared, ranchers once let almost anyone come in and shoot deer or elk, which munched haystacks and were considered a nuisance. Now hunters or hunting clubs that can afford it travel to the Rocky Mountain West to leased ranches for the right to hunt elk, white-tailed deer, pheasants, and so on, for prices ranging from $25 a day to $500 or $1,000 a season for a family pass. Fishing is part of the economy, too, and people pay $50 or more a day, per rod, for choice spring creeks. This is a big part of the New West—things that were always ignored or taken for granted by ranchers and other westerners are factoring ever larger into the economy.

A drawback has been the disenfranchisement of many local people who have neither the means nor the inclination to pay for something they consider part of their birthright. It's especially maddening because by law the wildlife belongs to the public, yet only a select few can get at it. And private ground is often the choicest habitat—along rivers and lakes, because the land that ended up in federal hands was thought unproductive and unwanted.

Not everyone who comes for wildlife takes the carcass home with him or her. There's a growing business in watching and photographing wildlife. This kind of eco-tourism is a big part of the New Western economy.

Tom Segerstrom was a district biologist with the Wyoming Game and Fish Department for six years. In 1987, seeing avid interest among the public for close encounters with wildlife, he quit the state and started a business called the Great Plains Wildlife Institute, in Jackson, Wyoming, designed to take people out to mingle with moose, elk, bald eagles and other species. He now employs three wildlife biologists. A single day's outing is $150 and is a biologist-accompanied journey to see wildlife. For a five-day trip the cost is $1,635, including lodging and most meals. Clients float a river to look for otters. Howl for coyotes. Search for grizzlies in the evening and morning. Now Segerstrom is hoping the wolf comes back to Yellowstone. "If there's wolves," he says, "I could capitalize on that quite a bit." A federal study on wolves in Yellowstone estimates that $19 million in additional tourism revenues might be generated in the three-state area by the presence of wolves in the park.

Those who throw in their lot with Segerstrom might also find themselves working at a labor of love: banding Uinta ground squirrels for a red-tailed hawk study, tracking radio-tagged elk calves or watching for bands of wild horses at watering holes.

Business doubled every year for four years and then leveled off in 1992, Segerstrom says. They take some six hundred people a year on one-day trips and thirty to forty on five-day trips, both winter and summer. "Some of the costs put this out of the reach of some people," Segerstrom says. "There's such a demand that eventually government agencies are going to have to get involved," in such tours.

Wildlife is big business in other ways, and the love affair with things wild is on the upswing. Travertine trout, bronze elk and paintings of any number of species can be found in galleries throughout the West. Elk antlers are made into chairs, chandeliers and cribbage boards. Even tea. Each May buyers descend on Jackson, Wyoming, to buy antlers that local Boy Scouts have plucked off the national wildlife refuge adjacent to town. Orientals believe that antlers brewed into tea are a tonic that, among other things, has aphrodisiac qualities. The Wildlife Art Museum in Jackson, a small but upscale gallery, features nothing but wildlife art. The prize for the most creative use of animal parts has to go to a woman in Jackson, Wyoming, who makes earrings and necklaces out of little round moose turd pellets that she glues to a setting. The line is called "Gems of the Tetons," and the card attached to each piece of jewelry says, "Yes, they're real."

Not all commercialization of wildlife comes legally. As wildlife numbers decline worldwide, the prices in the flourishing underground market for wildlife and wildlife parts merely go up. Commercial market hunting in the West—an industrialized form of poaching—has taken off. If it has a value at all, and wanders in front of a gun barrel, poachers have shot it and sold it or a portion of it.

Yellowstone, because it is remote and home to numerous species of wildlife, has a serious problem with poaching. Federal law enforcement agents have found sodium cyanide "getters" in the park. The homemade device is loaded with a .38-caliber shell, complete with gunpowder. But the bullet has been replaced with a lethal dose of sodium cyanide. The getter is driven into the ground, and the end of the trap is scented with meat or fish. When the trap is yanked, the shell explodes and the sodium cyanide is propelled into the animal's mouth, where it mixes with saliva and kills the animal instantly. All the poacher has to do is harvest the carcass. In one case, two Koreans were paying poachers $1,700 a piece for black bear carcasses. They would ship the animals off to San Francisco. Among some Orientals, bear gallbladders have a supposed medicinal quality, and bear paws are made into soup and considered a delicacy. Someone slaughtered four bull elk in Yellowstone, left the carcasses and sawed off their antlers, which are sold as an aphrodisiac in the Orient. Law enforcement officials arrested poachers working as outfitters who were taking clients on guaranteed hunts for bighorn sheep and elk in the park.

Poaching has become such a problem that the U.S. Fish and Wildlife Service, which manages much of the nation's wildlife, maintains a unit of federal undercover officers whose job it is to pose as poachers to set up sting operations complete with secret video cameras and hidden microphones, and get the goods on the real poachers. "We are the FBI of the wildlife world," says Terry Grosz, a Special Agent in Charge in Denver.

One of the more intriguing tales of the U.S. Fish and Wildlife Service Covert Operations Branch was Operation Falcon. In 1981 in Great Falls, a quiet, unassuming Montana falconer named John Jeffrey McPartlin began quietly letting colleagues in the small passionate world of falconry know that he had gyrfalcons for sale. Prized for their blinding speed, their beauty and their hunting ability, gyrfalcons are the sexiest of all raptors to those who hunt with birds.

On December 17, 1982, federal officials say, a chartered Falcon jet flew into the Great Falls airport to pick up packages left there by McPartlin. Two young brothers from West Germany, Marcus and Lothar Ciesielski, age nineteen and twenty-two, respectively, got out, went to a hangar and came out with several large boxes, which they loaded onto the craft. The boxes contained three gyrfalcons and three prairie falcons. The brothers ferried the birds to Washington, D.C., and then gave them to a man named François Messouadene, who loaded them into a trunk of a black limousine and had the driver take them to Kennedy International Airport in New York. There Messouadene purchased seven first-class tickets on Saudi Arabian Airlines—one for each bird and one for himself.

Messouadene had bragged to the limo driver that the birds were destined for members of the Saudi royal family, who were devout falconers. The problem was that the birds were captured by McPartlin, who was working as an informant for the U.S. Fish and Wildlife Service. Under federal and international law it is illegal to take these birds from the wild, and it is a federal offense to buy them or transport them across state lines.

In June of 1984, 150 shotgun-bearing, bulletproof-vest-wearing law enforcement officers burst into the homes of falconers around the country, arresting fifty-nine people who had bought birds of prey from McPartlin. Marcus Ciesielski was captured and pleaded guilty; his brother and Messouadene escaped. The birds they shipped to buyers were not recovered.

Operation Falcon was one of the agency's most controversial. Most of the falconers had never done anything illegal in their lives, yet were unable to resist the lure of a gyrfalcon. As one defense attorney put it: "It's like having someone bring Marilyn Monroe by and ask if she can spend the night."

"They're like the devil," said one falconer. "They entice you into breaking the law and then they punish you for it."

The undercover operation did not mean an end to the black market in birds of prey. In fact, law enforcement officials say, the same kind of illegal trapping and selling of birds of prey is flourishing once again.

The most serious threat to wildlife remains disintegration of their habitat. It is a continuing problem, and continues in large measure because it is difficult to see. Fragmentation is a key concept in wildlife biology these days, and perhaps the grizzly bear has received the most study of all. In fact, it was grizzlies that led Frank and John Craighead, twin brothers and wildlife researchers, to first propose the idea of a Yellowstone ecosystem in 1959 based on the wanderings of radio-collared grizzlies over a much larger area than just the park.

Bears simply don't understand boundaries, and they have needs outside the park, in the same way a plant is more than what grows above the ground. What happens and has happened, time and time again, is this. A section of forest is clear-cut—in itself, not a problem. But there may have been white pine nuts there that bears utilized in the summer. Nevertheless, the bears can still get by. Then an oil well is sunk, which pushes the bears out of an elk calving ground where they fed in the spring. A subdivision is built along the river, which wipes out the bears' access to succulents that grow in marshy areas. An early snow wipes out a huckleberry patch where the bears fed in the fall. A reproducing female—critical to the species breeding—is shot by hunters, another is hit by a car.

Bit by bit, populations of bears are isolated. Their nutrition gets poorer and poorer and their reproduction levels drop. Genetically they are too closely related, and recessive genetic defects—poor fertility, for example—begin to emerge with frequency in the population. Someday an island of 100 or 150 bears might not be able to survive over the long term. Once again it's the Death of a Thousand Cuts.

Fragmentation is graphically illustrated in Montana. Grizzly bears used to traverse freely the area between Glacier National Park in northwest Montana and the Selway-Bitterroot Wilderness Area to the south, in Idaho. While the wilderness area and the park are protected from development, the intervening land is not. Home building, logging, road building and other disruptive human activities between the two ecosystems continue apace and have thrown up a barrier to the bear. There is one three-mile-wide corridor left, a forested tract of land that allows some movement between the two reserves. But it is unprotected and homes are going in, timber is being cut, and so on. For all the millions of acres the bear has in two separate places, this strip of land may nevertheless mean the difference between a healthy gene pool and an unhealthy one—that is, between keeping the bear viable or having it go extinct.

A crack bicycle racer and runner, eighteen-year-old Scott Dale Lancaster was not fast enough to outrun the mountain lion that stalked him. In January of 1991, as the high school senior ran through the woods behind his school in the small town of Idaho

Springs, Colorado, just west of Denver, the lion padded unseen behind him. As traffic roared by a stone's throw away on Interstate 70, the cougar crouched and then uncoiled, killing the 135-pound athlete from behind. The Lancaster incident, wildlife experts say, was the first time the killing of an adult by a mountain lion was documented in North America.

In recent years, the behavior of the once secretive mountain lion, or cougar, has gone through a sudden and dramatic change. Throughout the West, fearless lions have been coming down from their mountain sanctuaries and paying a visit to the places where people live. And part of the problem is the accelerating fragmentation of their habitat.

There have been other tragedies. In May of 1990, a five-year-old boy in the rural town of Evaro, Montana, was attacked and killed by a lion as he played in his backyard in the woods. A Wyoming boy was attacked by a lion as he played on a beach in Glacier National Park. He survived. Dozens of dogs, cats, chickens, cattle and sheep have also fallen prey to marauding lions.

Lions were seen wandering by four-lane highways in Fresno, California. Two teenagers riding horses in Montana saw their pet beagle attacked and killed by a lion in front of them. Near Colorado Springs, one man came out of his house to find his cocker spaniel dangling from the mouth of a lion that was trying to make a getaway. Unfortunately for the lion, the dog was still attached to its chain, and as the lion struggled to get over a fence with its booty, the owner pulled out a pistol and plugged it.

What experts say is going on is that in the last couple of years, the number of cougars has greatly increased, a cyclical occurrence based on the abundance of lion prey, such as deer and elk. When a young mountain lion is old enough to go it alone, it seeks new territory. With a boom in mountain lions, the only place left to many juveniles is near or in urban areas. Emboldened by hunger, they are overcoming an innate fear of humans. "There's been an explosion of homes, vacation homes, ski areas and the like in cougar habitat," says Paul Beier, a University of California at Berkeley wildlife biologist who is studying mountain lion behavior and attacks in southern California. "There's a whole lot more people out there in cougar country."

No small problem. Mountain lions can grow as large as 275

pounds, are as strong as steel, with paws as thick as catcher's mitts. They are fast and agile and in one leap can cover more than twenty feet.

At the same time the lion's share of good habitat is getting chewed up by subdivisions, the people who come to live in wild country often know nothing more about getting along with wildlife than what they've seen in Disney movies. Near Boulder, for example, people have adopted wild deer, and attract them by placing salt blocks in their yard. "They even have names for them," says Todd Malmsbury, chief of information for the Colorado Division of Wildlife. "One's called Snuggles."

This is no way to run wild country, Malmsbury says. When hungry young lions come in to hunt deer, they find even easier prey, like poodles and chickens and occasionally humans. And because fewer people are hunting cougars, the animals learn they have nothing to fear from humans. It's part of the expansion outward of the city into wildlife habitat. And in one of the great themes of the West, the very thing people came here to enjoy is what they are destroying. People and the powers that be often don't know or don't want to know how the construction of homes and roads and other development affects the rhythms of nature.

It's not only the large, wide-ranging species like the cougar that are affected by sprawl. There are, for example, just seven sites left in the Greater Yellowstone where a plant called the yellow spring beauty grows. It is not yet protected, and one of the seven populations recently disappeared beneath a housing development near Henry's Lake, Idaho.

One of the things at work is an environmental theory of relativity. People moving to Boise from Los Angeles, from Miami to Billings, from New York to Santa Fe find that relative to where they came from, the new place is heaven, unspoiled, a piece of paradise. And so they proceed to build their home or a developer builds a series of condos along the river, thus beginning a slide down the slippery slope toward the destruction of paradise.

As development continues, as habitat disappears, as more and more species decline in number and the number falling under protection of federal laws is growing, pressure to change the Endangered Species Act to allow more development to occur is mounting. On the other hand, there are those who maintain the Endangered Species Act doesn't go far enough.

Tall, thin and intense, Jasper Carlton approaches his topic—biodiversity—with a religious fervor. He argues that people have no right to destroy other life-forms and he blames the Judeo-Christian ethic—which holds that the Earth serves at the pleasure of humans—for many of the problems. Few people think of this philosophy, Carlton argues, but it governs U.S. resource policy.

Carlton heads the Biodiversity Legal Foundation, a small, radical, nonprofit group in Boulder, Colorado, that is part of the Earth First! ideology. Carlton and others at the BLF are Deep Ecologists. While the traditional view taken by environmentalists is that nature is important to man's existence and should be preserved for that reason, Deep Ecologists argue that whales, grizzly bears, humpback chubs, Bruno hot spring snails and every other living species has an intrinsic right to existence. But Carlton does acknowledge that the importance of the natural world to humans is compelling. "We haven't even begun to understand what can be derived from plants or from the chemicals of insects, that may save human beings," Carlton says in a rapid-fire delivery charged with passion. "We have analyzed less than one percent of the species. There's no telling whether the cure of AIDS is tied up out there. To preclude that analysis before we do it is uncivilized, and I don't think future generations will forgive us for it.

"We don't know what role these natural systems play in the scheme of things. It would be unsubstantiated arrogance to say we have that answer. To say we don't have that answer is a reason for not eliminating those species. Look at how much we have learned about old growth in the last ten years. What we now know is that ten years ago we knew very little. Ten years from now the same thing will be true. Why preclude those options of understanding and benefits to human beings and the planet?"

The aim of the BLF is to protect as many different life-forms as possible, as soon as possible, by having their five attorneys (working pro bono) filing as many appeals and lawsuits as possible in several parts of the country, and especially in the Yellowstone ecosystem. Yellowstone, says Carlton, is a one-of-a-kind museum. "Yellowstone is one of the last places in this country to support a full array of species," he says. Because of the interrelatedness of life, Carlton says, allowing any plants or insects to go extinct could affect other life-forms. Everything must be saved. "You can't just pick some species to save, and ignore the others. It's easy for us to say we don't want a world without birds. Where's the singing, where's the beauty, where's the aesthetics? But nobody thinks about what the effect of what we're doing is on insects, which will have an impact on plant communities, and once those plants go, other insects go, and it goes right up the food chain and all of a sudden birds are gone."

The same thing may apply to grizzly bears. Millions of dollars have been spent to manage the bear in and around Yellowstone National Park. Critical habitat is protected, certain areas are off-limits to humans. It may be, however, that an unknown, unpredictable ecological interaction takes place, such as with the army cutworm moth, a native species. Army cutworm moths lay their eggs in wheat fields and the larvae emerge as they feed on the wheat and grow to their adult stage. They are a pest to farmers, who spray them with heavy-duty pesticides to protect their crops. The moths fly up to higher elevations in the alpine areas of Yellowstone, where they live on the talus slopes. At night they emerge, like bats, to feed on the nectar of blooming alpine wildflowers. They are a critical summer food source for grizzly bears, who feed voraciously on the swarms of moths. Should, as a method of pest control, sterile males be introduced to stop the moths from breeding, it could, in combination with other problems, jeopardize the existence of the bear. Since Yellowstone is the last biologically intact place, Carlton holds, and numerous unknown ecological interactions are taking place, why take a chance? Save it all.

"We are now at the point where we are destroying the last of the old-growth forest ecosystems in the contiguous United States, the last unique wetlands, the last biologically intact desert," says Carlton. "Look at Yellowstone: If we ask the American people, 'Is the public interest served to give emphasis in the Yellowstone ecosystem to natural diversity?', we would get an overwhelming yes."

Wilderness and wildlife, habitable places to live, these are all part of the ascending New West, as logging and mining and agriculture downsize. Environment and economy are usually considered at odds with each other; certainly in the Old West. The New West is the merging and marketing of those values. However, even as the New West begins to unfold, the underpinnings of this economy are imperiled. Wildlife and scenery are vital, the heart and soul and bottom line of the New West. People are coming to the West, from around the country, from around the world, because nature exists here. And they will pay a great deal for it. But the absence of grizzlies from Yellowstone, or the presence of air pollution there, or nuclear waste or mining or logging or subdivisions on the national park's border—these things begin to diminish the draw.

7
Gridlock in Paradise

FRIDAY, JUNE 9, 1989: SUICIDE WAS ON THE MIND OF BRETT Hartley, a twenty-one-year-old man from Baton Rouge, New Orleans, who took a hike up to Observation Point just above Old Faithful in the center of Yellowstone Park. He pulled a long-barreled .30-caliber Ruger handgun from his pack and pressed the steel against his head. He contemplated pulling the trigger, but couldn't. Instead, he thought, as he later told officials, why not let the rangers of Yellowstone National Park shoot him?

Hartley wandered down to the visitor center, which sits within view of the punctual tower of hot water and steam famous as Old Faithful. As tourists paraded by, wondering where the bathrooms were and what time the geyser erupted, the troubled young man with the gun came inside. He ordered women and children out, keeping eight men and two female employees as hostages. The word spread. Prowl cars converged on the visitor center. Dozens of bulletproof-vest-wearing members of the Park Service ranger corps and FBI agents surrounded the visitor center. Five tense hours later, after talking to a ranger on a phone for two hours, Hartley threw down his gun and surrendered.

Sunday, June 11, 1989: A "mental case from Oregon," as a ranger put it, broke into the water treatment plant at Old Faithful, the system that provides potable water for two thousand overnight visitors, 1,500 employees and the forty thousand visitors who swarm each summer day to the Old Faithful complex. The angry tourist mashed water-testing equipment, gauges and pumps with a ball peen hammer, spilled chemicals on the floor and stabbed knives into the screens on the windows. A trail of gunpowder was scattered on the floor, an attempt to ignite a pile of live ammunition. Before the man could touch match to the powder, however, rangers subdued him. After a vandalism spree that did $20,000 worth of damage, he was arrested.

Tuesday, June 13, 1989: The staccato chop of helicopter rotors sounded in the blue sky over Yellowstone as President George Bush and his entourage landed in a large meadow at Fountain Flats, seven or so miles from Old Faithful. As the president finished his speech about his environmental policies and climbed with a wave into his waiting helicopter, Old Faithful District ranger Debbie Bird felt a wave of relief wash through her. "It was a very memorable week," said the diminutive, blond-haired ranger, who is now the superintendent of Devil's Tower National Monument in eastern Wyoming. "But not that unusual in the Yellowstone I knew. I never had a summer that wasn't action-packed. It's mind-numbing activity at a rate that never ceases."

Once upon a time the national parks and wilderness areas were a world away from the cities, a natural paradise with breath-stealing views and absolute peace and quiet where people went to get away from it all. Now people are bringing the cities with them, and the problems associated with crowding are legion. From Yellowstone to Glacier, from Rocky Mountain National Park to the Grand Canyon, from Oregon's Three Sisters Wilderness Area to Colorado's Mesa Verde National Monument, America's premier natural areas are, say biologists, park managers and other scientists, overrun with people, automobiles and other trappings of civilization, overrun to the breaking point. Species are being lost, resources are being damaged, and the things that make America's wildlands wild are receding. Some call it "greenlock."

It's not just the natural environment suffering. There is a $2 billion backlog of repair work to the parks' infrastructure—such things as roads, sewers and bridges. Meanwhile, the pay for park professionals is caught far behind the cost of living. Morale is at an all-time low. In an unusually frank assessment of the problem, the

Park Service issued the *Vail Report* in 1992. "The ability of the National Park Service to achieve the most fundamental aspects of its missions has been compromised," the report said. "The agency is beset by controversy, concern, weakened morale and declining effectiveness." The so-called thin green line—the ranges and resource people and administrators that run and protect the parks—is growing thinner all the time.

Neither is the problem in protected areas—parks, wilderness, recreation areas, wildlife refuges—alone. Growth in the urban West has been phenomenal. From 1980 to 1990, Boise's population grew from 105,000 to 126,000, or nearly 20 percent. Las Vegas and environs went from 463,000 to 741,000, more than 60 percent growth. The Boulder-Denver grew by more than 20 percent (though the city of Denver itself lost about 10,000 people, or 1.6 percent). The city of Phoenix grew by 34 percent, while its suburb of Mesa grew by a whopping 76 percent. Salt Lake City went from 846,000 to over a million, an increase of close to 25 percent. Albuquerque went from 420,000 to 481,000, some 12 percent. As these cities grow, so does the damage. All of these things are pushing out into undeveloped and unprotected public and private land. The result, from impact of all stripes, is damage to the biological integrity of the land and a quickening diminishment of its long-term economic and ecological value.

The problem of greenlock is especially dramatic at the Grand Canyon, one of the most famous parks in the world and one of the most heavily visited. It is located in the northwest corner of Arizona, not far from either Utah or Nevada.

Human habitation of the canyon goes back at least five thousand years, and archaeologists have found split willow figurines of bighorn sheep and deer, likely talismans to ensure a productive hunt, for the figurines are split by a tiny spear, made from an agave thorn.

The Anasazi moved into the canyon area and occupied it for centuries, and hundreds of sites, with rock structures, pieces of pottery and other artifacts, are still found sandwiched in crevices throughout the canyon. The Anasazi developed irrigation and farmed ledges and flat spots throughout the canyon. It was the most extensive human habitation of the canyon in history.

The Havasupai tribe still occupies the bottom of the canyon, just to the west of the south rim development. The Havasupai—the name means "people of the blue-green water"—live in a village on a five-hundred-acre reservation along Havasu Creek, near a turquoise ribbon of water that drops into an emerald pool.

In 1540, explorer Francisco Vásquez de Coronado sent one of his officers, García López de Cárdenas, to check into reports of the large rock canyon. He is recognized as the first white man to see the Grand Canyon. Other Spanish missionaries and explorers would come and go, but the canyon seemed so impenetrable it held little fascination. One missionary called it "that calaboose [from *calabozo*, meaning prison] of cliffs and canyons."

With the signing of the Treaty of Guadalupe Hildago, the canyon fell into American hands. Lieutenant Joseph Christmas Ives, exploring the Colorado River in 1857, came upon the canyon and wrote, "The region is, of course, altogether valueless . . . after entering it there is nothing to do but leave. Ours has been the first, and will doubtless be the last, party of whites to visit this profitless locality. It seems intended by nature that the Colorado river, along the greater portion of its lonely and majestic way, shall be forever unvisited and undisturbed."

Major John Wesley Powell was the first white man to certifiably float the hellacious Colorado River through the Grand Canyon (sitting in an armchair lashed to the boat, no less). The one-armed Battle of Shiloh veteran and his party mapped the blank spot on the map, took in the geology and natural history, and officially named the chasm the Grand Cañon. He and his party named Dirty Devil Creek, after the mud and smell, and the clear Bright Angel Creek, to counter. Powell was among the first to see the West not just as a place to make money but as a true natural wonder. During one of Powell's visits, artist Thomas Moran would accompany him and take back drawings of the Grand Canyon and make it famous to the world. (Incidentally, Moran did the same with paintings of Yellowstone Park.)

As with most of the West, the railroad was the biggest agent of change for the canyon. Tracks were laid in 1882, and tourists, ranchers and other would-be boomers rolled west. Miners leading burros walked through the canyon, digging glory holes and sluicing the water for gold. Hermits and other characters crawled into folds and holes in the canyon. Before long, however, it dawned on people working to extract a living from the ground that there was more money to be made leaving the canyon together rather than pulling it apart. The first tourists came in 1884 and have been coming ever since.

The canyon is nothing less than astounding. Standing in one spot on the edge is amazing, and to think that the grandeur extends for hundreds of miles is mind-boggling. Small wonder that people flock here more than to any other park except the Great Smoky Mountains in Tennessee.

Come summer it is so crowded that "it's unreal," says John Reed, assistant superintendent of Grand Canyon National Park and a veteran park service employee who started as a seasonal at Yellowstone in 1964. "We have 1950s-era facilities with twenty-first-century crowds. There's insufficient parking, which means people park wherever they can, off the road and in the trees. We have three public restrooms for millions of people. And people have to wait several hours to eat."

In 1991, roughly four million people streamed through the entrance station into the Grand Canyon National Park. Ten years earlier, that number was 2.6 million. The number of visitors to all the parks has doubled in the last twenty-five years, to 267 million. Thirty thousand people a day funnel through the small, congested area at the South Rim of the canyon in the summer. On a good day in the summer, traffic crawls; on a bad day, it doesn't seem to move at all. Parking is a nightmare, and the sound of idling engines and sour smell of blue diesel smoke from tour buses hangs in the air. "Flight-seeing" planes and helicopters from Nevada, California and the Grand Canyon National Park Airport just outside the park drone incessantly overhead. And there is crime in the park—increasingly violent crime, as years go by.

Ranger Brian Smith puts on his black sunglasses and slips into his white Park Service prowl car with the Park Service arrowhead emblem on the door. A black shotgun is bolted to the dashboard. Radio static hisses. Smith makes a slow loop through Grand Canyon village, along the south rim of the canyon, the urban center of the park. Pushed by the wind, heavy white clouds cast mottled shadows that ride the contours of the carved canyon features. "Any kind of criminal activity you can think of goes on here in the park," explains Smith, a dark-haired, intense ranger who has been with the Park Service for more than a decade. "We have homicides, assaults, burglaries, drunk driving and illegal drugs."

Smith and other rangers are fire fighters and paramedics as well as cops on a decidedly urban beat, making four hundred arrests a year here, many of them among the three thousand people who work here for the park service and the concessions, and live on the rim.

Other parks have similar problems. Roving gangs of "car clouters" work Yellowstone, Yosemite and other crowded parks, including the Grand Canyon, breaking into cars and stealing cash and cameras. Mobile amphetamine laboratories have been set up in Joshua Tree National Monument. In 1990, there were eight murders in the national parks. In 1991, there were sixteen. The sixteen-cell jail at Yosemite is full all summer. Smith, who in his ten years with the Park Service has worked at Sequoia–Kings Canyon national parks and the Chattahoochee River and Glen Canyon national recreation areas, say things are tough. But he also says he loves his job. "Where else," he says, "can you jog after work on the edge of the Grand Canyon?"

A white, twin-engine Otter aircraft taxis down an airstrip with nineteen passengers at the Grand Canyon National Park Airport, picks up speed and is airborne over a carpet of green forest. The lip of the Grand Canyon comes into view, and suddenly, as the plane flies over the rock formations, the ground falls dramatically away beneath the plane. Far below, a shiny black raven soars with unflapping wings over the convoluted canyon, and farther down still—over a mile farther down—a ribbon of coffee-colored river, the muddy Colorado, the creator of this spectacle, oxbows through the sheer canyon walls, the buttes and the sagebrush-studded mesas.

Crowding at the canyon is not confined to the ground. Few ways of seeing the seven-thousand-foot-deep, 277-mile-long Grand Canyon are as thrilling as soaring over it, and some fifty thousand flights a year carry hundreds of thousands of people over the canyon. Such heavy air traffic has created a conflict. Thousands of people also come here to hike the steep trails into the depths of the canyon, to camp along the river, or to float the rambunctious rapids of the Colorado and soak in the solitude. For them the constant buzz of airplanes and the *whop-whop* of helicopter blades are an invasion of the wilderness experience, the very thing they came to escape.

And it is not only happening here. Officials at one hundred parks, from Glacier to Hawaii Volcanoes, say overflights are a problem. One of the primary reasons these areas were set aside was for the solitude, "a vignette of primitive America," a place where people can remember what pre-Columbian America was like, which makes the impact all the greater. In fact, park officials measured the "quiet" at the Grand Canyon when planes weren't flying. What they found was that in the bottom of the canyon, far from anywhere, the lack of man-made noise is so absolute they had to come up with new measurements. Fact is, however, that there is no law against flying over a park or wilderness area, no matter what altitude.

Environmentalists complained long and loud about the "invasion," and a few radicals took matters into their own hands. In 1987, a helicopter pilot was hovering over prehistoric Indian ruins at Point Sublime in the canyon, a favorite spot to take tourists. Suddenly a group of radical environmentalists—one ranger said they were members of Earth First! —hidden behind the walls of the ruins, stood up and began throwing rocks at the chopper. Fearing damage to the helicopter's rotor, the pilot veered away.

In 1985, former Grand Canyon National Park superintendent Dick Marks and U.S. Senator John McCain, then a congressman from Arizona, were backpacking to the bottom of the canyon. As they stood at a place called Tip Off Point on the South Kaibab Trail about two thirds of the way from the rim to the canyon floor, they heard a noise. They looked down to see, about five hundred feet below them, and three thousand feet below the south rim of the canyon, a huge C-130 military transport plane flying between the intricately textured red and brown canyon walls, just above the Colorado River. "I wondered what the hell he was doing down there," recalls Marks. "Military aircraft have no business flying that low." It was apparently just a joyride.

Problems with aircraft at the canyon were nearly constant. Air Force fighter pilots often zoomed through the two-hundred-mile-long chasm. "A lot of them flew upside down," Marks said. "You can take better pictures that way." One Air Force officer claimed there was a "canyon club" among pilots who had flown in the canyon. Commercial flights were a headache as well. Without restrictions, airplanes flew deep into the canyon, and helicopters hovered, like giant dragonflies, above prehistoric ruins and the canyon's most scenic areas. Marks once came out of his office to be greeted, at eye level, with a Braniff Airlines 727 passenger jet—filled with passengers—that was flying at rim level.

But this time a congressman was along on the trip, and the incredible sight of the huge aircraft flying so low led McCain to introduce a bill that would restrict flights.

Change finally came, as it often does, on the tail of tragedy. On June 18, 1986, a sight-seeing helicopter lifted up into a Twin Otter aircraft that was landing at the Grand Canyon airport. All twenty-eight people aboard the two craft died. It was the thirty-second air crash in and around the canyon since 1965. (The worst crash in the canyon was on June 30, 1956, when two commercial airliners collided overhead, killing 128 people. Pieces of the wreckage still lie scattered across the rugged terrain at the bottom of the canyon.)

The 1986 accident "accelerated things," says Mike Ebersole, the Grand Canyon's flight operations officer. A pilot himself, Ebersole knew safety was a problem. He was once the first on the scene of a plane crash on the canyon's rim in his plane and flew circles over the downed aircraft and with his radio guided rescuers to the crash site's remote location.

Grand Canyon officials adopted an SFAR: a special federal airline regulation. Now some 44 percent of the Grand Canyon is off-limits to aircraft that fly under 14,500 feet above sea level or a little over a mile above the top of the canyon. That flight-free designation, says Ebersole, keeps rim-level sight-seeing aircraft away from all visitors to the rim and 90 percent of the back-country users. In the rest of the canyon airspace, helicopters must fly at rim level or above and fixed-wing craft must fly five hundred feet above the rim. Flights may no longer dip into the canyon. Yosemite National Park in California and portions of Haleakala National Park in Hawaii have since adopted similar restrictions.

That doesn't mean things are perfect. Hikers in busy areas near the "Dragon Corridor"—a route that brings tour operators across the canyon and into the airport—might hear and see as many as forty flights an hour. As Reed puts it: "If you think you'll hear nothing but your own heartbeat, you'll be disappointed."

Environmentalists are pushing for more restrictions, but air tour operators think things have gone far enough. Tom Kelley, a customer service manager for Papillon Grand Canyon Helicopters, which provides air tours over the canyon, thinks conservationists aren't being fair. "Take handicapped people," he says. "It's difficult for them to get on the back of a mule. There are a lot of overweight people who don't have the ability to hike the canyon, or to ride a mule, because the mule has weight limitations. And a lot of people fly so they don't have to spend time walking along the rim or driving."

The military makes its contribution to the invasion of air space over natural areas. Take the case of VR 1257. *VR* means "visual route" and number 1257 takes the cream of the fighter crop from Lemoore Naval Air Station just south of Fresno over Joshua Tree National Monument, a prime piece of southern California desert. The country is made up of beautiful granite canyons and odd-shaped Joshua trees, which grow with thorny balls on the end of the branch. This desert country is populated by desert bighorn sheep and cougars.

"When the route was laid out," said recently retired Joshua Tree superintendent Rick Anderson, tongue-in-cheek, "they made a mistake. They somehow missed a campground. We have ten campgrounds here; they only fly over nine." The flyovers happen one or two times a day he said, and generally involve two or three aircraft. One of his rangers was forced off the road by a plane that looked like it was going to collide with his vehicle. "I'm an airplane nut," Anderson said. "I love to fly. But they don't belong over the national parks. Not at that altitude." Anderson spoke to officials at Lemoore, and they were sympathetic, he said, but didn't change the route.

If the military would respect the limit of two thousand feet above ground level limit over parks and wilderness, he said, it would greatly reduce the noise and visual impact.

The military is not always intransigent when it comes to the thunder created by its aircraft. Giant B-52 bombers used to fly low and slow over Petrified Forest National Park, occasionally just five hundred feet over the administration building. "It's like someone is driving a hot rod through the middle of your office," said Ed Gastellum, former superintendent of the park and now assistant superintendent at North Cascades National Park in Washington. "The windows rattle and the furniture shakes."

After much disagreement with Air Force officials on a local level, Gastellum said, Gary Vest, the Air Force deputy assistant secretary for environmental safety and occupational health, traveled to the park and had the bombers fly over. After the test, the Air Force agreed to move the flight path to just over the park boundary.

The most often voiced complaint about aircraft is that they are grossly incompatible with a primary quality of a natural area: tranquillity. Tranquillity is valued because it provides an opportunity for reflection. A mandate for parks and wilderness areas is that they be maintained as "vignettes of primitive America," and aircraft, especially low-flying military aircraft, destroy any sense of primitive tranquillity. "I've been in canyons in Utah and felt the whole world was coming to an end," says Terri Martin, regional representative for the National Parks and Conservation Association in Salt Lake City. "It's bizarre. You're communing with nature and all of a sudden a huge symbol of our military-industrial complex comes screaming low overhead. It's not only disturbing, it's depressing. It's a desecration."

It can also be painful. Some people describe the impact of some sonic booms, which come as a surprise, as similar to a slap in the face. Noise affects wildlife and domestic animals as well, which scatter pell-mell beneath low-flying aircraft or sonic booms.

It has become more difficult to reconcile military training with the need for solitude, says the Air Force's Gary Vest, because the nature of warfare has changed in recent years. "If there was a war in Europe," he said, "all access to the target would be at low level to avoid radar. Your ability to survive is based on being low and fast. That's the way our crews survive. But flying that low is tricky. It requires a level of proficiency and you have got to go out and fly." Nonetheless, he said, "if we can make changes, we will. These are two valid national interests."

"It was," says ranger Joe Evans as he adjusted his flat-brimmed Smokey the Bear hat, "quite a haul." A charm bracelet. Nails. The hinge from an outhouse door. Sunglass lenses. A couple of dozen coins. He nods to the orange and green colors in Morning Glory Pool, and says, "It's the wishing-well syndrome." Tourists had tossed so much junk into Morning Glory Pool that the stuff had clogged the vents that feed hot water into the pool. When hot water can't get into the pool, the temperature drops. Algae dies. And the beauty of the pool is diminished. So rangers steam-cleaned the "honey wagon" that they use to pump out septic tanks, and used it to reduce the water level in the forty-foot-deep pool. With a spoon on the end of a long stick they fished out what they could find. "Except for the white fisherman's hat," Decker says. "It came floating up to the top, but then sank down again before we could get it."

The love affair visitors have with the park's geothermal features has not always been a healthy one. In the early days, concession employees washed clothes in some of the hot springs near Old Faithful. It was common for visitors to cast a handkerchief into Handkerchief Pool and watch the natural movement of the water swish it back and forth. Even the Park Service toyed with them. Near the century's turn, when dignitaries came to the park, rangers would dump a box of laundry soap into the geysers, a hot spring emetic, causing them to erupt on cue. The soap hardens the bubbles, which increases pressure inside the rock chamber where the water simmers. Voilà: instant eruption.

For causing permanent damage to the environment, there is nothing that can match crowds of people on the ground. The 22,000 people a year who raft and camp in the Grand Canyon have strained the ecology. Vegetation gets trampled. River guides carry human waste off the river, but disposing of it at the end of the trip has created problems with disposal logistics. Human waste is also a problem along Bright Angel Trail. Thousands of people climb into the canyon via this route, often after breakfast, and the Park Service can't put enough outhouses on the rocky slope.

In some parks, visitors feed the rodents and birds so much junk food they no longer eat fragile alpine vegetation and drop the seeds so the plants spread. Native plants are dying out.

Automobiles are probably the biggest part of park crowding, a problem that affects almost every park. The Yosemite Valley fills in the summer almost every day, and after five thousand cars have arrived, no more are allowed in. One goes out, one comes in. Mount Rushmore in South Dakota could be called Mount Crushmore: it was closed some twenty-five times one recent summer because no more cars could fit. The Park Service is considering a reservation system for day use of the parks—a radical but necessary step, officials say.

The continuing growth in visitation—and projections are for rapidly increasing growth for the next several decades—puts park managers in a double bind. More people create the need for such things as hotels and parking lots, which, however, impact on the natural beauty and can displace wildlife or fragile park features, as it did in the case of Fishing Bridge in Yellowstone.

Fishing Bridge is a rustic tourist hamlet in the heart of the park, with log buildings from the 1920s painted pastel shades of green and yellow. In 1981, Yellowstone then-superintendent John Townsley authorized construction of another tourist complex—Grant Village—smack in the middle of critical grizzly feeding ground thirty miles from Fishing Bridge. The park maintains it did not know how important the habitat was at the time. Environmentalists were outraged, so park officials made a deal: when Grant Village was finished, Fishing Bridge would be bulldozed flat and the land given back to nature, specifically the bear. A biological quid pro quo.

Yellow dozers never rumbled into Fishing Bridge. After Grant Village was finished in 1982, merchants in Cody, Wyoming, complained to the Wyoming Congressional delegation that campers at Grant Village were too far away from their shops. U.S. Senator Alan Simpson, a Republican, came down on the side of the purveyors, and the Park Service backed off closure plans, instead closing down only a portion of Fishing Bridge, despite the fact that the Park Service itself called the complete closure a matter of "some urgency."

Environmentalists were livid. "You have politicians making biological decisions. That's wrong. The Park Service should put itself between the politics and the resource," says Michael Scott, director of the Northern Rockies Office of The Wilderness Society. "As bears filter in here to feed, they're going to get in trouble with tourists."

"Parks are religious to many people," says Terri Martin. "People use parks to get away from urban society. Yet the Park Service responds to increased visitation by building more parking lots, more roads, more sidewalks. Parks have become a place of profit rather than preservation. There are a lot of people who won't go to parks anymore, a lot of displaced people."

Not everyone sees crowding as a problem. Concessionaires, those who run the businesses in the parks, think the problem of crowding is one of perception. "It's been exaggerated," says Allen Howe, Washington representative of the 150-member Conference of National Park Concessionaires. "Some parks on peak weekends might be overcrowded. The rest of the time it might be crowded, but it's manageable."

Lorraine Mintzmeyer was regional director for the Rocky Mountain region of the national parks, based in Denver, and responsible for the finest of the parks—Yellowstone, Zion, Rocky Mountain, Glacier, Mesa Verde and others. Mintzmeyer had worked her way up from a position as a secretary and spent thirty-two years devoted to the Park Service. She claims she was harassed and forced out in 1992 by officials in the Bush administration. After she left the Park Service, she criticized the agency for its failure to limit the number of visitors. The trouble, she contends, is that the Republican administration was so aligned with business interests and an anti-environmental mentality that such closures were impossible. In fact, she says that the strong-arming of biological values by politics is a chief cause of problems at the parks. "Closures should have happened by now, but they haven't. Yosemite reached saturation a long time ago. Zion has reached the saturation point. Yellowstone in the summer is overcrowded." The problem is not the Park Service, she says, but politicians who force the agency to do things that run counter to its responsibilities. It remains to be seen what the Clinton administration will mean for the parks.

Another kind of visitor is a serious threat to the parks these days. Imagine walking to the precipice at the edge of the Grand Canyon, having just driven three days to vacation there. The kids jump out of the car and run to the railing. "Where's the canyon?" your kids ask as you approach. The canyon, the spectacular, yawning abyss you've heard about all your life, is filled—to the rim—with a blue smog. It looks like a lake.

It is, a ranger explains, a "haze episode." Those famous crystalline western vistas are no longer so crystalline. Air pollution from coal-fired power plants and places like Los Angeles gets caught up in prevailing winds and makes its way to the Grand Canyon, where, because of temperature differences, it often sinks and stubbornly sits. "The canyon," says Carl Bowman, an air quality specialist for the Park Service, "is a catch basin for pollution." He has a picture on his office wall of the canyon filled to the rim during a haze episode.

Even though days when the canyon is not visible occur only a few times a year, there are many more days when smog obscures but doesn't quite block the striking reds, browns, purples and grays. An average of one day in ten a visitor cannot see the other side of the canyon, ten miles across at the South Rim Village. "There's a lot of color and texture that gets washed out with pollution," Bowman says. "That feeling of immensity is gone."

The Grand Canyon is not alone. Many more of America's most famous vistas are disappearing behind a veil of pollution. Kings Canyon National Park and Sequoia National Park, adjacent to each other and located in eastern California, suffer some of the worst pollution in the country, stuff generated in the populous Central Valley. The haze virtually smothers the park and looks as if someone pulled a layer of white or gray gauze over the mountains, so that only a dim, indigo silhouette of the nearest mountains are visible. Taking scenic photographs is almost impossible. On the rare clear day in Sequoia—eight or ten days a year are considered clear—a visitor can stand on Moro Rock, a popular viewing spot, and see one hundred miles and eleven mountain ranges, including California's coastal mountain range. Most times the visibility is less than ten miles, with only two of the eleven ranges barely visible through the haze. "It's an aerial sewer," says Dawn Vernon, a park service interpreter at Sequoia who explains air pollution to visitors. "You wouldn't swim in it, and you certainly wouldn't drink it."

The interesting thing is that many people don't notice the problem, again the theory of relativity at work. However poor things are in the parks, the air seems good compared to that in many parts of the country. "We get a lot of people from L.A.," says Vernon. "They get here and think the air is wonderful. When we tell them it's not, they're shocked."

The biological diversity the parks protect is also at risk in the aerial assault. The parks are vital as storehouses for plant and animal life that is going or gone elsewhere, but scientists have begun to see ill effects to the flora and fauna within the parks, primarily from ozone and acid rain. (In the upper atmosphere, ozone is beneficial: it filters out harmful ultraviolet rays from the sun, and depletion of upper-atmosphere ozone is a concern. At ground level, however, where ozone is created by a chemical breakdown in automobile exhaust, it is, ironically, harmful.)

Both ozone and acid precipitation show up in high levels in Sequoia and Kings Canyon. Ozone has contributed to the death of Jeffrey pine trees in Sequoia and has caused visible damage to ponderosa pines. How ozone will affect the giant sequoias is not yet known. Studies in which sequoia seedlings are encased in plastic and fumigated with ozone show that at levels just higher than they are now, ozone adversely affects root and shoot growth. The old trees, like the almost 2,700-year-old General Sherman, are too big to wrap and fumigate. But there is concern, for in humans air pollution causes the most severe effects among the very young and the very old. In some parks, including the Santa Monica Mountains National Recreation Area and Indiana Dunes National Monument, high levels of ozone have wiped out a number of lichen species.

Air in the West, according to the Environmental Protection Agency, is expected to get worse, and it is more and more likely that when people come to the parks, they won't be able to see them in all their glory. "Every place we've monitored we've seen degradation of visibility from man-made sources," says Christine Shaver, former chief of the Policy, Planning and Permit Review Branch of the National Park Service's Air Quality Division in Denver and now with the Environmental Defense Fund. "No place is immune." The Park Service says that more than 90 percent of the time, scenic vistas in the parks are affected by man-made pollution.

"It's the destruction of the heritage that the parks were set aside to protect," says Bob Yuhnke, an attorney with the Environmental Defense Fund in Boulder, Colorado. "If you go to the Grand Canyon and can't see 50 miles, you can't see the Grand Canyon. It's 160 miles long. Part of the majesty is being able to take in this work of creation at one time. What we're seeing is a graying of the West."

Air pollution is a good example of the growing number of problems that originate outside the parks, and which park managers are nearly powerless to do anything about. Parks are green islands, at the mercy of the outside world, everything from global warming to a gold mine just over the border. Commercial drilling for hot water or oil and gas outside of Yellowstone, for example, may disrupt the hot water flows to Mammoth Hot Springs and other hot spring features. In the Grand Canyon, a change in river flows caused by the construction of Glen Canyon Dam in the 1960s outside the park has restructured the ecology of the river, wiping out several species of fish. The Colorado has always carried a lot of sediment, giving it its ruddy appearance. The Glen Canyon dam traps sediment behind it, and clear water runs through the canyon, wiping out sandy beaches but carrying nothing to replace them with. Nonnative species have moved in to occupy the changed habitat. The list goes on and on.

Reptiles and amphibians are causing concern in the West these days, or more accurately the lack of them. Populations of frogs and toads are blinking out all over the West (as well as the world). In Sequoia National Park, the foothills yellow-legged frog is gone. In the Laramie Basin of Wyoming, there is a single population of the Wyoming toad left, where there once were many. The leopard frog is gone from 85 percent of its Colorado range. The numbers of the western toad in Grand Teton National Park are greatly reduced. "I haven't seen twenty adults in two years," says Charles Peterson, a herpetologist from Idaho State University who studies the Teton creature. "Forty years ago you could see that many in a morning."

Sensitive to the climatic change, acid rain and other ecological changes, reptiles and amphibians indicate by their decline in numbers that something dramatic is happening to the environment, but no one knows for sure what is causing the die-off. Drought? Acid rain? Too much ultraviolet radiation? Pesticides?

While the nature of threats to the parks from outside are widely recognized, some critics say some of the wilderness parks are suffering at the hands of an unlikely perpetrator: the Park Service. The problem, critics say, is natural regulation. Humankind's tinkering with nature has always been analogous to the story of Brer Rabbit and the tar baby. Coming down the road Brer Rabbit says hello to the baby made from tar. It, of course, does not respond. Brer Rabbit hits the rude tar baby and gets his paw stuck. He hits it again with the other paw so it will release him. That paw gets stuck. Pretty soon Brer Rabbit has a real mess on his hands.

Why make changes in nature, the Park Service theory holds, when every time changes are made more problems crop up? Nature knows best and should be left to its own devices. Grizzly bears, threatened or not, should be treated as wild animals, and left to fend for themselves in the wild. Elk and bison numbers should be determined by hard or mild winters and wet and dry summers, not a formula of wildlife biologists or a troop of rangers with rifles. If lightning starts a fire in the park, the fire should be allowed to burn, for in a dry climate like Yellowstone, nutrients return to the soil primarily through ash, not decomposition.

But critics say natural regulation is contributing to the decline of the grizzly bear in Yellowstone. In 1983, Charles Kay, a biologist, did a study of aspen and willow trees in the park. What he found was that, unlike in areas around the park, there was extremely little regeneration of these species. Kay says it is because the elk deprive the beavers of food and so there are very few left in the park, though it appears to be prime beaver habitat. Beavers dam rivers and streams, create ponds and increase the growth of succulents and forbs for grizzly bears to eat in the spring. No beavers, no bear food. Poor nutrition could lead to the eventual dying out of the bear. The park, essentially, stands accused of the same kind of overgrazing leveled at many ranchers. To benefit the grizzly bear, author Alston Chase holds, reduce the number of elk in the park by hunting. That, however, would not be a natural thing to do, and so the park has refused.

Chase wrote a book called *Playing God in Yellowstone* and has long been a stone in the shoe of the Park Service, constantly criticizing its natural-management philosophy and advocating active, hands-on management. Without it, he predicts, Yellowstone will be ruined.

Chase's book came down hard on the park's philosophy, and cast the Park Service as the chief cause of the park's perils. The slight, gray-haired, mustachioed Chase, who lives in the Paradise Valley just north of the park, says such management is ridiculous in light of the fact that the parks are bombarded with the effects of humans, especially the fact that the park is some sixteen million acres shy of a full ecosystem. Federal managers are a few bricks shy of a load if they think they can manage Yellowstone as wilderness, he says. How can the park function as a wild region if its most impressive features—grizzly bears, geothermal displays, elk, bison—can't exist without surrounding lands, and those lands have small towns on them, or dozens of bomb shelters built by a cult, or are being logged pell-mell? Or when politics, disregarding biology, calls the shots? Moreover, river bottoms, the most important wildlife habitat in the park, have been paved over with asphalt, and small towns in the park are invaded by more than three million tourists each year. The natural aspects of the park need compensation for the problems humans have caused. Shoot elk and feed bears, Chase argues.

Chase says the fires of 1988 damaged the park more seriously than the Park Service admits. Problems with soil erosion have been serious in some parts of the park. What may bring the greatest change over the next decades, he says, is that so much of the park burned at once. Instead of hundreds of small fires burning a million acres over many years—as with prescribed burning—a few big fires burned nearly one and a half million acres all at once. When the vegetation grows back, it is all the same age, and the plant communities are far less diverse than if the fires had occurred over a longer period of time. "We won't know for a long time," says Chase, "but we can speculate that the effect will be less biological diversity." Again, Chase faults the Park Service for its failure to consider man, in any way, an element of nature. Indians managed the West—including Yellowstone—for thousands of years with fire, he says, burning grass and forests every twenty-five years or so to create forage for game. "Yellowstone still needs fire," Chase says. "You need frequent fires. Prescribed burning. That's the kind the Indians produced."

John Varley bristles at Chase's accusations. As far as a loss of diversity from the fire goes, "it flat out isn't true. There's been an explosion of diversity. Every species we've monitored has taken the fires in stride. I don't know any knowledgeable scientist who would challenge me on that. Chase is not a scientist. And none of the credible fire ecologists believes prescribed burning in these lodgepole pine forests will buy us anything. It will not prevent the next summer of 1988. The concept of natural regulation in the scientific world has been revalidated by the fires. It proves nature cannot destroy herself."

Many independent fire experts say prescribed burning probably would not have prevented the fires of 1988. The forest was simply too dry. But Chase's argument raises an interesting philosophical question that has implications far beyond Yellowstone: when should people be considered part of the natural world? It's a question that has yet to be answered.

One of the things at risk as the parks begin to come apart is the role that parks play in the study of natural processes in their relatively undisturbed state. As environmental problems in the world grow, the parks are the laboratory where people are learning how they work and how they can be put back together. "The national parks produce two commodities," says Varley. "Inspiration and information." They also provide a baseline against which change on other lands can be measured.

Yellowstone, for example, has fourteen full-time researchers and three hundred who work only in the summer. University and industrial researchers also conduct a large proportion of study in the parks. There are more than 370 ongoing experiments and studies.

Yellowstone is where much of the book on wildlife management has been written. The knowledge gathered here on grizzly bears and elk, for example, has been applied to the management of these animals worldwide.

The grizzly bear, which for many years teetered at the brink of extirpation in Yellowstone, is probably the most studied feature here. Researchers are looking at how large a territory the bear needs, its diet and favored habitat. There is also a study with the goal of determining why hibernating bears don't suffer from osteoporosis, a condition characterized by brittle, easily fractured bones. Humans, especially older women, suffer from this crippling affliction, and researchers believe the bear study might someday lead to a cure.

The uniqueness and diversity found within a park—often the reason it was set aside in the first place—is a prime draw for scientists. "There's twenty-eight researchers who come here to study life in boiling water," says Varley. "You can't do that in Kansas." In fact, Yellowstone's geothermal area is the last intact geyser field in the world.

Yellowstone's geothermal collection has been the subject of an array of research looking at everything from industrial applications of certain microbes to the origin of life on the planet. Mary Bateson, a research associate at Montana State University in Bozeman, has been part of a research team funded by the National Science Foundation looking at microbial mats—a layer of slime that grows on top of the water in Yellowstone's hot pots. Because it's hot, "this is one environment where other organisms, like flies, can't graze on the slime layer," she says. "Big mats of algae can form and tell us what it was like on Earth billions of years ago, when single-cell organisms were the only life on the planet."

Scientists have only recently come to realize how vital microbes are to the Earth's ecosystem. "Microbes decompose the garbage of the world and give nutrients back to the soil," Bateson says. "They provide oxygen. Algae does all of the photosynthesis in the ocean. All the processes that keep us alive happen with microbes. Yet we're still in the dark ages when it comes to understanding them."

Yellowstone's hot springs were also the source of the recently discovered *Thermus aquaticus*, a tiny organism that duplicates DNA molecules. Combined in a test tube with DNA, *T. aquaticus*, in a matter of hours, creates copy after copy of the molecule, until the DNA is large enough to be read under a microscope. This technique is widely used for DNA fingerprinting in criminal cases, and replaces a cumbersome technique that took weeks.

Fire behaviorists are carrying out a series of extensive studies of the park's fire-scarred landscape. "The most interesting aspect of the fires is the scale," said Varley. "They are the only truly large-scale fires in the West since there was a science of ecology. The fires behaved in ways that have never been seen. Marshes and swamps burned, green willows burned. These things had never burned before. Fire behaviorists with thirty years of experience are going to have to scrap all of their models," Varley says. "They became obsolete in 1988."

The park also serves as a kind of genetic safe deposit box. The grizzly bear does well here, and may someday be the stock from where it is returned to former range. In Yellowstone Lake, the offspring of lake trout big enough to eat ducks off the water, which came from Lake Michigan by railroad car in the late 1800s, are being returned to their former home. The huge trout in Lake Michigan died out. To return them, biologists turned to the best-adapted stock, which had flourished since their transplant to Yellowstone.

On a fiercely windy day on the Blackfeet Indian Reservation in northwest Montana, a group of Blackfeet traditionalists emerged from a sweat lodge made of animal skins and, chanting and drumming, made their way with a simple wooden box toward a large, freshly dug grave. Ninety-seven years after they were stolen from their reservation in northern Montana, the skulls and other remains of three child and thirteen adult Blackfeet were returned from the storeroom of the Smithsonian Institution to their home beneath the sawtooth range of the northern Rocky Mountains.

To the Blackfeet, the return of the human remains is more than just a victory in a long-standing debate over who controls ancestral remains. It is, they say, the start of a process of reconstructing the morale, cultural identity and spirituality of the Blackfeet nation, which like many Indian tribes, has been devastated—first by disease and the U.S. Army and later by losses to a very different set of foes they continue to battle—high rates of alcoholism, drug abuse and unemployment.

Rediscovery of traditionalism is going on in many tribes. However, as the western tribes struggle to rebuild their culture with the help of their traditional religion—which is tied inextricably to the land—they are finding that many of the places once a part of their traditional ceremonies, such as vision quests and sweat lodge rituals, are gone or under assault. To the Blackfeet and other tribes in Montana, the Sweetgrass Hills in northern Montana have always been a place to seek visions, and there are still rings of rock where men would sit for days at a time without drinking or eating and wait for a message. Traditionalists still seek visions in what is believed to be a powerful site. However, mining companies want to search the Sweetgrass Hills for gold, and when it comes to a showdown between gold and native religions, there is little contest.

The clash between development and deities is taking place throughout the Rocky Mountain West. Uranium mining is planned for the rim of the Grand Canyon, near the Havasupai's holy Red Butte. The U.S. Forest Service wants to turn the Big Horn Medicine Wheel in the Bighorn Mountains of northern Wyoming into a full-fledged, developed tourist site. Such development, tribal traditionalists say, robs sacred sites of their power. One estimate places the number of conflicts in the West at more than sixty. "Every part of this Earth is sacred to my people," said Seattle, chief of the Suquamish and other Indians near Puget Sound in 1851. "Every shining pine needle, every sandy shore, every mist in the dark woods, every clearing and hummingbird is holy in the memory and experience of my people. . . . Where is the thicket? Gone. Where is the eagle? Gone. The end of living and the beginning of survival."

The landscape of the mind and spirit is being bulldozed figuratively as well as literally. The whole concept of wilderness and wildness, how people think about those things, is eroding. Solitude is becoming rarer and rarer, natural sound increasingly polluted. Animals are becoming more and more managed. There are bears and elk and eagles and individuals of other species that wander the West, all the time with a radio transmitter beaming their whereabouts to a satellite 22,000 miles into space and back to a scientist with a receiver somewhere. Fish swim rivers with beepers in their bellies. In Yellowstone, there are numerous bears wearing beepers, and if they get close to people, appropriate action can be taken. The depths of rivers are monitored by satellite, the current depths always known by a computer operator. The Forest Service recently developed a hand-held geopositioning instrument, which can, through signals coming from orbiting satellites, provide constant information on a person's whereabouts. Every inch of the West is mapped by satellites.

The sense of history that is arguably more alive in the West than anywhere else is also under assault. As cities continue their sprawl, the feeling of history imparted by the landscape is smothered. How great a sense of mission-era California or the Battle of Gettysburg remains, when the battlefield or mission is surrounded by tract homes or shopping malls? Yet go to the Custer Battlefield in Montana or Chaco Canyon in New Mexico or South Pass in Wyoming and history, nourished by a timeless landscape, lives on.

Real adventure is also waning. Reservations for the parks must be made a year or more in advance with Ticketron or a similar agency. No more getting into a car and bombing around the West, a spontaneous trip in which a course is charted as you travel. Much of the experience of wilderness is in the idea of it. A hundred years ago a person who was in the wilderness was there on his or her own. No helicopters could fly in for a rescue. Cabins near the wilderness boundaries had no phones or radios. You couldn't drive from the trailhead into a town for help. Now a visitor in a wilderness area knows that if the going gets tough, a modern Park Service or Forest Service ranger force is there to make a rescue. And that alone changes the nature of the experience—how a visitor thinks or behaves. A good example of how wilderness and the place of people in it have changed is found in the rescue procedures in the Grand Teton Mountains in the last twenty or thirty years.

The glacier-carved peaks of the Tetons, which lie in Grand Teton National Park in the southern portion of the Yellowstone ecosystem, rise up from the plains so suddenly that from the distance they look like a startling, snowcapped illusion. Their beauty, however, harbors a cruel statistic. Out of the some eight thousand climbers a year who come to climb the Tetons, four die and many more are injured. Given the fact that no one can be turned down for a climbing permit, it's a wonder there aren't more fatalities. One reason is that in the past few years an elite group of climbing rangers using new helicopter-rescue techniques have drastically shortened the time it takes to pluck injured climbers from the mountains.

Headquartered in a little cabin at the foot of turquoise Jenny Lake, the men and women climbing rangers at Grand Teton make some of the most dramatic rescues in the United States. The crew, with eighteen people in the summer, and three year-round, are highly trained, and most are emergency medical technicians, who can give IVs, perform surgical procedures, cut a trach, or administer drugs.

Two years ago, for example, a climber just three hundred feet shy of the summit of the Grand Teton, or the Grand, fell into a remote, nearly inaccessible crevice. Using the new techniques, five rescuers reached the climber and flew him out, all in about three and a half hours. "A conventional evacuation would have taken eighteen people eighteen to twenty-four hours to get him to the closest place to land a helicopter," says Pete Armington, the supervisory park ranger who heads the climbing rangers.

Contrast that with the rescue in August 1967 of Gaylord Campbell, a climber who took a tumble near the summit of the North Face of the Grand Teton, a difficult place to reach without helicopters. "It was a big, forbidding face on a big mountain, white-knuckle all the way," recalls Rick Reese, a climbing ranger at the time who later received a Citation of Valor for the rescue.

Campbell lay writhing in agony on the ground for twenty-four hours before the rangers could climb to him. When they reached him they administered morphine, strapped him in a sling and began lowering him two thousand rocky and dangerous feet, some three hundred feet at a time, on the end of a quarter-inch steel cable. For three days, six climbers worked to get Campbell down, fighting for every inch and spending sleepless nights on ledges not much bigger than a tabletop. They lowered him to the steep Teton glacier, rendered more icy by the summer sun. The rangers had dug a trench on the glacier, so that when the chopper landed on the ice and slid down, it was stopped by the trench. Campbell survived.

Things were much more difficult before jet helicopters. In one famous episode in 1963, rescuers went to the aid of a group of climbers suffering from hypothermia, a condition in which the body loses heat and the victim becomes delirious. As the rangers approached wearing headlamps, some of the climbers thought they were one-eyed devils and fought them off. Rangers fought to subdue them, and tied them up to be rescued.

Because Grand Teton rescue sites are often vertical with nowhere for a helicopter to land, climbing rangers use three helicopter-rescue techniques. In the heli-rappel, a helicopter hovers fifty to two hundred feet above the victim and climbers rappel down ropes to the site. In an insertion rescue, a helicopter picks up rescuers who are clipped to the end of a long line and flies them to the site to "insert" them. In the third technique, the short haul, a cot is helicoptered in, the climber is fastened into the cot and then, in a tricky, wind-tossed ride, the cot is carried above the mountains as it dangles a hundred feet below the helicopter, sometimes to a site miles away, where the helicopter can land and pull the climber aboard. "It's definitely an E coupon ride," joked Armington, referring to the most stomach-churning rides Disneyland has to offer. The new techniques have eliminated the need for risky helicopter maneuvers called "toe-ins" or "one skid" landings. In these moves, the chopper slowly landed the front end or one side of the helicopter on a rocky ledge so rangers could hop out.

But the danger, no matter what technological changes are made, will always remain. One of the most dramatic and tragic rescues in the Grand Tetons took place in September of 1986. Five climbers making their way up the Grand were stranded by a late-winter storm. Drastic and rapid changes of weather are the major factor in Teton climbing "wrecks," as rangers call them.

There are times when even helicopters are useless and things are done the old-fashioned way. The rescue helicopter was unable to make any headway against strong winds, so two rangers took off in the afternoon, hiking six hours through snow and gale-force winds to find the route the climbers took. They hiked to the 12,500-foot level and examined the couloir, or crevice, where the climbers were supposed to be. No sign of them.

Darkness swallowed the snowy mountain range, and the two rescuers turned back and made camp at 11,000 feet. Getting ready to go to bed, one of the rangers went out to get snow to melt on his stove for drinking water and saw the faint glow of a single dying headlamp in a couloir to the right of where the climbers were supposed to be. Hurriedly the rescuers packed up their belongings for a dangerous climb in the dark. Bone weary, at 1 A.M. they reached the fallen climbers. Only two of the five men were still alive. Both survivors were in advanced stages of hypothermia and had frostbite, and lay unmoving in the fresh snow. "They had lain down to die like the other three," said one ranger on the rescue. Quickly the rangers bundled the dying men into sleeping bags and crawled in with them, warming the men and saving their lives. By first light, other rangers made their way in and carried out both the wounded and the dead.

Questions of wildness and how it should be managed are among a long list of serious philosophical questions about the New West. What should the "western experience" be? Is the goal to attract as many people as possible, or to provide for an experience of a certain kind of quality? How much taming is in order? Should things be allowed to go "backward," and become more wild? Questions like these are at the heart of the West, and need to be answered soon, for as the economies of Yellowstone and the West move away from resources, they are moving in other directions so fast it may soon be too late.

8
Comes a New West

AT THE BASE OF THE ABSAROKA AND WIND RIVER MOUNTAINS of central Wyoming runs the Dunoir Valley, also known as the Valley of the Warm Winds, with the dusty, minuscule town of Dubois at its center. The silvery, tree-lined ribbon of water called the Wind River oxbows through the broad valley. This is Wyoming ranch country, archetypally so, with sprawling cattle and sheep ranches that run on over swells of prairie grass for tens of thousands of acres. It's called the Valley of the Warm Winds because even in the worst of winters, balmy winds often sweep it free of snow, though a drive several miles to the west, toward Togwotee Pass, takes you up in altitude and quickly into deep snow.

Dubois is little more than a couple of dozen buildings clinging to the highway that brings tourists and travelers through this remote part of Wyoming, many of them happy campers on their way to Yellowstone. A town a lot like Jackson before the money flowed in. There is a gas station, a drugstore, a hardware store, a cafe called the Wild West Deli and two bars, the Rustic Pine and the Ramshorn. The buildings are covered with frontier facades of rough-cut timber, and the sidewalks are wooden. As in many small western towns, the hunting season is to the merchants here what Christmas season is to businesses in other locales, and there are several motels and log tourist cabins—the kind popular in the 1950s—scattered along the highway. Dubois is also the county seat for Fremont County, a rambling chunk of real estate of 9,300 square miles with just 33,000 people. That's down from 38,000 in 1980, when uranium mining was a going concern.

On the southern end of the Yellowstone ecosystem, Dubois is in the heart of wildness. There are four wilderness areas nearby. Grizzly bears wander down into the woods just outside of town, elk vastly outnumber the 895 Duboisians, and herds of bighorn sheep graze the windswept ridges.

Until the spring of 1988, Dubois was a mill town—"a banana republic based on timber," said one Duboisian—with a sawmill owned by the giant Portland, Oregon-based timber company Louisiana Pacific, which employed 165 people who fashioned two-by-fours at an old mill on the edge of town. The workers made between $18,000 and $30,000 a year, good wages in a place where many people live on the edge of subsistence. The average annual salary in Fremont County in 1990 was $12,730. When the mill closed, citing a lack of available timber, many people felt Dubois would dry up and blow away over the hills with the next stiff breeze, like a dust devil, following the same path of any number of small towns in the West.

It didn't.

It is basking in a shaft of golden light from above, a sanctified economic blessing in the form of the service industry. Tourism, second-home development, and people moving to the rural Rocky Mountains to escape a city are at the heart of the New West economy, and it appears to be taking off in Dubois. It is the same salvation that other towns around the West are down on their knees praying for these days. As the ore plays out, as the ranches close down or are converted to a playground, as farms dry up and the logs get cut and carted away, towns are turning to tourism as a way to keep tumbleweeds from taking over Main Street. Welcome to the New West, the marketing of charm and myth and landscape.

Many of the Old West types eye this new economy warily, not really trusting something that isn't pulled out of the ground with lots of sweat and blisters and cursing. But the money is welcome.

One of the things that Dubois is trying to market, for example, is the Whiskey Mountain bighorn sheep herd, more than a thousand bighorn sheep that graze on a windblown bench overlooking the town. Wildlife has become a major league tourist attraction, and charismatic species like bighorns are as good as gold. Duboisians hope to bring people to town in the fall when the sheep are down low, which will help extend the summer tourist season. They've bet $1 million on it, in the form of a new bighorn sheep interpretive center.

But it's not just tourism anymore, not just people coming through to stay at a dude ranch and buy potato chips and gasoline. Tourism also turns into second homes and primary homes for retirees and other people who no longer are constrained by place. There is a burgeoning group of real estate entrepreneurs trafficking in a way of life and scenery and wildlife and the grand myth of the West. This has been especially true of the Yellowstone ecosystem. Because of the landscape and wildlife and small towns and Yellowstone itself, people are coming from all over the country to relocate here, in the world's last intact ecosystem. "It's becoming more and more attractive," says Ed Lewis, director of the Greater Yellowstone Coalition, "as the rest of the country becomes less and less attractive." There's an old saw that says you can't eat the scenery, but the tourist industry has found a way to do that. Indirectly, of course.

Tourism has exploded in recent years and is now the largest industry in the country, generating $700 billion in revenues a year, employing nine million people for 8 percent of the nation's jobs, ten times the number of jobs in the auto industry or the steel industry. The annual payroll is $200 billion. A study of six Montana counties near the Greater Yellowstone in 1989 showed that tourism created 25,000 jobs and pumped more than $1 billion into the economy there.

The West is finding out, however, that tourism is not everything it's cracked up to be.

Tourism is not new. It was a business even before the West had been fully wrested from its previous owners. In 1877, the federal government, carrying out its policy of forcibly shrinking Indian lands, ordered some Nez Perce Indians (named by the French who believed they pierced their noses) in Idaho to leave land they had occupied for generations. They were nontreaty Nez Perce, being held to a treaty signed by other Nez Perce, who U.S. authorities claimed spoke for all.

Before the Nez Perce left, three warriors snuck off to kill four whites, claiming it was to avenge an earlier killing. More renegade Nez Perce joined in, and in two days fifteen whites lay dead. The entire group of Nez Perce, knowing that the Army would make no distinction between the guilty and the innocent, were forced to flee, and a tragic 1,700-mile odyssey began.

White settlers demanded retribution. On June 17, 1877, an army of 110 white men surprised sixty or so Nez Perce men, at White Bird Canyon in Idaho Territory. The battle left thirty-four whites dead, and just two wounded Nez Perce. The race was on. With recruits joining, the Nez Perce grew to eight hundred men, women and children. With dogs, a large herd of horses, travois and elders, the Nez Perce headed east, hoping eventually to reach the sanctuary of Canada. During the three months it took the Nez Perce to travel to northern Montana Territory, they engaged ten separate U.S. commands in thirteen battles and skirmishes, fighting so skillfully that their tactics are still studied at West Point.

Part of their journey, which they hoped would get them to Canada, took them through Yellowstone, its designation as the first national park five years old. With several thousand horses and the belongings they could carry on horse and travois, they rode into the park from the east, past Henry's lake, over Targhee Pass and up the Madison River. For two weeks, the Nez Perce worked their way through the herds of elk and fields of boiling hot springs, geysers and steaming fumaroles. One author called it "warfare in wonderland."

The Nez Perce ran into two groups of tourists: the Radersburg party, who were from the territorial capital of Helena and Radersburg, Montana, a small mining town south of Helena. This party had made their way by wagon into the lower geyser basin, and there spent the first part of their vacation "geyser jamming," which consisted of stuffing Old Faithful full of stones, tree branches and rubbish and sitting down to watch as the geyser blew the detritus high into the sky. They also stuffed the geyser full of their dirty socks and underwear, which exploded as "nice and clean as a Chinaman could wash it with a week's scrubbing," according to one of the party.

Another, separate group of ten men, all from Helena, were camped near the falls of the Yellowstone.

The Nez Perce rode into the park and came upon a lone prospector, John Shively, and held him captive for two weeks and used him for a guide, as they moved through the park. Meanwhile, a small band of Nez Perce rode up quietly and watched as two members of the Radersburg party—A. J. Arnold and William Dingee—went for coffee water in Tangled Creek. The Indians followed the men back to camp and asked for coffee, bacon and sugar, which they were given. One of the men, Frank Carpenter, asked if harm was in store for them. "Don't know, maybe so," said one of the Nez Perce. Growing fearful, the tourists tried to leave, but were barred. The Indians took their horses and guns, disassembled their wagon, and told them to leave, but to stay off the trail.

The fearful tourists obeyed for a while, but tired of the rough going through downed timber. When they returned to the trail, they were attacked. Several scattered into the woods. One man, George Cowan, was shot in the head, and fell to the ground. Several hours later he came to, and was shot again, this time in the hip, by a different Indian. Left for dead, he snuck away by crawling into the forest. Another man, Albert Oldham, was shot through both cheeks and his tongue. He also was left for dead. Both men survived.

Three of the Radersburg party joined Shively as hostages; the others had managed to sneak off. The hostages spent the night in the camp of Chief Joseph, who sat staring somberly into the fire, "foreseeing in his gloomy meditation possibly the unhappy ending of his campaign," wrote hostage Ida Cowan.

Meanwhile, the Nez Perce raided the camp of the Helena party. One man, Charles Kenck, was killed, and another, John Stewart, took a shot in the hip and leg, and when the Indians approached him he bought his life with $263 and a watch. Stewart and several others from this party eventually made their way to McCartney's, a log hotel in Mammoth Hot Springs, where they met Ida Cowan and others from the Radersburg party, who had been released.

George Cowan, who crawled across the Yellowstone terrain a total of nine miles, was found in the brush by a scout from O. O. Howard's column (the one-armed general who convinced Patty Kluver's ancestors to come to Montana). But his adventure was not over yet. Left by the scouts before a blazing bonfire, Cowan was seriously burned when the fire touched off his bed of moss. When he was found again by the troops, Army surgeons, operating by candlelight, took the bullet out of his skull. Meanwhile, one of the Helena men, Richard Dietrich, who had been stalked by the Nez

Perce on Otter Creek but had escaped, had made his way to McCartney's at Mammoth. When he came to the door of the hotel to investigate the sound of hoofbeats, he was killed by a shot from a group of Nez Perce. He and Kenck were the two fatalities in the park.

The Nez Perce moved to Tower Junction, up the Lamar River over the Absaroka Range and down the Clarks Fork of the Yellowstone. There were no major engagements with the Army in the park, and the Nez Perce kept moving north, eventually into the Bearpaw Mountains, in north central Montana, for what would become their last stand, some thirty miles from the Canadian border. In the snow and cold of late September, after five days of sporadic negotiations and fighting, hungry, tired and overpowered, the Nez Perce surrendered. It was in the Bearpaws that Chief Joseph made his famous speech that culminated with the words "Hear me my chiefs, I am tired; my heart is sick and sad. From where the sun now stands I will fight no more forever." The tribe was held prisoner for a while in North Dakota, during which time many died from disease. Eventually the survivors returned to the Northwest, where the Nez Perce live today. Charles E. Wood, an aide to General Howard, summed up much of what happened when he wrote, "I think that, in his long career, Joseph cannot accuse the Government of the United States of one single act of justice."

Now even the flight of the Nez Perce has become a tourist attraction. In 1992, Congress created the Nez Perce National Historical Park, thirty-eight sites along the entire route the tribe followed, sites that mark everything from where the Nez Perce lived and what their culture was like to the Battle of the Bearpaws.

Tourism has always been thought of as a clean industry, an alternative preferable to mining or logging. Dudes are herded into town or to the ranch, and they spend their money on hats or boots or souvenirs. Fall comes and the summer people go home, and the town goes back to sleep until the next Memorial Day. The topography still rolls along, original and uninterrupted. What is different these days is the scope of things. It's not just a few people who are coming to visit anymore. It's large numbers. The number of visitors to Yellowstone, for example, has doubled since the 1960s and is now over three million annually. People who live in the places that cater to tourists are finding there is indeed an impact from people who come to see the scenery, and townspeople are worried about what their hometown will become. "We don't want to be like Jackson," one nervous Dubois resident said, having seen real estate values skyrocket in recent years and people from around the world move in.

Not wanting to become a town that has been given over to tourism and the rich is a common theme in the New West. Luring outsiders to the community is a sword that cuts two ways. They may leave their money. But more and more people who live in tourist towns complain that tourists don't always know when it's time to go home. A few who set down roots are fine, but it seems that more and more are staying, and many people are finding themselves strangers in their own town. Dispossessed, disenfranchised strangers.

"There is little or nothing moderate about the state of Montana," wrote a historian named K. Ross Toole. "It has ricocheted violently down the corridor of possibility. What is good in reasonable measure is often bad in full measure and Montana has been a place of full measure." He was talking about the Old West and resource development—but he could have also been talking about the New West as well. What many towns and cities are now looking for is "reasonable measure."

In some communities, the influx of refugees has, for some, taken on nightmarish proportion. Many people who work for a living in Jackson, Wyoming, in Aspen, Colorado, or in Santa Fe, New Mexico, have found that they can't afford to stay in the town their grandfather or father may have come and settled. The town is now full of "swells" that have turned the local drugstore into a Ralph Lauren factory outlet, the local cafe into a fern bar, the coffee shop into a cappuccino bar. It is just beginning to happen in Dubois. In many ways the West really was an egalitarian place. Now many "natives" are finding two distinct classes in the hometown, with themselves the "lower" class. (Ironically, it mirrors the treatment accorded those who lived on the land before the white men came.) It's just getting off the ground in Dubois. Some of the ranches here have been owned for years by famous families—the Disneys, the Guggenheims, the Schwinns and the Duponts. Now there are investment bankers and lawyers from New York and Los Angeles buying property. The Brooks Lake Lodge in the mountains near town was recently bought by a Santa Monica developer who caters to the Hollywood set. And in the summer of 1992, actor Kevin Costner was spotted in downtown Dubois. Rumor had it he was shopping for a spread. Ironically, many of the people coming to the West are fleeing from California, the place that was built on its unparalleled quality of life.

Over a century ago the siren call went out to America, a call that has only recently begun to fade. California is "The West"—a promised land, a mythical place, a golden, halcyon, sun-drenched place where summer lives the year-round. Paradise. The sweet perfume of orange blossoms floats intoxicatingly on gentle ocean zephyrs. In the late 1800s, in an ad for subdivisions around the San Diego Peninsula's Hotel Del Coronado, promoters captured much of the charm of southern California: "There is not any malaria, hay fever, loss of appetite or langor in the air; nor any thunder, lightning, mad dogs, cyclones, heated terms or cold snaps."

Today an estimated thirty million people live in California, up from twenty-four million in 1980, the fastest decade of growth of any state in U.S. history. Predictions hold that the population will reach fifty million by 2010 or 2020. More than fourteen million people live in the Los Angeles area alone, more than any other state except for New York or Texas.

There may not be any mad dogs or cyclones, but there is unmitigated gridlock. People commute for three or four hours a day. Smog chokes the blue skies of southern California and turns the setting sun a blood red. Housing prices have gone through the roof, and the five cities with the most expensive housing in the United States are in California. Nature has disappeared beneath pavement. There is chaos spawned by poverty and the difficulties of multiculturalism, particularly in Greater L.A., where a hundred different languages are spoken. The riots after the first Rodney King verdict were frightening. Almost everything people migrated to the Golden State for, the quality of life, has been squandered, mined out, evaporated in the heat of uncontrolled growth. No one ever bothered to find a way to preserve it. You can eat the scenery, but then it's gone.

"The dream is over," says Bill Seavey, founder of the Greener Pastures Institute, which, for a fee, helps people who are fed up with the urbanization of California find a new life in some small- or medium-sized town elsewhere. "It's not like it was in the fifties and forties. California is becoming a Third World country."

And now the California experiment is being replayed in communities throughout the Rocky Mountain West. Allied Van Lines tracks the number of its moving vans going into a state versus those leaving. In 1990 and 1991, for the first time since the company started keeping records in the 1940s, the number of vans leaving were greater than those coming. Approximately 58 percent of the people who use Allied's vans left, while 42 percent arrived. Meanwhile, the top "magnet" states are Oregon, Washington, Montana, New Mexico and others in the West. Evidently, the people who are coming to California are not hiring moving vans.

Again the theory of relativity is at work. To many people emigrating to Greater Los Angeles from other countries, southern California really is the promised land, the land of opportunity with jobs, beautiful homes, and substantial public assistance programs. To many people that already live there, the place is in a steady downward spiral. As taxpayers leave for more promising horizons, those who collect services are increasing. By 1995, state officials hold, tax receivers will outnumber taxpayers. Housing prices have slumped in California and sales have slowed; however, it doesn't seem to have affected the leavers. In fiscal year 1991, there were thirteen thousand more Californians who requested their driver's license be changed to another state than vice versa, the first time in twenty years.

But the people coming to the West—and to Dubois—are not just coming from California. As urban areas throughout the country suffer problems, people are fleeing. From New York, Denver, Philadelphia, Seattle, Miami and everywhere else. They are in search of a place where traffic is tame, houses and land affordable and recreation out the back door. From Las Vegas to Las Cruces, Missoula to Moab, Saratoga to Sedona, Bozeman to Boulder, Telluride to Tucson, Hurricane, Utah, to Henry's Fork, Idaho, people from all over the failing urban areas are cashing in the equity in their homes and looking for another home or summer home. Or they are inheriting money. As the parents of the baby boomers pass on, their accumulated wealth will be passed on to the children, the largest transfer of wealth, it is said, in American history. And so the search is on. A little ranchette on twenty acres or forty acres or forty thousand acres with a couple of horses, a pair of spurs, and a mile of river teeming with chubby trout. "It's a fresh start," said one longtime observer of the Rocky Mountain West of the recent migration to the rural West, "almost with a sense of desperation."

"It's a back-to-basics movement," says Seavey. "There's a lot of unmeaningful, technological jobs in the cities, and people are being forced to separate from their communities and families to make a living. The kids are being raised by nannies or nobody in particular. That way of life is a false god. People want to be in the country, closer to the land, involve their kids in a home business. The urban and suburban environments don't let you do those things."

"People are scared shitless living in the cities," says Bill Bryan, owner of Off the Beaten Path, an upscale travel booking company in Bozeman. "The gap between the haves and have-nots is so great that people are scared of people of color. They come here and it's all white people. They can stop here and smell the roses." Dubois is no exception. The last census found of the 33,000 people in Fremont County, fifty-one are black, and a thousand or so are Hispanic. The militant racism that was so much a part of the settling of the West in the nineteenth century seems to have been replaced by a new, different kind of racism, some of it intentional, some of it not.

One of the things that has enabled the West to be discovered in such a big way is the advent of the electronic cottage—people who work at home, wherever that might be, with computers, fax machines, cellular phones and Federal Express. One man in Dubois runs a business that takes people camping in remote locations around the world. His clients are also from all over the world. ACW, the phenomenon has been called: Another Computer in the Woods. People have been freed from their office to work at home or even halfway across the continent and commute by bouncing signals off a satellite or sending them through the telephone lines. For occasional business trips, all that's necessary is that an airport be an hour's drive away or so. In fact, there are people who commute once a week or more from places like Santa Fe, Phoenix and Denver to southern California.

Refuge and redemption are the great themes of the Rocky Mountain West, seen as a place where convention and social stratification are minimal, where people live and let live. Like any western myth, it's overblown, though it has elements of truth.

While the influx of outsiders to Dubois is nascent, there are other places urban refugees have "discovered" during past exoduses from the cities. One of those is Santa Fe, New Mexico. One person's discovery, of course, is, as the history of the West amply illustrates, another person's invasion.

At seven thousand feet above sea level and at the southern end of the Rocky Mountains, Santa Fe is indeed, as its motto claims, The City Different. From the highway, it is difficult to tell there is a city of 56,000 nestled in the valley. The southern tip of the Sangre de Cristo Mountains, quilted with green forest, rises up around the city like a natural cathedral. The sky is a crystalline, bottomless blue, the light strong and deeply illuminating. The perfume of pine and pinyon trees fills the air during the abundant warm days, while during the crisp high-altitude obsidian nights, the sweet woodsmoke from juniper and pine scents the darkness and stars swarm over the mountains.

Downtown Santa Fe, the heart of the place, shows a city whose scale serves humans, rather than having humans serve the city. The buildings are all adobe brown, none taller than several stories. User-friendly. Buildings are small, human-sized. A plaza is the center of town, where shops face onto a park, a place where people still gather beneath huge trees, a nucleus for the community. Streets are narrow, easily and unthreateningly traversed by pedestrians. The architecture works together, instead of clashing. Wood and adobe, natural materials, make up the buildings. In fact, it's illegal to build with anything except adobe in the historic district of Santa Fe.

With automobile traffic restricted and reduced to a crawl on the narrow streets, Santa Fe is relatively quiet, studded with huge shady trees and birds that sing in the morning. Dress is informal. All of these things combine to create a summer camp feeling, a refuge, a spell, a town that seduces. Travel magazines have waxed eloquent about Santa Fe. "An enchantress among cities" according to *National Geographic.* "A real-life Shangri-la" said another. "You feel like you could be in another country in another century," says Sharon Woods, president of the Santa Fe Historic Design Review Board.

Something about Santa Fe appeals to the avant-garde. Cafes abound. There are 254 art galleries in Santa Fe, 51 acupuncturists and numerous psychics, including one woman who, for a fee, will tell you what your dog or cat is thinking. Meanwhile, there are more than 650 realtors, one for every hundred people.

The rugged and sublime, even mysterious, country around Santa Fe is held by some to be one of the Earth's "power spots." Wheeler Peak near Taos, for example, is allegedly home to a Great Deva Angel that lives atop the mount and emanates a brilliant (though invisible to the untrained eye) blue light that Santa Fe basks in. Whatever the reason, Santa Fe draws New Age groups. The Light Institute. A Sikh sect led by Zen Master Rama. John Rogers, who holds something called Insight Training Seminars. There is even an Old Age group there called the Mighty I Am. A cult that flourished in the 1930s and '40s, it all but disappeared when Donald "Daddy" Ballard died instead of ascending, and Edna "Mama" Ballard, a.k.a. "Little Dynamite," was charged with mail fraud.

"There's a lot of channelers, a lot of small cults," says Joseph Szimhardt, who came to Santa Fe as an artist seventeen years ago and now makes a living "deprogramming" people who he says are victims of cult mind control. "Cults are drawn here because Santa Fe has always been an outpost for Bohemians, artists and esoteric groups. And because religious themes are strong. The Indian religions and the Catholic Hispanic religion."

The earth beneath Santa Fe, on the banks of the Santa Fe River, was first used by Pueblo Indians, who built mud apartment buildings and grew corn. Prolonged drought struck the area in the 1400s, and the Indians abandoned the small villages of Ogapoge and Arroyo Hondo, though they remained in the area. Small groups of Spanish soldiers began to wander into territory in the late 1500s, but La Villa de Santa Fee, as it was called, or the Village of the Holy Faith, was not officially founded until 1610, by Pedro de Peralta. At that time, many of the Spanish homes were built on top of the Indian ruins, or even incorporated the ancient structures into their architecture.

Relations between the Spanish colonizers and the Indians were usually strained, a strain compounded in the 1670s by famine and epidemics that ravaged the colonial outpost. Apaches, meanwhile, launched savage assaults on Spanish and Pueblo Indians alike. The spark that set the tinder burning, however, occurred when the Catholic Spanish tried to stamp out the Pueblo ceremonies, claiming they were an abomination in the eyes of God. On August 10, 1680, the Pueblo Revolt began. Indians slaughtered hundreds of Spanish who lived outside of Santa Fe, and lay siege to the city. The rest of the Spanish, some 2,500, fled to El Paso. Once in the city, the Indians smashed Christian statuary, discarded rosary beads, occupied the Spanish buildings and tried to wipe out all trace of the hated Spanish and their God. "The God of the Spaniards is dead," they cried, "but our Gods will never die."

In 1692, Diego de Vargas retook Santa Fe. For a long time to come, Santa Fe flourished as a capital of Nueva Mejico, a Spanish city of culture and money in what the Europeans viewed as wilderness. It was a closed city, and the Spaniards maintained tight control. In 1821, Mexico earned independence from Spain, and the Mexican governor of Santa Fe, Facundo Melgares, threw the city open to anyone who wished to come. Traders came in droves from the East, along a 770-mile pathway called the Santa Fe Trail, which wound across the high plains from Independence, Missouri, across Kansas, through the southeast portion of Colorado and into New Mexico from the north. The trail opened a lucrative trading route first into Santa Fe, and then into the Mexican provinces. Traders brought a whole new world with them, things unheard of in nineteenth-century Santa Fe: velveteen, flannel, paper, tools, books, medicine and champagne. It was a harrowing trip for traders, a wide-open seven hundred miles, and Indian attack was a constant threat.

On May 12, 1846, following boundary disputes over Texas and heady with the idea of Manifest Destiny, the U.S. Congress declared war on Mexico. By August 18 of the same year, Brigadier General Stephen Watts Kearny marched into the plaza of Santa Fe, where, meeting no resistance, he raised the American flag. In 1848, Mexico surrendered and signed the Treaty of Guadalupe Hildago, which turned New Mexico, Texas, California and Arizona over to the Americans.

The United States held the city until February of 1862, when, during the War Between the States, much of New Mexico fell to Confederate Texans, including Santa Fe. The Stars and Bars fluttered over the capital, but only for a matter of weeks. On April 14, the city came under Union control again.

Big changes came in 1880, when the railroad reached Santa Fe. It brought large numbers of tuberculosis patients seeking a hospitable clime, and the Atchison, Topeka and Santa Fe began to create the Santa Fe mystique with travel posters about the Pueblo Indians. It also brought the beginnings of a tourist industry, as well as a new element—American artists—to Santa Fe's long established reputation as an Indian and Spanish arts community. Adding to the mix was the fact that the governor at the time was Lew Wallace, author of *Ben Hur.*

All of these elements—the Pueblo Indians and their culture, the rich Spanish heritage, the dramatic and romantic history, the artists, the architecture, the landscape—have combined to create a city irresistible to tourists. In short, Santa Fe has character, a strong regional identity when so much of the country has become a monoculture, a series of long congested strip developments populated with chain restaurants and motels and stores, with no center of town, no real character, little to distinguish it from anywhere else.

Santa Fe passed a milestone of sorts in 1990. Hispanics, the majority in The City Different for 350 years, were officially made a minority. Census figures show that there are now about 27,000 Anglos and 26,400 Hispanics. And that does not make Debbie Jamarillo a happy woman.

Energetic and strong, Debbie Jamarillo has jet hair, a firm voice and a husky, frequent laugh. "This house," she says, gesturing to the beautiful Southwest-style home she is standing in, "is how it all got started." On a small rise on Santa Fe's west side, the property looks out over the pinyon-covered hills of Santa Fe and the surrounding mountains. It is a classic adobe home, which Jamarillo and her husband Mike built themselves over an eight-year period. Inside the house it is cool and dark, a refuge from the middle of a warm New Mexico afternoon. A triangle-shaped fireplace adorns both kitchen and living room. Wood beams, or vigas, hold the wooden roof on the adobe walls, and in the kitchen a clerestory provides soft, warm light. A blood-red chile-pepper *ristra,* a sign of welcome to Hispanics, hangs outside the home, and several more hang from beams in the kitchen. The floors are smooth stone. A crucifix is affixed over the front door, a replica of the Last Supper on a kitchen wall. A poster on the refrigerator, meanwhile, says "Fuck Housework."

"We built this house ourselves," Jamarillo says. "It's beautiful. But we're always one paycheck away from poverty, even with a combined family income. We were going to sell our place and move north to Mora where we have family. But after two months I saw the kind of people who were coming to look at the house. Wealthy Californians who could lay the money down on the table just like that. I didn't like it. Uh-uh, I told my husband. Let's not be part of the exodus. Let's stay and fight."

Jamarillo had been watching for years as Hispanic friends and families left Santa Fe because they could no longer afford rent, taxes, groceries or other exaggerated costs of living in Santa Fe. Some people moved to Albuquerque, sixty miles away, or smaller towns, and commuted back to jobs in Santa Fe.

In 1986, Jamarillo, having decided to stay, organized a battle against a highway-widening project through her part of town which would have gobbled up affordable housing and improved access to the predominantly Hispanic neighborhood, setting it up for gentrification. The project galvanized much of the anger against the "invasion" of her town by wealthy Anglos and rapid growth, and Jamarillo and her troops beat the project back. Encouraged, in 1988 the combative Jamarillo ran for city council, which was dominated by Anglo real estate interests, and won. She ran and won again in 1992. Each time, she was fought tooth and nail by the real estate powers that be. "They did not," she says, grinning, "want Miss Radical in there."

Miss Radical, however, is what they got. She is working to make changes in the power structure, specifically as it regards the tourism industry and the damage she perceives it has done to Santa Fe. "Tourism is killing our town. Responsible growth is my platform. Growth that benefits all. I want the developers to give something back to the community. We don't want to be like Aspen."

The City Different has become different all right, she says. It has now become a community for the elite, most of them Anglos. She maintains there is a difference between entertaining tourists and handing over the soul of a town to them. "They painted the downtown brown and moved the brown people out. If you go downtown, that's not Santa Fe," she says referring to the high-priced specialty stores that sell astronomically expensive paintings, clothing and numerous objets d'art. "It's God knows what. We've promoted Santa Fe in a false way, turned it into Disneyland. People want to come and see the Hispanics and Indians and live among them. Yet they [the Hispanics and Indians] can't afford to live here. I'm sick of the lies, the lies that convince you there's something more for you in more growth and expanded tourism."

In 1994, she says, she will be an antigrowth candidate for mayor, a position now held by a real estate developer.

Tourism does strange things to a town. There is a thin line between reality and fantasy, and tourist towns, hungry for tourist money, often fall to the fantasy side. Some people feel tourism causes towns to become something they're not, to become what people think the West was like from watching cowboy movies. In White Sulphur Springs, a small, dusty, central-Montana ranch town, away from the interstate and its economy flat, local businesses floated a plan to attract tourists by placing false "western" fronts over authentic western buildings. Director John Ford's words come to mind again: "Not the West as it was, but as it should have been."

"People come here and say they're trying to escape places like California, but they're not," says Joel Bernstein, a rancher and writer who lived in the Bitterroot Valley, in the southwestern corner of Montana. "They bring the world they come from with them. Since I've lived here I've seen more fences go up. You can't do business with a handshake anymore. They have money the locals don't have and the ranchers get squeezed out. It becomes too valuable not to sell to celebrities. You've lost that sense of community."

There is a feel of a theme park to "meccas" like Santa Fe, Jackson, Sun Valley and Aspen, and other towns that have had their complete makeover. (Aspen is by far the most severe; what was done to the town has been immortalized in western vernacular as a verb transitive: *to aspenize:* to displace people in a town with other people, of higher economic standing.) Santa Fe's distinctive southwestern look was created by people who built adobe because that is what they had and what they knew and who they were. Everywhere you go these days, people are striving to achieve the Santa Fe look. And everywhere in town are pictures, sculptures, buttons, T-shirts and coffee cups in the shape of or covered with the image of a howling coyote. To the tourists, the coyote is a symbol of the Southwest; to some locals, it is a symbol of too many tourists.

Jackson, Wyoming, is a good example of a cowboy theme. There are wooden sidewalks and stores that sell designer western wear, at prices far beyond what any working cowboy could afford. There is cowboy coffee, and lodgepole furniture, used on dude ranches and in ranch houses, has become a pricey collector's item. Telluride, Colorado, and Park City, Utah, meanwhile, are mountain mining-theme towns. A town becomes a theme town when all of the real cowboys, miners and Hispanics are gone or going and the people left there re-create the old effect.

Some argue that the closure of the mill in Dubois was the start of that town's themeness. "The real Wyomingites were chased away," from Dubois, said Fremont County superintendent of schools Jim Robinson. "They were what Wyoming was. Now we're going to be eastern folks who entertain other eastern folks and simulate the former Wyoming economy. That's the real irony."

There is always the question of how far the theme should be taken. Devout Hispanics in Santa Fe grew angry when state tourism officials promoted Catholic holy day processions in national magazines as part of the local color.

Hispanics are not the only Santa Feans who complain about change. There are people who, years ago, fled to places like Boise or Jackson or Santa Fe for the quality of life, who don't like what America has become and now have been found out and are worried. "It's heartbreaking," says Susan Hazen-Hammond, a free-lance writer in Santa Fe who came from the Pacific Northwest. "The home we rent may be sold out from under us because we can't afford to buy it. It's an occupied city. The only difference between Santa Fe and Kuwait is that no one has come in and pushed the bullies out."

Occupation, of course, is another theme in the West (and especially in Santa Fe). Spaniards came and seized the Southwest from Navajo and Pueblo Indians, often violently. Indians also fought bitterly over territory. What people like Jamarillo and Hazen-Hammond ask is why such occupations don't let people and their life-styles remain, an enlightened or benevolent occupation.

In its own small way, Dubois is beginning to feel similar pangs of economic growth. "A lot on the golf course that went for eight thousand dollars," says Pat Neary, Dubois Town Manager, "now goes for fifteen thousand. Someday the people who live here won't be able to afford to anymore. We're going to be steamrolled by people who don't like where they are living now."

No one really blames people for wanting to get out of California.

"We want a better life-style," says Steve Mellinger, who with his wife Debbie has been to a Greener Pastures counseling session. Mellinger, who lives in a suburb of 14,000, seventy-five miles east of L.A., says gangs and pollution have followed his family's move to suburbia. "What we see happening isn't good for our kids. We want to live in a neighborhood where you can talk to your neighbors. We want to move to Oregon or Idaho, but we're not sure where to go. That's why we're taking classes."

Bill Seavey built a successful business exit-counseling California refugees. Options from Greener Pastures include a year's subscription to the gazette, which comes out four times a year for $25, provides such tips as how to make sure you don't move next to a nuclear missile silo, and even features a Western State of the Year award based on quality of life. Idaho won in 1991.

A ninety-minute class on smart departures is $15 for one person, $29 for two, and personalized exit counseling with Seavey costs $60 an hour. Greener Pastures also has Hinterland Hosts, who live in different western states and assist people once they start to settle in.

Seavey, who runs the business with his wife Laurel and twelve-year-old son Eric, says teachings in classes and in counseling run the gamut from urging people to visit their chosen refuge in the winter to how to hide the fact you are a refugee from California. "Maintain a low profile," Seavey says. "Change your license plates, don't buy the biggest house on the block, and get involved in the community."

There is reason to lie low. As Californians bail out for medium and small cities around the West, locals have seen real estate prices shoot up, traffic problems grow, and jobs get scarce. Cars with California plates often get damaged or their drivers verbally harassed.

Not everyone stays in the western outpost of their dreams. One estimate holds that eleven of twelve people who move to Santa Fe are gone within two years. In fact, in these charming little towns, these comings and goings are important to the economy. People move to the capital of their mountain dreams, buy a house, buy furniture, try to make a living or find a job, and burn up their savings. Then they move back to a more practical place. "The charm in their head," says Hazen-Hammond, "doesn't match what's on the street." The weather is cold. Distance from family and friends is too great. Isolation is more difficult to handle than expected. Jobs are tough to find.

Jamarillo has a message for tourist towns. "Everybody charmed by your beautiful city will want a piece of it, for that's the way rich Americans think. After them will come developers ready to build fancy new homes and condominiums. That will mean new roads, extended sewer and water lines, more police and fire protection, larger schools and a need for more school buses. And who will pay for all of these expanded services? You will."

Jamarillo says she does not begrudge newcomers who want to settle in Santa Fe. People have come here since the 1920s. But there is that problem of attitude, she says, one that leaves less-well-to-do neighbors feeling like they have their nose pressed up against the glass. Feeling like they are a distinct underclass. "What has happened is that people do not come here to assimilate. They've come here to make it into the place they think it should be, with restaurants we don't dare go into and stores we don't dare think about shopping at. They live in gated communities, put up their walls, and say keep out."

There is a serious impact on local economies from "equity exiles." The average price of a home in Santa Fe in 1975 was just under $44,000. Ten years later the average was $78,000, and in 1992 it soared to $183,000. Nancy Fisher has owned a real estate firm in Santa Fe for fifteen years, and now has eight salespeople. She says it is not unusual for raw land to go up 30 percent a year. One lot changed hands three times in a year and a half: at $35,000, two months later at $49,000 and again at $65,000. "Fifteen years ago people would say I would like an adobe fixer-upper on the East Side [one of the city's nicest neighborhoods] for fifty thousand and I would laugh at them," Fisher says. "Now they say they want it for two hundred thousand and I laugh at them."

This in a state where the average annual wage in 1991 was $18,933, the lowest for a state in the Rocky Mountain West.

Tax policy has played into the growth of the meccas in a couple of ways. As a neighborhood in a mecca city is discovered, and prices rise, property taxes soon follow. Working-class families, whose homes were valued at $50,000 a few years ago, find that because of the discovery of their town, their home is now valued at $150,000. Property taxes are tripled.

The federal government is helping subsidize this growth. Interest and tax payments on second homes are deductible from federal income taxes. If someone owns a second home and is paying $10,000 a year in interest on the mortgage, and $2,000 a year in taxes, up to 31 percent of that amount comes off income taxes—a $3,720-a-year subsidy. "Resort areas like Scottsdale and in the mountains near Denver are very much dependent on all of the tax incentives that relate to second homes," says Bill Frenzel, a former Republican congressman from Minnesota who served on the House Ways and Means Committee and the Budget Committee, and is now a guest scholar on financial matters with the Brookings Institution in Washington, D.C.

Michael Kinney, wearing a neon-green King Ropes hat and nursing a beer at the Rustic Pine bar in downtown Dubois, talks about the changes in Fremont County. A technician for a small local phone company called Dubois Telephone, he has watched the change firsthand. "A lot of people are getting a second line for a computer or fax machine," he says. "When I came here in 1980, we had 637 lines between here and Crowheart"—a town twenty-nine miles to the southeast. "Now there are 1,200."

"It's a mailbox economy," the long-faced, mustachioed Kinney says. "There's a lot of retirees moving in, early active retirees, and a lot of people who made a lot of money in the eighties. They come from the East or Midwest or California, buy five or ten acres and build big fancy houses. A lot of them go to Arizona in the winter."

Dubois is just beginning to feel some of the impacts that places like Santa Fe are well acquainted with. One of the big changes caused by an influx of tourists, says Kinney, is the creation of two distinct and often widely separated classes, especially evident in a small town like Dubois. "I'll have a beer with the haves or have-nots. I don't treat either level different." A great equalizer, he says, is the town's festivals: a square dance, a buffalo barbecue, the pack-horse races. That brings out the upper-class folks. "I've seen 'em down here after four or five toddies," he says with a grin, "and they're good and normal."

The change in the social fabric is a chronic complaint among people whose town is discovered. There is an unwritten code of ethics in small western towns and rural areas. Step up to cross a busy street and more often than not a car will stop in the middle of traffic to allow you to pass. Businesses take not only out-of-town checks, but out-of-state checks as well. On rural roads, people wave to each other or stop to help someone with a stalled engine. "You might have a cabin up in the mountains, with a sleeping bag and tools and stuff," says Pat Neary. "You don't lock it because someone might need it in a storm. They won't steal it. That hasn't changed yet. But I think it might." There are a myriad little things that are part of everyday small-town life that are diluted or disappear when a town is subject to rapid influx of people who live by different rules.

There are more impacts from growth than just social ones. Environmentally, growth is almost always destructive, in large part because no town ever wants to make planning and zoning a priority until it is already a problem—especially in the West, where the notion of freedom means the right to do anything with your land you see fit, even if it's building a Kentucky Fried Chicken next to a historic church, or building houses or a mall on land that might be important wildlife habitat. One planner in a rural county in Montana says that he had three death threats from people who felt his suggestions about land use were "socialistic."

And many of these small towns now being discovered have never known the taste of real money, and it's too much to resist, and perhaps diminish, through the regulation of growth.

The impingement on wildlife habitat is the overriding concern regarding subdivisions, which are often in valley bottoms and along rivers, the choicest habitat. The conflicts with cougars are a good example. Subdivisions also contribute to runoff entering streams, pollution from septic systems and erosion. Dogs chase wildlife. Many archaeological sites lie along the rivers, and homes go on top of them. Some western valleys are meteorologically unequipped for large populations. Missoula, Montana, has such a serious problem with air pollution from wood stove smoke, for example, that children and pregnant mothers are sometimes warned not to go outside.

Jack B. Wright, a former county planner and now a conservation geographer at New Mexico State University in Las Cruces, is the author of *Searching Country: Conservation, Land and Life in the Rocky Mountain West,* a study of the differences between land conservation in Colorado and Utah.

Wright contends that how land is developed for homes in the

West is a policy of the past that is being applied to a present in which it is no longer relevant. "The Homestead Act, the Desert Land Act, the mining law and others, were essentially a way to fill up the West. They were passed when the land was empty of people, not for now when the land is filling up with people. Subdivision laws contain massive exemptions, and are de facto homestead acts. Laissez-faire, step-out-of-the-way, let things happen."

Planners facilitate growth, Wright says, but never ask the fundamental question: should growth take place? "The question of what you do with urbanization has never been asked," he says. "Remember the Los Angeles Basin has had planning since the 1920s."

Wright did a study in Missoula County, Montana, and found that in 90 percent of the county, growth was taking place without review by county officials, a percentage he says is echoed throughout the Rockies. If growth continues, he says, the West will suffer many of the problems now afflicting California. "The West," he says, "is up for grabs."

Neary has seen wildlife impacted in Dubois, even though growth is in the early stages. "A lot of the winter range is down along the valley bottom," he says. "That's where people want to build. Even places where we saw wildlife just a year or two ago, they are no longer there. People are pounding hammers and moving dirt, and wildlife are not coming down."

Jack Lessinger is the author of *Penturbia.* His theory, based on census data from 1790 to the present, is that there have been four great migrations in American history, the last one being from urban to suburban areas. The fifth migration, he says, is just getting under way: a migration from urban and suburban America to penturbia—rural places fifty to one hundred and fifty miles beyond suburbia. And it is a psychological as well as physical move. It is a fundamental, back-to-the-land movement, Lessinger says, a deep yearning for the basics of life. A movement away from a consumer society to an ecologically conscious society, a rejection of urban and suburban America with its pollution and crime and depersonalization. Small-town virtues. "It's too bad it's happening now," he says, "because the laws aren't in place to protect the land."

The director of the Montana Travel Promotion Unit, the state agency whose duty it is to attract tourists to the state with $3 million in advertising each year, thinks tourism is getting too much of the blame. "People are looking for a scapegoat and they are picking on tourism because it's visible,'' says Matthew Cohn. "It's too simplistic to say people come here because of tourism. It's part of the equation, but just one of many factors.''

In 1992, Cohn says, tourism brought $900 million directly into the economy in the form of retail sales, lodging and food, and more than $80 million in revenue from gas and payroll taxes.

Michael Cerletti is the secretary of tourism for the state of New Mexico, a cabinet-level position that illustrates the growing importance of revenues from visitors. Tourism is the largest industry in Santa Fe and the second largest in New Mexico. "There have been changes,'' Cerletti says. "But there's nowhere around where there is prosperity that there haven't been changes.'' Tourism is too important to the economy to be limited. "What do we do instead?'' he says. "No one ever has an answer.''

Bayard Fox is part of the vanguard of the New West, one of the people who lives in the Dubois area and communicates with the world—quite literally—by computer and fax. Tall, rangy, with a bushy mustache and long, strong fingers, Fox retired from the CIA in 1970 after an accident in Virginia when a horse somersaulted on him. He came to Wyoming and bought the Bitterroot Ranch, four miles from the nearest neighbor. "This country suits me,'' Fox says in his office, which is in a little 1960s ranch house on the outskirts of Dubois. He strokes a cat that sits in his lap. "The freedom and emptiness are great. You can be freer here than anywhere else in the world.''

The Bitterroot Ranch is a guest ranch, and four hundred people a year come to stay and ride in the mountains of Wyoming. But with several computers, a toll-free 800 line, a fax machine, and three employees, Fox also runs Equitour International, a company that books seven- to sixteen-day horseback tours with forty to fifty outfitters anywhere in the world—Australia, Egypt, Morocco, India—for a global clientele.

Running a business in Dubois has its problems, he says. The closest commercial airport is in Jackson, more than an hour away; the pool of educated labor is small; and it is difficult to bring in married people to work for the company because the spouse can seldom find good work. But clients from Paris, London, New York, Los Angeles and, once in a great while, Wyoming, keep calling. As if to underscore a point, Fox answers the phone. While the warm wind of the Dunoir Valley howls outside, Fox says, "I see. You're not interested in fox hunting, just horse tours in Ireland. How much is that in Swiss francs? Fifteen hundred."

The migration of outsiders to a community is far from all bad. It can be sustainable and have beneficial impacts. In fact, migration to the Rocky Mountains has been a shot of diversity and other worldviews into communities that are often isolated and narrowly focused. It has injected new life into dying or static towns. Bozeman, Montana, a small, picturesque community of just 25,000, hosts an opera with players from the New York Metropolitan Opera, because tenor Pablo Elvira married a local girl. Jerome, Arizona, was a tumbledown mining town that clings precariously to the north side of Mingus Mountain, in the central part of the state. A dreamlike place with an incredible panorama in front of it, it was discovered by a Bohemian community, and now the ghosts rub shoulders with artists, cappuccino makers, and shopkeepers who moved into the old banks, houses and stores and brought the town halfway back to life. Top-notch doctors practice in towns with good skiing or fly-fishing. And the relocation of small businesses to small and medium-sized towns and cities also brings the diverse economy that economists say is vital to long-term economic health.

People who move from a megalopolis to a small or medium-sized town often find their batteries recharged and realize that in a small community, they have a voice; they feel like participants in a real democracy. They can call the governor at home or have lunch with a legislator. "A lot of ex-urbanites have become disenchanted with government and don't participate," says Bill Seavey. "It's understandable. In a megalopolitan area the problems are hard to deal with, are hard to solve in a simplistic way. One community can't control its own airspace. The smog blows from one town to another. Regional transportation authorities will shove freeway systems down local governments' throats. That doesn't happen in small communities. People get involved, though some people do want to drop out and hide out."

The influx also replaces out-migration from the Rocky Mountain West, a substantial factor, since people find employment opportunities in many western states very limited, especially in the resource industries. In fact, population in Montana grew so slowly between 1980 and 1990—790,000 to 800,000—that it lost one of its two congressmen to other, faster-growing states. But immigrants do not exactly replace the emigrants. There is a redistribution of population going on in the West, which is borne out by census figures. As some parts of the agricultural and resource economy decline—oil and gas extraction, uranium mining, coal mining, logging—rural parts of many states are declining. Medium or large urban areas and resort towns are gaining.

The influx of outsiders, with very different value systems from urban life, also places a market value on things old-time residents take for granted—views, homes at the end of the road, ambience, water in the rivers, Forest Service land as a neighbor, and so on. The New West is a valuation of things never seen in that light before. It also often creates an indigenous constituency for protection. Many people who are moving to small towns or who live there are asking, How much growth do we need? That wasn't much of a question thirty years ago. But as people flee from America's urban sprawl, some come determined to keep things the way they are, the reason they moved there. That poses a problem for resource-dependent employment. Not that long ago, timber operators would cut their trees up in the hills and no one would say ah, yes or boo. Now there are people using the woods, or fishing the stream or climbing the mountains.

The appearance of tourists and scenery lovers also changes the power structure in town, sometimes dramatically. For a long time, the town council in Dubois was resource oriented, what you would expect in a town where people make their living extracting resources. But as it dawned on outfitters and motel operators and others on Main Street that their bread was buttered on the side of tourism, they challenged timber sales in the mountains, filed lawsuits. The Forest Service halved the timber quota and Louisiana Pacific folded its tent.

Resource extraction's Waterloo in Dubois, the sign that things were really different, came in 1990. Conoco, the oil giant, had leased public land to explore for oil near Brooks Lake, a beautiful high-mountain lake with a giant log resort on its shore on the edge of the Washakie wilderness. It is surrounded by a palisade of rock called The Pinnacles, which looks like the skyline of a major city.

The Dubois town council voted to appeal the decision. The mayor, Bob Baker, a former officer of Louisiana Pacific and owner of the town's hardware store, vetoed the decision, which the council promptly overrode. An era had passed. The transition was not easy; rather, it was often bitter. Kinney, for example, an outspoken environmentalist, had his windows soaped and tires shredded. Dubois is a microcosm of the change that is being played out again and again where Old West meets New.

The change to a "bed and breakfast" economy has not made everyone happy, especially Bob Baker. Tight-lipped, still a little angry, Baker, who wears an Abraham Lincoln–style beard, says Dubois lost more than jobs when the mill closed. "The diversity is gone," he says. "As well as the high-paying jobs. The jobs you end up with are dishwashers, waitresses, chambermaids and handymen. Are all my kids going to be forced to work at Burger King or McDonald's, flipping hamburgers? If not, they will be forced to go elsewhere. When you take timber and grazing away, it limits the list. My heart is deep in this state, and by limiting resources you have less opportunity." And while people who work for the mill live in Dubois year-round and are part of the community, Baker says, "People who are here three months a year, here today and gone tomorrow, don't care if there's a sewer system."

That may be so. But tourism is the only game in town and better, as the saying goes, than a poke in the eye with a sharp stick. Throughout the West, many town fathers and mothers are grudgingly coming to realize that wilderness and parks and scenery are more than just some cockeyed notions of a bunch of granola-eating, Volvo-driving, white-wine-sipping, Synchilla-wearing, wind-kissing environmentalists. It is indeed the light of salvation, a big part of new life in the New West, and a way to mitigate the impacts of an Old West in its declining years.

As parts of the West fill up with new people, now is the time, many say, to do it right. The last chance to save the last refuge. Then again, perhaps there is a fundamental contradiction at work in the peopling of the West—the destruction of a place by the people who love it. This contradiction was summed up by Robin Wilson, a widowed Utah ranch wife who spoke to a *Denver Post* reporter in 1991. "You can't possess the West," she said. "When you buy a piece you buy an illusion, because as soon as it is under control you have lost that which is the West—the open, untamed geography of hope."

9
Creating a New Society?

At the end of a narrow, rutted logging road, Woody Barmore has set up his turquoise-and-white aluminum house trailer. A couple of dogs run through the woods yapping. Outside, Barmore, who is an independent logger, looks like a small child as he stands behind two giant black Percheron draft horses, named Gypsy and Milo, each weighing about 1,600 pounds, with hooves the circumference of dinner plates. Surrounded by a forest of pines near Togwotee Pass on the Bridger-Teton National Forest in the southern part of the Yellowstone ecosystem, and bathed in the cool, green light that filters through the canopy, Barmore wraps a chain choker around a bundle of trees, each eight inches or so in diameter. As his wife and infant son watch, he urges the powerful horses on and runs behind them as they drag the logs down a skid trail through the woods.

Barmore makes his living cutting small logs for firewood and house logs, charging $60 a cord in Jackson, for which he pays the Forest Service $5 to $16 a cord. If he splits the wood and delivers it, it costs the customer $115. It takes about twenty acres to produce 130 cords. He drags his logs over the ground on skid trails, about as wide as a city sidewalk, to a pickup area, where the logs are loaded onto a truck. The horses run through trees, over deadfall and over other smaller trees.

Wearing a worn-out cowboy hat, heavy leather gloves and black logger's boots, Barmore talks about the advantages of horse logging. "The horse forces me into certain techniques that are better," Barmore says. "I jerk out twenty-foot lengths instead of forty-foot lengths," he says. "Forty-foot lengths crush the little trees." Barmore can turn the horses around with little damage to the forest; a "cat," a name for a large logging machine, crushes trees and seedlings to make a turn. He leaves behind a "biological legacy," downed timber and slash, seeds and seedlings, snags and live trees, insects—the material from which the forest can rebuild itself, material that is not left behind at a clear-cut. When he's gone, though the fact that it was logged is not a secret, there is still a forest. Moreover, the waste is far less. "The Forest Service wastes more on large sales than me and another logger can use in ten years," Barmore laments. "The trees you see in my truck would have been in a slash pile."

This is horse logging, a relic of history that some environmentalists and loggers see as part of the future of timber harvesting in the Greater Yellowstone ecosystem, and perhaps in much of the West. These are the kinds of practices the Greater Yellowstone Coalition believes the ecosystem needs. Accordingly, the GYC has set up a project to bring people together to discuss and use and promote these kinds of practices. The project is called Yellowstone Tomorrow.

Using the Greater Yellowstone ecosystem as kind of a laboratory, the GYC is looking for ways of preserving diversity: social, economic and biological diversity. It is hoped that diversity can be preserved by helping communities maintain old jobs and provide new jobs, by keeping stories and myths and subcultures alive and, most critically, by not destroying the naturalness of the ecosystem. The Yellowstone Tomorrow project does not seek to ban logging or ranching or mining, or to turn the area into wilderness or a bigger park; instead, it seeks to integrate humans into the ecosystem. It hopes to bring New West and Old West together in a way that ensures a future for both.

Rather than taking a short-term, often one-time profit at the expense of the resources or other people, we should strive for the goal of "ecosystem friendly" management, the GYC argues, to sustain communities and businesses, to break the West's boom-

and-bust cycles, to write a new kind of future, a new kind of land ethic, for the West. Something that makes sense on every level—economic, environmental and social. It's a recognition that humans are part of a larger system, and that what they do, however small it may seem, affects that system. Know the land, the GYC says, and manage according to how nature works. It might mean less profit for a timber company or mining company, but it will mean less cost to the taxpayer in subsidies such as road building or the reclamation of acidified streams.

When Yellowstone was created as the national park, it was a global prototype. The GYC sees an ecosystem approach in the same way. If it works here, this integrated approach as a new way of doing business can be applied anywhere in the West, or the world. Sustainability is not a new concept. It is a growing phenomenon in many countries, especially in Africa and in Central and South America. But success in Yellowstone could give the idea a higher profile.

While to some the move toward a society predicated, first and foremost, on a sound environment is a movement forward, an evolution, to others it is a revolution, the seeds of change having been sown in the radical sixties. To these latter people, it is the kind of change that runs counter to free enterprise, to country and even to the notion of God in heaven, and threatens to undermine reality as they know it. That is the mindset of much of the Old West, and there is no way to overstate the anger that falls between the two worldviews.

The Wilderness Society, a national environmental group and a constituent of the GYC, with its offices in Bozeman, took a first step toward a new way of looking at the Greater Yellowstone economy in 1992 when it published a short report with a red cover called *The Wealth of Nature.*

In the report, Wilderness Society Ph.D. economist Ray Rasker studied twenty counties that are wholly or partly in the Greater Yellowstone ecosystem, in Montana, Idaho and Wyoming. The report came up with surprising conclusions. From 1969 to 1989, the number of jobs in the ecosystem counties increased 68 percent—if they were a state, the twenty counties would be the fastest growing state in the U.S.—and personal income doubled to $2.2 billion. Ninety-six percent—and this is critical—of the new jobs and nearly 90 percent of the growth in labor income took place *outside agriculture, mining and logging.* The growth occurred in construction, in transportation, in utilities, in the federal government and in such services as retail trade, finance, insurance and real estate, business, education, social care, and law. Nearly 80 percent of the new jobs and 65 percent of the increase in total personal income were generated by these kinds of services.

In essence, the growth and economic adrenaline for the Greater Yellowstone comes not from cutting logs and digging ore and riding herd on beeves, the report says, but from people who have come there or live there for things usually considered to have little economic value: scenery, small-town values, wildness, wildlife, and other amenities that add up to a way of life. As a matter of fact, recreation generated the vast majority of new jobs on six of the seven national forests in the last twenty years, ranging from a low of 76 percent of new jobs on the Targhee National Forest to 99 percent on the Custer. Meanwhile, the total number of jobs tied directly to commodity extraction in the region is 5 percent of the total employment.

The Greater Yellowstone is a beating heart of the New West. The market for "naturalness" is muscling resource extraction out of the economy.

And yet, The Wilderness Society says, the Forest Service continues a rearview-mirror approach to the economy. In 1990 and 1991, respectively, the Forest Service spent $12.8 million and $12.6 million of taxpayer money to subsidize the private timber companies so they could cut logs in the forests of the Greater Yellowstone. That is because the western economy has always depended on jobs processing resources to be sold, and the unquestioned assumption is that the economy still depends on those jobs. The inertia of tradition. That's Old West thinking, The Wilderness Society says. The organization argues that its analysis supports the New West and the protection of the West's most valuable asset. To continue to dismantle the ecosystem, piece by piece, and ship it off to Japan or New York or elsewhere will hurt the core part of the real Yellowstone economy. Commodity extraction, the report indicates, is doing damage far out of proportion to its benefits. "If there is going to be a rural renaissance," says Rasker, "it will be in the communities that protect assets that attract people from the global economy."

What are the businesses that make up this new economy? Everything from Bayard Fox's Equitour International, to a company in Red Lodge that makes backpacks, to a sawmill in Livingston that makes furniture for Japan, to a company in Jackson that makes quality winter clothing, to a woman in Moose who makes jewelry from elk turds, to a company that reclaims damaged streams and rivers, to the Buffalo Bill Historical Center (a world-class museum in Cody), to a wildlife touring company in Bozeman, to doctors and lawyers and stockbrokers and insurance companies and ski areas and hotels and restaurants.

Many environmentalists favor banning ranching on public lands. Or logging. Or mining. The GYC sees things differently. Its proposal is not to ban commodity extraction, but to convince loggers and miners and ranchers and real estate developers and those involved with tourism to operate on a scientific, sustainable basis that will allow them to continue generation after generation. It has to happen in a way that stops the destruction and squandering not only of the New West economy, but of the Old West economy as well.

Call it living on the interest, says the GYC, and not on the principal.

Based on the accumulation of the last three decades of new knowledge of how natural systems work, the goal of many new proposals for managing the Earth is to get humans to become part of the natural systems and play to their strengths, instead of fighting against them, being a burden on them, and eventually destroying them. The proposals look at how people can do more than burn up in the blink of a geologic eye what took millions of years to create—soil, trees, water, wildlife and minerals. Without these new approaches, advocates of ecosystem management say, Yellowstone and its wild wonders, the finest of the last handful of remaining essentially intact ecosystems in the world—and an increasingly vital part of the economy—will disintegrate.

Dennis Glick, project director of the GYC's Yellowstone Tomorrow project, flashes a series of slides on the screen in the back of an

Italian restaurant in downtown Red Lodge, Montana. On hand are members of the local chamber of commerce and other community leaders.

The slide program illustrates the eighteen million mountain and prairie acres of the Greater Yellowstone ecosystem, describes what the ecosystem is and how it works, shows what makes it unique, and demonstrates the role it plays in everything from people's lives to the region's economy. After the slide show is over, GYC staffers ask people to articulate what is important to them about their community, what they want to keep, what they want to change. They urge them to think about the future in a specific way. In a sense it's counseling for these small communities, to give them a strong sense of who and where they are. The GYC has a road show that it takes to places like Dubois, Wyoming, Ashton, Idaho, and Red Lodge, Montana.

The communities in the Greater Yellowstone ecosystem have also worked with an outfit called the Sonoran Institute, near Tucson, Arizona, as part of a similar program called Successful Communities. Citizens talk about ways their homes and the attributes of their community they value most can be protected—through economic and tax incentives, through county planning and zoning, through federal or state legislation.

The idea of both programs is to teach about the ecosystem by pointing out its component parts, to have people recognize what is special about where they live, and to show them how to preserve the ecosystem through careful planning and analysis.

Working at the local level is vital to any change, says Glick. "If environmental groups are making unilateral decisions in a conclave in Washington, D.C., they will be open to charges they are elitist and don't care about communities." Many people, in fact, even some environmentalists, say national groups are guilty of that fault, so the thrust of the environmental movement in recent years has shifted away from Washington, D.C., to regional groups like the GYC, and to local, grass roots organizations.

One of the first steps in the process of managing Yellowstone as an ecosystem is a redrawing of the maps. Political boundaries are often a barrier to ecosystem management. Yellowstone needs to be thought of as an eighteen-million-acre, dynamic, living entity rather than two million acres in a box whose lines were drawn before anything was understood about ecology. The ecosystem and its functioning must be foremost in mind. To that end, the mapping of the plant and animal life of an ecosystem is critical, an inventory that allows managers to make decisions on where, when, and if logging or ranching or mining should take place. If a river corridor is critical spring habitat for the grizzly bear, then logging there might take place in the winter to reduce impacts on the bear.

Since water is so precious in the West and fundamental to almost every other activity, many of the new, sustainable strategies are focused first on maintaining the flow, both in quantity and quality. From the time the first raindrop hits the ground or the first snow melts in the mountains, water should receive protection. The plan of the GYC is to protect the high country, the natural reservoirs, the peaks of the Centennial, Gallatin, Wind River and other ranges with federal wilderness designation that prohibits such activities as mining and logging.

Down lower, water management of all kinds is going through a rethinking. Heeding the call of the New West, the management of dammed rivers is changing. The generation of electrical power for cities and the storage of water for irrigators are no longer the sole concerns of managers of the Glen Canyon Dam on the Colorado, for example. The drastic change in flows that came from releasing water to meet power needs—as much as thirteen feet in a day—flow changes that ate away beaches and archaeological sites, destroyed fish spawning grounds and wiped out species of plants, are no more. New guidelines allow fluctuations in flow only a third to a fifth of what they were, a precedent expected to change the way many other dams are managed. On the Columbia River, fish screens have gone up on dams to protect fish as they swim downstream to the ocean.

University of Colorado professor of natural resource law Charles Wilkinson, the author of a book called *Crossing the Next Meridian*, which advocates changes in federal law to help solve the West's problems, would like to see fundamental changes in water management. "Place a tax on the extraction of water. Right now every drop comes out of the stream free. That's extraordinary. We use water at twice the rate of the East and several times the rate of foreign countries. If we charge, in the same way loggers pay a fee or ranchers pay for grazing, it would encourage conservation." Wilkinson also advocates retiring senior water rights as they are abandoned, and leaving that water in the stream for the health of aquatic ecosystems.

Land is the watershed, the catchment for all of the water that collects in rivers and streams and aquifers. If the catchment is stripped of cover by logging or ranching or mining, the water that washes into streams will be fouled and thick with sediment, which wipes out spawning beds for fish or causes the fish to suffocate. So the goal is to find new techniques for these resource activities, techniques that minimize or eliminate the disturbance, since present-day practices often do not take this into account.

This is the basis for Seattle scientist Jerry Franklin's proposals for overhauling the way forests are managed for timber. A "kinder, gentler logger," in Franklin's words, one that recognizes the ecological needs of the forest. "We've got to stop this billiard-table cutting," he says. The U.S. Forest Service must manage for long-term health of the forests as well as a range of values other than timber—everything from fisheries to recreation to wildlife.

Instead of a large area with patches of trees and patches of clear-cuts—which essentially kills the entire forest—old-growth and even old second-growth forests need to be carefully logged so the biological diversity is left behind. So bugs and birds and plants can rebuild the forest, as equally diverse as the one that was torn down. Franklin points to places where trees have fallen naturally, such as in a blowdown, or where the forest has burned. When trees come back to such a clearing, they come back with the diversity intact.

Kinder, gentler logging means going into a site, cutting some trees but leaving perhaps 10 to 15 percent of the trees standing, so the forest isn't wiped out, and so a new forest has something to build with. It is a tactic that mimics nature. "You hit 'em hard, leave them alone, get out and let them recover," Franklin says. It also means not logging ecologically sensitive areas, such as stream corridors and owl nesting sites. And instead of cleaning all the slash or tree branches and rotten logs up, much is left behind. Messy forests are rich, happy forests. It is not only ecologically sound, but taking *all* things into account it is far more economical. Soil from these forests isn't exposed and doesn't wash off the ground and into the streams and rivers where it chokes the very life out of them. People can still fish for salmon. Flooding of homes and businesses is less of a problem.

In practical terms, environmentalists believe in the message of the New Forestry, but fear it will provide an excuse to allow the cutting of more old growth. Instead, they feel it should be practiced on second-growth forests that are 100 or 150 years old.

The New Forestry doesn't do much for some loggers. "There's a danger factor," says Jerry Leppell. "You drop one tree and weaken the roots in another or crack the top and someone's going to get hurt. You've got to cut them all down. It sounds good. But it don't work." Even Franklin admits the companies will not find logging nearly as profitable, but others who depend on the forest will find extra benefits, and that may ease the political pressure to end logging.

Woody Barmore and others like him are important to the new kind of forestry. But replacing clear-cutting with selective cutting by small outfits like his is not an easy transition. Barmore says it is difficult for people like himself to get contracts to cut wood, because the Forest Service thinks in terms of large-scale sales—which produce more money for Forest Service coffers.

The Forest Service has also been geared toward big sales, some say, because companies like Idaho Forest Industries wield economic and political power and have the ear of their congressman. The Forest Service responds to that kind of pressure, says Ed Lewis. "The large mills have political power, while the little guys have never been organized and are at the whip and mercy of the big guys."

Many conservationists believe small-scale logging provides more jobs, a healthier forest and a healthier economy than the corporate kind. Small-scale logging may be the future anyway, because so many of the forests in the Greater Yellowstone have so little timber base left, and the large companies will not find logging profitable.

In addition to changing the way the forest is cut, there's an emphasis these days on changing the way the wood is used. "Value-added" is a buzzword in building a sustainable economy. Shipping raw logs to Japan or two-by-fours out on a flatbed truck does not create many jobs, except for loggers and sawyers. But turning lodgepole pine into furniture or wheat into bread or butchering and selling beef locally creates another layer of manufacturing and more jobs. Doug Crandall is manager of the Brand S sawmill in Livingston, Montana. Because of the difficulty of getting enough timber to cut into two-by-fours, Brand S is now turning lodgepole pine into garage doors for the British and frames for the paper doors that the

Japanese favor. While the sawmill has 125 employees, the mill-works part of the business has 65. "We're trying to be a survivor," says Crandall.

Allan Savory is an unlikely character to be playing a central role in the debate over Western Inestock grazing. From Zimbabwe (formerly Rhodesia), the dark-haired, charismatic Savory was a game ranger, tracking down man-eating lions and poachers. Rhodesia's civil war was heating up and Savory was drawn into the conflict as a commander of a unit trained in behind-enemy-lines guerrilla warfare. Tracking nationalists across the Rhodesian rangeland, Savory noticed great differences in land grazed by Europeans and that grazed by African natives. Europeans allowed animals to forage continuously, as ranchers do in the West, while natives herded their animals across the range, a technique that kept the vegetation in far better shape. Savory felt that the native approach approximated the action of wild animals on the soil, which moved from place to place, churning the soil, planting seeds that fell from grasses and never staying in one place long enough to hammer vegetation or compact soil to the point where it couldn't recover. "I hated cattle," he says. "I would have shot every damn cow and their owners too, if they had resisted, because of what they were doing to the land." Savory left Rhodesia in 1975 and came to the United States, and took up residence in Albuquerque, New Mexico.

Instead of shooting ranchers, Savory is trying to teach them to mend their ways. Everything depends on the land, Savory says. The health of a country is related to the health of its resources. And so Savory brought to this country a new kind of cattle-grazing technique, Holistic Resource Management, which he developed and which recognizes the scientific principles of an ecosystem and utilizes them to improve the land.

Because with traditional grazing livestock are allowed to feed continuously, choice plants never go to seed, or store food during the critical periods of the dormant season. Grasses that cattle eat stop reproducing and die out, and with ground cover gone, soil is lost to erosion. The problem is compounded by the action of cow hooves—cattle move slowly and, in concert with rainfall, compact the soil, causing it to cap, or form a hard surface. Rain runs off the land instead of percolating into the underground water table. Aquifers are not adequately recharged, and water stored in the upper level of the soil itself is wicked to the surface and evaporates in the West's arid environment.

The hooves of cattle can be used to mimic the action that native animals like bison or elk had on the land, Savory says. They just need to be managed properly, to replicate the effect of wild animals, by such things as moving them around more. Cattle can even be used as a tool to help a stream return to health or improve habitat for an endangered species.

Without a change, he says, cattle will turn the West into a desert. People can come to a rich new continent and mismanage for a century or two without serious problems. However, at some point, he says, the damage will catch up with them.

Savory's HRM is not just about cattle; it includes the rancher and his worldview, and such things as values, belief systems and the need for a vision beyond ranching, land and cattle, to include society as a whole. He tells ranchers that if they do not clean up their grazing, and make it more efficient, they will lose the political and economic battle, and their way of life.

HRM is not universally accepted, by any means. It has been criticized by many ranchers and some environmentalists as mumbo jumbo and too complex to ever be widely implemented. And Savory has been criticized as arrogant and high-handed—a statement he agrees with. "I know I'm a bastard," he says. "But I also know I'm right."

Change toward a more natural kind of resource development seems to be catching on. In Oregon, for example, some ranchers are discovering that by leaving the beaver dams that block the streams on their ranch, instead of dynamiting them out, the level of the water table beneath the ground rises and subirrigates lush meadows and encourages the growth of nutritious plants.

Some ranchers are turning to bison. As an animal native to the western ecosystems, many people feel the vegetation does better under the hooves of bison, hooves that are sharper than cattle's and churn the soil up and naturally replant grasses, rather than compacting the soil. While cattle often congregate along streams, mill about and damage riparian areas, bison spend more time off the streams and move around more.

The idea of nature as a partner is being applied to farming as well. In Salina, Kansas, the heartland of America and the center of farming culture, Wes Jackson has founded the Land Institute, which is trying to stop, and even reverse, the tremendous damage Jackson says has been done to the soil and water in the name of farming. "The plowshare," Jackson said, "may well have destroyed more options for future generations than the sword."

One of Jackson's maxims is, "Wilderness is the standard against which agriculture should be judged." Translated to farming, that means instead of a monoculture of wheat, plowed and planted each year, and sprayed to fend off insects and weeds, it would be a crop of edible-seeded perennials, with four or five different and hardy varieties, which because they are wild would be able to survive drought, wind, frost and fire. It might be plowed and renewed once in five years. The plants would find moisture and hold the soil in place, and reproduce on their own. And like many wild plants, they would naturally be pest-resistant.

A new kind of plow, in fact, is moving farming in the same direction. With the traditional moldboard plow, each spring the farmer would slice open the earth to plant seeds, at the same time exposing the soil, allowing it to be swept away by wind and water. It's estimated that in Iowa, two bushels of topsoil are lost for every bushel of corn grown. The new plow—the technique is called residue management—leaves the remains of last year's crops in place, and chisels holes in the soil amidst the mulch, which serves to protect the seedlings and provide compost. Soil and water are held on the field instead of running into streams or being blown away. The crops are rotated to thwart insects. And though some herbicides are used for weeds, they are a new kind that break down quickly.

While there are a great many disagreements and criticisms with the solutions offered by Allan Savory, Jerry Franklin, Wes Jackson and others, there is no question that they have helped launch resource management off into new directions.

Perhaps there is a way for long-established farming communities like Olney Springs, Colorado, which are faced with extinction, to survive without large amounts of imported water, or expensive herbicides and pesticides. Perhaps logging towns like Forks, Washington, don't have to cut themselves out of trees—sustainable forestry may hold an answer that enables loggers and mills to rotate their cut so that in fifteen or twenty years they can come back where they started, and begin the cycle over.

In some places an even more radically different approach to agriculture might be appropriate, especially in areas of low rainfall, frequent drought and poor soils.

Frank and Deborah Popper are two academics from Rutgers University in New Jersey who advocate rescuing portions of the rolling prairie and grasslands from the plow blade to return it to the native bison, sixty million of which once roamed the plains. Since the towns that dotted the plains are dying, the answer may be a merciful death for some. "We tried to force waterless, treeless steppes to behave like Ohio, and got three or four boom and bust cycles for our trouble," Frank Popper says. "Now the classic plains cycle of drought, financial woe and depopulation is rolling again, and this time it may go all the way. Thirty years of water-table depletion, S and L's collapsing right and left, whole rural counties voting with their feet—and still no one's thinking ahead." If trends continue, in thirty years two thirds of the prairie and plains communities will vanish.

The Poppers' Buffalo Commons would encompass parts of Kansas, Nebraska, Colorado, Montana, New Mexico and Wyoming.

The bison, the Poppers say, would create an unparalleled tourist attraction, and do away with destructive agricultural practices in favor of an animal that is native to the ecosystem. Buffalo could even be harvested and sent to slaughter. Some towns would flourish as jumping off points for hunting or photo safaris into the heart of Buffaloland, which would, the way the Poppers envision it, affect 109 counties and about 413,000 residents.

The idea has ignited a prairie-fire-like hatred of the Poppers from one end of the Great Plains to the other. Popper, who speaks to prairie peoples only with security guards, has called himself the Salman Rushdie of the plains. One Wyoming state legislator, Patrick O'Toole, a Democrat, said having Popper speak in Wyoming was "like bringing in someone from Nazi Germany to talk about population control."

Hard rock mining, coal mining and other kinds of mineral extraction pose different questions for the West than do agriculture and logging. According to the Mineral Policy Center's Phil Hocker, there are no environmentally safe mines. Some are better than others, but no matter what precautions are taken, cyanide leaches into groundwater, mountains are torn up, tons of hazardous waste are left behind. No one has found a way to mine without problems, he and others say, and they advocate a change in the General Mining Law of 1872. Most important, Hocker says, is making sure that federal agencies have the power to say where and how mining will happen. "We'll still say yes to mining activities," says Hocker, "where it's appropriate. The Noranda mine at Cooke City is not appropriate." Secretary of the Interior Bruce Babbitt, the Mineral Policy Center and others, advocate a 12.5 percent hard rock mineral royalty, the same amount paid on oil and gas, so public minerals are no longer granted to corporations free of charge. The substantial costs of reclamation should not be passed on to the taxpayers, Hocker says, and the patenting aspect, which transfers property from public to private ownership without charge, needs to be a thing of the past.

Some kind of change in the 1872 law is likely in the near future. In 1992, a reform bill passed the U.S. House of Representatives, but never made it as far as the Senate. It will be introduced again.

The Mineral Hill Mine at Jardine, just north of the park's northern entrance at Gardiner, is the kind of operation environmentalists point to as the direction mining should take. John Hoak, administrative superintendent of the mine, says that the air and water at the mine are carefully monitored to catch problems early on. The tailings, or the mixture of water and soil that constitutes the mine's waste products, are dried before they are dumped, so contaminated water won't leak through the lining of the tailings pond. Cyanide is removed from waste water and chemically neutralized. But the most important part of the mine, Hoak says, is the fact that "everything and anything is open to the public. We created dialogue, a forum for people to bring their questions and concerns to us."

Nearly everyone preaches the gospel of diversification for western economies, and says a mining town or logging town should be a thing of the past. If a town loses a sawmill or mine with one hundred workers, and it is the largest employer, the shutdown can be devastating. On the other hand, if there are ten small businesses, each with ten employees, the economy is more resilient and the power of any one company is reduced. So the search is on for small businesses.

One thing the GYC would like to establish in the ecosystem, says Glick, is a pool of available money that can be loaned to "green" or sustainable kinds of businesses for start-up. Rural development banks, similar to inner-city development banks, are also being created to provide capital for small, diverse businesses in some parts of the West.

As the West's primary raison d'être changes from resources to services, states, counties and communities need to come up with a way to deal with the impacts of tourism, not only on the environment, but on the people who call the West home. Santa Fe councilwoman Debbie Jamarillo has been trying to derail a growing tourist industry there for several years, claiming it lines the pockets of a few and works against many in a town. "We need to quit the way we promote this town, asking people to come and live here," Jamarillo says. "We need to quit spending lodging tax funds on promotion. We should use it in the community. Everybody in the world knows of Santa Fe. Let it attract people with its own charm, not charm we create."

The city also increased its fees for real estate development, so-called impact fees that make developers pay up-front costs for things like sewers and roads. "We figured if we imposed a tax on everything that's done, it pisses off enough developers so they end up going elsewhere," she says. Next on her agenda, Jamarillo says, is a 0.5 or 1 percent fee levied on homes above $250,000, money that can "help us bring back some of the things we're losing. Such things as affordable housing, economic development or a school that teaches traditional Hispanic art."

In Bozeman, Montana, Bill Bryan of Off the Beaten Path would like to see tourism overhaul itself, and think about what it's doing and plan, instead of blindly rushing ahead with a "K Mart approach" to the industry, attracting as many people as possible—quantity, he says, without thought to quality. "Tourism is managing a herd of people through the park, and that frustrates me," he says. The notion of eco-tourism doesn't go far enough, doesn't take into account the impact on people and culture. He favors, instead, something he calls "appropriate tourism." "If you look at tourism, there are limits," Bryan says. "Limits to the number of people who can be employed, limits to the number of tourists who can visit a park because of impacts. Tourism is exploiting the worker and the environment. People have to set limits." Bryan favors an emphasis on education for tourists, spending time with a guide who teaches about the biology or the culture of an area.

Some argue that tourism can have environmental and social impacts that are different, but just as severe as a mine or a timber sale. Why shouldn't an environmental impact statement be required for tourism? Or at least some kind of planning process?

Getting a handle on park visitation, limiting somehow the impact wildly growing numbers of people are having, has always proven difficult. There are ideas as to how it could be done, and again, instead of a single magic bullet, the approach is multifaceted. Lorraine Mintzmeyer, who was regional superintendent of the National Park Service in Denver for many years until she was forced out, says a carrying capacity for parks should have been done some time ago. "The Park Service has to say that when we reach a certain number, the gates will close. It should have happened by now. Visitation to Yosemite should have been limited a decade ago," Mintzmeyer says. "Yellowstone is at a saturation point in the summer and approaching saturation in the winter."

Some towns, like Jackson, are shifting their promotion. No longer do they advertise Jackson in summer, but in fall, spring and winter to distribute the tourist burden more evenly.

One way to ease overcrowding, Mintzmeyer says, is to create new parks. There is obviously a demand. "I would love to see [portions of] the Wind River [in Wyoming] added as a park, along with the Maroon Bells Wilderness Area in Colorado." Grand Gulch, a canyon in Utah with the remains of a once thriving Anasazi culture, should be made a national park, she says, along with the Bob Marshall Wilderness Area, which could be added to the acreage of Glacier National Park, just to the north.

On the outskirts of Tucson, at the end of long, six-lane boulevards that carry the city's traffic, are the two units of Saguaro National Monument, islands of wilderness in the path of an approaching wave of urban America. They are packed with an array of unusual desert wildlife and vegetation: tall, green saguaro cacti with spined, fluted trunks and giant creamy yellow flowers, which blossom in the summer. Peregrine falcons slice through the cyanic skies, and javelinas, cougars and black bears wander the Dragoon and Santa Catalina Mountains.

Tucson is growing rapidly, luring snowbirds from the north and refugees from California to a warm and sunny climate. Between 1985 and 1990, growth here averaged a steady 2 percent a year.

When they were founded in 1933, these national monuments were twenty miles from Tucson. Now the city has finally reached them.

It would seem the destiny of these two national monuments, one on either side of Tucson, prime real estate and highly prized as a neighbor, would be to be swallowed up by the sprawl. Their ambience and their ecological integrity would be lost to urbanization. Species could vanish. However, a new kind of project is planned here, a project that may create a blueprint for an "eco-sensitive" development that will marry private land outside a national park with the biological and aesthetic values of the parks. Conservationist Luther Propst is the director of the Sonoran Institute in Tucson, Arizona (which also conducts the Successful Communities program), and has been a principal in this new kind of real estate development.

The question is this: how do you protect the saguaro ecosystem, the movement of wildlife in and out of the park, precious water supplies and critical parts of the ecosystem, yet allow growth to continue? The Rincon Institute (created by the Sonoran Institute specifically for this project), working with a developer, the Rocking K Development Company, and officials of Saguaro National Monument, came up with a plan. Six thousand homes, two resort hotels and two golf courses planned for nearby would be built not based first on the best view or location on the bank of a creek, but in places designed to best accommodate the movement of deer and peccaries. In addition, two and a half miles of riparian areas, perhaps ten times as productive in desert ecosystems as in upland habitat, will be reclaimed by the developer, after damage suffered at the hands of farmers and the hooves of cattle. Meanwhile, 3,540 acres of especially ecologically sensitive land—including 1,900 from the Rocking K Ranch—are being purchased to add to the monument.

The Rincon Institute will hold comprehensive environmental, natural history, and cultural history programs about the desert area for Rocking K residents, tenants, employees and guests and will be a permanent part of the development. The importance of such things as native vegetation and conserving water is taught. In essence, these programs are about how people can be part of the environment.

A similar development Propst has been working on, in California and near the Santa Monica Mountains National Recreation Area, will take the idea a little further. In addition to the features of the Rocking K, the Santa Monica village will be built on a pedestrian scale, with bike paths and sidewalks so that 70 percent of the homes are within a ten-minute walk to schools, a library and a transit station that takes people by bus to commercial areas in the San Fernando Valley. All of the 2,700 homes (which include 500 for low- and moderate-income people) are wired with fiber optics so people can work at home.

The eco-aspects of the development are ensured by deed restrictions and paid for with fees from the developer, which are passed on to the landowners, as well as bed fees (50 cents a night per room at the Rocking K) from the resort hotel at the development. When built out, it's estimated the development will fund the Rincon Institute to the tune of $200,000 to $300,000 a year. "The key," believes Propst, "is that it fits into the profit system." Otherwise, he says, it will be rejected by business, which holds the power to develop.

There are other ideas. Glacier National Park supervisory biologist Cliff Martinka is an advocate of "cluster developments," a group of houses built together rather than spread all over. "Ten people on ten acres is better for wildlife than ten people on a hundred or a thousand," he says. Jack Wright, the geographer from New Mexico, says the old European idea of "long lots" bears looking into. Instead of a lot as wide as it is long, each homeowner has a long, narrow lot that runs from the road to the river's edge. The house is built near the road, leaving a long stretch of open land near the river. "The idea is that that way you're not covering up that fine agricultural land." Or important riparian area.

Protection is also found in the tax codes, and is being brought to bear in the Yellowstone milieu, as is land protection through a conservation purchase, or what's called an easement. An easement is a donation of development rights to a nonprofit group such as The Nature Conservancy, the Montana Land Reliance or the Jackson Hole Land Trust. Say a conservation-minded buyer has a ten-thousand-acre spread, and wants to keep it a ranch. The buyer agrees to forgo his or her right to develop the ranch for a subdivision or anything else, restrictions that are written into the deed. If the property is sold or passed on to heirs, the restrictions stay with it. As a result of forgoing some uses, the land has lost value and the owner can make a deduction of that value from his or her taxes. The local land trust is a nonprofit organization set up to hold and oversee the conservation agreement.

Easements are also a way to protect the erosion of the agricultural economy. Many farmers are land rich and cash poor. Inheritance taxes often break up a ranch and force it to be sold into subdivision because the inheritors must sell it off to pay the tax. The last crop, a farming maxim holds, is houses. What happens as the New West grows is that some agricultural land near town takes on a value as a subdivision or investment property for someone in a different economy, far beyond what a farmer or rancher could make growing peppers or wheat on the property. If a farmer declares, through a conservation easement, that he or she will keep the property in agriculture in perpetuity, it can reduce the value of the land by as much as 50 percent, which means inheritance and property taxes are far less than they would have been. It makes it less likely a rancher or farmer would be forced to sell.

A conservation group may simply buy property for protection. The Nature Conservancy in Montana owns eighty acres of key wetlands habitat along the South Fork of the Madison River in the Yellowstone ecosystem. It was subdivided, and ready to be sold, when The Nature Conservancy stepped in. It's home to sandhill cranes, ospreys, bald eagles and, possibly, reintroduced Arctic grayling. The Nature Conservancy also bought Gray's Ranch in the bootheel of New Mexico, the largest outright conservation purchase in the United States. It is 502 square miles of hot, dry desert, and full of life. Boulder, Colorado, in an effort to keep the city from losing much of its character, has purchased more than thirty thousand acres of open space around the city.

It's estimated that 90 percent of the West lives in urban areas. To try to fix what takes place on undeveloped lands, without dealing with the cities, is folly, for eventually many people abandon the cities as uninhabitable. Los Angeles is a case in point. Some residents of Phoenix, the huge megalopolis that shimmers in the heat of the desert in Arizona, are trying to come to grips with the city's impact, not only on the 444 or so square miles of desert it sits on, but on the huge area around the city that has been dewatered and denuded.

The city of Phoenix is sometimes called "City Without a Soul" because it has little charm, no center of town, has simply spilled higgledy-piggledy into the desert. Not only that, it has been constructed with little regard to the fact that it is in the middle of the driest part of the American desert. The buildings and homes of Phoenix, with their air-conditioned offices, green lawns and fountains and swimming pools, are the same kind as the ones in, say Minneapolis, which gets twenty-five inches of rain a year. Phoenix gets less than eight.

Phoenix had a civic group called the Future Forum, which was examining a new direction for Phoenix, how to make the city *a part of* the desert instead of *apart from* it. To give Phoenix, in essence, some soul. To make it grow according to the limits of its environment, to make it sustainable. In the late 1980s, as many as four thousand citizens came together under the umbrella of Future Forum and put together a long-range plan for the city. "Phoenix had grown so extremely rapidly," says Rod Engelen, recently retired director of Future Forum, "that the community is unsettled and so is its sense of self and where it wants to go." One idea was to carve up the sprawling mass into ten urban villages that would each have its own planning council and give people some sense of belonging. The plan also addressed such issues as eliminating noise and air pollution, protecting open space, easing traffic congestion, teaching people through museums and education programs about the desert, promoting arts and culture and decentralizing government.

After Mayor Terry Goddard was defeated in his bid for governor, Future Forum waned and has since been absorbed into a nonprofit group called Community Forum. Future Forum found it tough, says Engelen, to go up against the powers that be even with goals that seemed so modest. "The dominant industry in Phoenix, Albuquerque and elsewhere is building, and builders do not support planning, research and goal setting. They are a threat to what builders want to do."

A group in San Francisco called Planet Drum has tried to drum up the acceptance of "green cities," inviting nature back into urban America, a formula that includes such things as more plantings of native plants, which makes the cities more aesthetic, cools these islands of asphalt and concrete in the summer and stems runoff and pollution from roads and parking lots. The group has promoted the reclamation of urban streams, the construction of alternative transportation to ease traffic, and the creation of greenways to connect the city to outlying natural areas.

Restoration will play a central role in the future of the West, with federal and private money being directed away from subsidies to reclaim overcut forests, mine waste damage, overgrazed land and ruined rivers and streams. As nature intact becomes increasingly valuable, a service economy that restores nature is springing up.

A curious reclamation phenomenon is now sweeping parts of the West—reestablishing trout in rivers and streams that meander through ranches owned by well-heeled fishermen. A common problem in the West, where the mountain-fed streams are world-class fly fisheries, is that too many cattle, too much plowing, and too much stream-straightening along roads by the highway department have choked the very life out of good trout streams.

That's where stream doctors like Dave Odell come in. There are numerous river reclamation companies around the West, ranging in size from one-man outfits like Odell's Curlew Consulting, near Hamilton, Montana, to larger companies like Inter-Fluve, which enhanced the streams on Ted Turner's Flying D Ranch in Montana. Inter-Fluve, a large company with offices in Bozeman, Denver and Portland, has twelve employees, and does millions of dollars' worth of work each year, not only in the West, but in places like Scotland, Wales and New Zealand.

Odell was brought in to diagnose the problems with Mitchell Slough, a quiet, inauspicious thirty-foot-wide stream that runs through a 360-acre ranch in western Montana's Bitterroot Valley. The ranch had been purchased by rock-and-roll singer and fly-fisherman Huey Lewis, and Lewis had become concerned about the stream's paucity of trout. Odell, who also consulted with discount stockbroker Charles Schwab in this valley, found that an irrigation dam at the stream's headwaters on the Bitterroot River had choked off high-water flows that occur in spring. High flows charge down a river and flush out silt that collects through the year. Without this annual purge, silt covers trout eggs laid in the gravel beds, and nascent trout suffocate.

After studying aerial photos and walking the mile or so of stream several times each season, Odell started the reclamation. Heavy equipment rumbled in to dig sand and silt out of the stream channels and create islands in the middle of the stream. Since the same amount of water is now moving through a narrower space, it moves faster, scouring silt from the channel and delivering more oxygen to the trout and their eggs.

Streambanks were fenced off to keep cattle from knocking soil into the stream and eating streamside vegetation. Rope nets were fastened to eroding banks to hold soil in. Cottonwood logs were dropped into the water along the shore and anchored to the bank with heavy-duty stainless steel airline cable, both to keep the bank in place and to provide a place for trout to hide from airborne predators, such as great blue herons and osprey. And with the strategic placement of small islands to direct the flow, the stream was encouraged to meander. Winding streams cut away banks and provide dark hidden places, with overhanging grass and shrubs where fish can grow old and big.

"There were four holes [by "hole" he means a deep spot in the river] that held fish here before we started," Odell said as he waded noisily through the stream, pointing out an occasional pair of trout lips as they surfaced long enough to sip in a tiny insect. "That's a small number for a mile and a half of stream. There's thirty holes deep enough now to hold trout." This single one mile of work cost about $20,000, Odell says, though a badly damaged stream can go $50,000 a mile. Inter-Fluve, meanwhile, reclaims streams at a cost of between $5 and $20 a foot, excluding travel.

Come summer, Odell plunges into the stream with a mask and a snorkel to count and measure the fish. Rainbow trout grow up to five pounds here, he says, and brown trout as high as eight pounds, resembling little speckled footballs. "Nature does the work," he says. "I just help it along."

Two years after the project began, Mitchell Slough looks healthy. The man-made islands are thick with vegetation, and in the summer, clouds of insects swarm on and above the water. The rumps of diving ducks waggle as they feed head down beneath the water, and white-tailed deer bound like four-legged dancers over barbed-wire fences. "People love their trout streams," said Odell, explaining the boom in stream reclamation work. "When they look out their window and see a big trout porpoising to mayflies, this really turns people on."

Professor Patricia Limerick lowers her sunglasses to read a bronze plaque fastened to a monument alongside Independence Rock, a red rock formation about the size of a city block on the prairie of central Wyoming. "To all unknown pioneers who passed this way to win and hold the West," the plaque reads. It was placed there by a troop of Boy Scouts from Long Island in 1931 and sounds fairly innocuous, even laudable. But the single sentence represents an idea that Limerick is trying very hard to disabuse people of. "The people celebrated as winners are not winners," she says. "There are any number of questions about how long this empire will hold."

For things to change in the American West there must be an admission that the Old West is riddled with mistakes. That's the argument of people like Limerick. She claims Americans suffer from a kind of societal dysfunction. They have been living a racist, sexist, environmentally ignorant, and generally wrongheaded myth about the American West for the last century, yet they believe the myth is glorious and honorable. Western history, the way films, television and other parts of the culture have written it, Limerick says, is largely responsible. The myth is so seductive and powerful it stands in the way of a hard look at the past. It's time, she says, for a New Western History.

The standard view of the West, says Limerick, is of a wild, useless "virtually uninhabited" place that white men visited, wrestled with and then tamed, taking it from the grasp of people who did not know how to use it. They made it productive and therefore better. In the process, the land and the life-style turned drab Europeans into uniquely American characters. Miners and cowboys. Loggers and roughneck oil well drillers. Independent. Stoic. Romantic. Lovers of the land. And everyone has lived happily ever after.

This myth is so loved, so pervasive and so well told by the likes of John Wayne and Louis L'Amour, she says, that it has blinded most Americans to what has really gone on in the wide, open spaces. The Indians were the victims of genocide. Hispanics were driven out. Women were ignored. The rugged and romantic landscape, meanwhile, has been ripped apart for its treasures and left that way. Now, Limerick says, it's time to face up to that past. "It's the difference between going through life thinking you were the lost son of the king of England versus who you really are," she says. "If you weren't the lost prince and were responsible, you'd want to know it."

At stake in who controls the territory of the past is how we chart the course of the future. Limerick's recipe: First off, she says, forget the notion that the West was a "frontier"—a term Limerick calls the "F word." "The frontier is the name for the place where white people get scarce," she says. "Instead of seeing it as a frozen continent with Indian people and Hispanics waiting like stage furniture for the play to begin when the white men came out, you must look at them as living people. The term frontier only makes sense if you're a white person standing in the East with white people."

Another barrier to an honest view, she says, is the happy ending myth—especially when it comes to the land. "They did not tame it," she argues. "They seemed to tame pieces and parts. But earthquakes and wind and drought were not tamed. Those things are fundamentally untamable. And things they thought were progress—plowing the land and planting crops—seemed like a good thing. But if you wait around and see a dust bowl and weeds and pesticides, you wouldn't say you mastered it. You changed it. You didn't master it."

A sacred cow that Limerick loves to grind into hamburger is the notion of independence. The federal government subsidizes ranchers with reduced grazing rates, and the result has been overgrazed land. The feds have paid the bill for water that flows to farmers and ranchers in the West and in the process destroyed rivers. The government sells federally owned timber at a loss to keep timber companies alive, and it literally gives away publicly owned gold, silver and other metals to miners, large and small. "These people weren't inept bunglers who couldn't do a thing for themselves, a bunch of Barney Fifes," Limerick says. "But the federal government made the whole party possible by paying for the Army, managing the land and paying for the railroads. It's not hardy folks creating a life of their own."

Now the feds are paying to clean up the party, she says. "In the old view of western history, miners came in and prosperity radiated out of the mines. Now there's fifteen thousand mines in Colorado radiating toxic chemicals. Even if an individual miner went home making a profit, he left the bill for the next generation to pay," she says. "I hated westerns because they always smashed up the saloon, and broke mirrors and bottles and then rode out of town. I'm still back in the saloon saying, 'Hey, wait a minute. Somebody has to clean up this mess.' "

It's an attitude born of the view, she says, that the West is infinite, uninhabited landscape. "That sense of endless open space says, If you make a mess, there are many more miles untouched to forgive. It exempts you from regret or consequence."

The New Western History strikes some people as absurd. Before his death in 1991, A. B. Guthrie, Jr., the eighty-nine-year-old author of the Pulitzer-prize-winning historical novel *The Big Sky* and the screenplay for *Shane,* and a host of other novels about the West, responded to Limerick's notions, claiming the New Historians dwell on the negative. "It took courage to pull up stakes and venture into an unknown land," Guthrie said. "That was heroism. She's so intent on making a case, she ignores anything that opposes it."

Richard Misrach is a revisionist himself, a photographic revisionist who swings his camera lenses in different directions than most. Not toward the unspoiled mountains of Idaho. Or the red rock cliffs of southern Utah. But onto a Navy bombing range on public land in Nevada which he favors turning into an unusual national park. The land is covered with shrapnel and unexploded bombs the Navy calls "ugly babies." Craters pockmark the sagebrush landscape where bombs have exploded. Misrach envisions a "Boardwalk of the Bombs" that weaves among the destruction, and a road that tourists can motor on with the kids called "Devastation Drive." Then they can stop in at the visitor center, which is built in the style of a munitions bunker with a museum on military abuses of the land. Although it sounds like a joke, Misrach is serious. He wants people to see what the "real" West looks like. Misrach's photos of military abuses of the land and his detailed plans for a new park are contained in his fifth book, called *Bravo 20: The Bombing of the American West.*

Misrach's landscapes contain bomb craters in front of a range of desert mountains, twisted metal on a bombing range and a group of horses found mysteriously dead in an area used by the military. They've been called "landscapes of consequence." They are a new way of seeing the West, yet they are beautiful and haunting with a sophisticated composition on light and landscape. Misrach came to his own conclusion on the problems of a mythical West, and like Limerick, he seeks to bring honesty to the vision of the West with what he calls cultural landscapes. "The beautiful things are still there," he says, "but it's a fiction that you can go into the West and find pure untrammeled wilderness. It's hard to go anywhere without running into dune buggies and dumps and people target shooting."

Misrach says the traditional western landscape photographer, by shooting the same cliché landscape hundreds of others have shot, has done a great disservice. "I have a lot of trouble with the *National Geographic* and *Sierra Club* photos," he says. "They take a picture between the power lines and Winnebagos of a 'pure view' of Half Dome in Yosemite. Yet it's really so smoggy and so crowded." Such work, he says, also fosters the idea that only beautiful areas should be protected, "and the subtle message is you can trash everything else and set aside these areas to be nice to."

This is much of what the notion of sustainability is all about. It's no longer enough to draw a box around the park and let the rest go to hell. People must find a way to live on all of the land.

The environmentally minded envision the next West as one of true redemption, a way to correct the mistakes people have made, and are still making, by logging and mining and ranching, and to restore it to a more natural state. It is a new way of living on the land in harmony with it and cleaning up well-intentioned mistakes of the past.

However, remaking the West, criticizing longtime practices, tinkering with a proud and righteous history, moving the settling of a harsh country from the win column to the loss column, does not set well with all of the people whose lives depend on the status quo. And that's an understatement. Sawmill workers, loggers, miners, farmers and ranchers see their worldview and economy under assault from many quarters, crumbling before their eyes, with people making a living by attacking them and claiming their whole way of life is dead wrong. If the changes environmentalists, fiscal conservatives, easterners and far westerners, celebrities and wealthy people would like to visit on the West are a revolution, then the recently organized resistance to the changes is a counterrevolution. Participants in the battle for preservation of the Old West, who refer to themselves as the Wise Use Movement, include people from such organizations as the Western Public Lands Council, a conservative group that formed a smaller organization called People for the West!; the right-wing Center for the Defense of Economic Freedom; the National Cattlemen's Association; the Trail Bike Riders Association; The Blue Ribbon Coalition; Grassroots for Multiple Use; and so on.

It is a pitched battle, far beyond any disagreement over policy, with both sides casting it as a struggle for survival, even a holy war. People for the West! is one of the most prominent and successful of the counterrevolutionaries, a new breed of conservative activist in the West. For the past twenty years, environmental groups have laid sole claim to masses, calling themselves "public interest" groups. People for the West! claims that that characterization is dishonest, and that environmentalists, most of them headquartered in Washington, D.C., are out of touch with the reality of life in the West. These environmentalists are so extreme in their view they would cause hardship to a large segment of the public and destroy a western way of life based on commodity extraction on federal lands. "They're talking about dessert," said one activist of environmentalists who want protection for wilderness, national parks and such things, while well-paying jobs are growing fewer. "We're talking about meat and potatoes." Groups like PFW! are tapping into the deep-rooted fear of dramatic changes taking place these days.

"People are being rubbed out one at a time," says Troy Mader, of the anti–Endangered Species Act group Abundant Wildlife of North America. "The rancher. The little sawmill operator. They [environmentalists] have killed the economy in lots of ways."

Leaders of Wise Use groups rail about efforts by conservationists to reduce or cancel longtime subsidies for timber companies, mining companies and ranchers who run cattle on public land. They denounce what they call excessive environmental regulations that dampen the spirit of free enterprise.

The Old West has taken a chapter from the environmentalists' manual, hiring staff in each state to organize people who have traditionally been difficult to organize, directing letter-writing campaigns and protests toward politicians, working the press, and getting the faithful out to rallies and hearings on controversial topics. "It's empowerment for people who don't know they have the power," says Barbara Granell, the blond, articulate executive director of People for the West!

With an annual budget of $650,000 (compared to $700,000 for GYC), Granell runs PFW! out of an office in downtown Pueblo, Colorado, a symbolic place for their headquarters, for Pueblo is a steel town, and at its peak the mill here employed five thousand people. Now a thousand or so work here, and their future, along with the future of the mill and Pueblo's future, is in doubt.

"People say to me, 'What in the world can I do, Barbara? I can't do anything,' " Granell says. "I say, 'Are you going to roll over and play dead, or are you going to fight back? Environmental elitists are saying they know what's best for you, intellectually pontificating about what's best for you. That's not how America works.' "

While Granell champions the cause of the people, a look at the board of directors shows that the group is dominated by mining companies, which have more at stake in current efforts to change nineteenth-century resource practices than any other industry. Mining company board members—which make up almost two thirds of the PFW! board—include people from such industry giants as Homestake, Hecla and Noranda. That doesn't mean there isn't a grass roots involvement in these groups. There is, in People for the West! and in numerous other organizations.

Another prime mover in the Wise Use Movement is the Center for the Defense of Economic Freedom, based in Bellevue, Washington. This organization has gone on the offensive with an extremely conservative philosophy. Run by two men, Ron Arnold and Alan Gottlieb, the CDEF favors mining or logging in wilderness areas and parks; requiring environmentalists to pay industry damages if they stop or slow a project; and weakening the Endangered Species Act. At rallies around the country, Arnold tells loggers and ranchers things like, "We're going to destroy them, like they're trying to destroy you." But it's more than just an anti-environmental movement. Well-funded, with a sophisticated, computerized direct-mail system that brings in millions of dollars a year, the CDEF is building coalitions between groups that are angry over changing resource policy, and in the process is putting together an effective conservative political base, largely in the West.

Not all of the conservative notions being offered in the marketplace of ideas are rejected by environmentalists. Groups to the right, such as the Political Economy Research Center in Bozeman, among others, advocate something they call "free-market environmentalism." Simply take the government out of the picture and base everything on the profit motive. Sell the public's land and resources to individuals and corporations who, in their own self-interest, will protect their investment.

At least part of the philosophy has fallen on friendly ears in the environmental community. The Defenders of Wildlife, an environmental group based in Washington, D.C., for example, has established a fund to reimburse ranchers whose livestock has been killed by wolves, a species the Defenders of Wildlife want protected.

Even Jasper Carlton, the biocentrist, believes the free market should figure in protection of endangered species. "I'm all for positive incentive," he says. "Why not pay these private owners to raise prey base for the wolf, to raise grizzly bears instead of cows? They can have their privacy, their ranch and their way of life. Why not build in extra funding for these things? That makes people part of the ecosystem and gives them a stake. The rancher could still have cows, if he didn't put them out in grizzly bear habitat. He could ride his horse, chase his cows. Fine. Just don't shoot or poison grizzly bears."

Backing off on environmental requirements and regulations, say leaders of the Wise Use Movement, will revitalize the West, will call up pioneer gumption and unfetter the strong arms that made the West what it is. Don't change the system that made America great. Make it lean and mean and make it work again so we can produce our way out of trouble. "Rural America contains the roots and values that make America," says Granell. "Rural America does not want to die."

Environmental groups, however, see the hand of big business cynically directing the "grass roots" campaign, manipulating those who work for a living by raising the specter of widespread unemployment and deserted main streets in small towns throughout the West. They claim the real threat comes from corporations that, because of mechanization, are using fewer and fewer people. And which are cutting all the publicly owned trees, mining publicly owned ore and using federally subsidized water. When the resources are gone, they say, the jobs will go with them. As well as any long-term hope for the future. "It's not grass roots at all," says Bob Ekey, communications director for the GYC, who calls the group "People for the Past." "It's a transparent front for corporate America to further its agenda."

As vitriolic as the politics are, this is more than a political debate. The differences go much deeper, often to a religious bottom, with both sides believing their vision of nature and God is the true celestial design.

Many environmentalists believe a deep spirituality can be found in nature, and that by protecting nature they are somehow defending a universal force, of which humans are a part. All life is sacred, not just human life. It's called Deep Ecology. (It's not just radicals that believe in Deep Ecology; many of those in mainstream groups hold similar personal views, yet it is not an obvious part of their environmental politics.)

No group is more up front about the religious aspects than Earth First! "It's not terrorism, it's not vandalism," says Dave Foreman of the campaign of sabotage aimed at stopping the conversion of the natural world into goods by disabling bulldozers and the like. "It's something very deliberate, very thoughtful, that is undertaken as a last resort with full appreciation of the consequences. It's nonviolent, because it's directed toward inanimate machines. And monkeywrenching has to be looked at as being fun. We always believe in having fun. Yet it's very serious. It's a form of worship toward the Earth. It's really a very spiritual thing to go out and do."

Earth First!ers really see themselves as an *intifada* of the western woods. Foreman wrote *Ecodefense: A Field Guide to Monkeywrenching*, which spells out precisely how to sheer off the cogs of progress. Section titles of the 308-page book include "Burning Machinery," "Flattening Tires," "Billboard Burning," "Fence-Cutting," and finally "If You Are Arrested."

For humans to live a long-term, sustainable life-style, the philosophy holds, their activities should not separate them from nature. The whole planet is a spiritual aquifer for humans; a cool, clear drink for a society dying of thirst. Some call it "Gaea" after the Greek goddess of the earth, and believe it has a consciousness.

The Earth First!ers vision of an idyllic planet includes drastic reduction of the number of people on the Earth through birth control, setting aside 50 percent of the Earth as off-limits to resource extraction, dismantling places like Los Angeles, New York and Denver and the eventual creation of small, sustainable communities that are designed according to the environment in which they're located. The world's societies must be predicated first on a sound environmental policy. Earth first. "You can't get there from here," Foreman says. "The system has to collapse first."

Earth First! has paid for its extreme views. In 1989, as three Earth First!ers attempted to topple a power tower that fed electricity to a pumping station that kept water flowing through the Central Arizona Project aqueduct, the FBI arrived. The FBI arrested Foreman, claiming he contributed $680 to the action, though apparently he was drawn into the whole thing by an undercover informant. The arrests were the result of a $2 million, eighteen-month undercover investigation and sent a chill through Earth First! Sentences for those involved ranged from thirty days to six years. Foreman pleaded guilty to conspiracy and received five years probation. Nonetheless, Earth First! is still active.

Earth First!, and even the more moderate groups, are, in the opinion of people such as former secretary of interior James Gaius Watt, a kind of Antichrist. "They stand for pantheistic control of our well-being," says Watt, a self-described fundamentalist Christian. "It is a religious struggle." Watt says that Congress has been co-opted by environmentalists. "They have been misled by zealots who do not share the values of Western civilization. There is no way to have compromise under those conditions."

"I call it Manifest Destiny II," says Mader, who believes conservationists have a hidden agenda. "Manifest Destiny was the destiny of the white man to control the continent [in the 1800s]. The Indian was called a savage so they could be removed and the people who moved in are the ranchers, farmers and loggers. Now it's come full circle. The people from the East are pushing in again. They are dictating public policy by removing farmers and ranchers. They call us exploiters and want us off the land, and say they have a higher use. It's the battle between the Judeo-Christian ethic of conservation by man and the New Age movement, which holds that nature is God."

One of the battlegrounds for the two opposing philosophies has been Yellowstone, for both sides understand the symbolic nature of what happens in the nation's first, finest and highest-profile national park.

In 1990, the Park Service and U.S. Forest Service, at the direction of Congress, put together a document called *Vision for the Future: A Framework for Coordination in the Greater Yellowstone Area.* The report was planned to move management of the Yellowstone ecosystem in the very direction that the GYC and other groups are proposing over the next fifty years. The report, called the vision document for short, was a soft, very general look at the idea, and specific ways to achieve the goal were to follow. The primary management goal would be the health of the natural systems, with a focus on grizzly bears and geothermal features. Like many of the initiatives and ideas that come out of Yellowstone, it was viewed as a pilot for national and international parks.

Lorraine Mintzmeyer, the National Park Service regional director in Denver, a taciturn woman in a predominantly male world, was the consummate bureaucrat, having spent thirty-two years in the Park Service, working her way up to regional director of the service from an entry-level position as a secretary. She administrated the cream of the Park Service crop, the Rocky Mountain Region.

In October 1990, shortly after the document was released, Lorraine Mintzmeyer was in Washington talking up the report to members of Congress, federal officials and members of the conservation community. Unbeknownst to Mintzmeyer, a storm was brewing over the white marble buildings of Capitol Hill. In October, a meeting had been held between Senator Alan Simpson of Wyoming, one of the most powerful Republicans in the country and a close friend of former President Bush, and Malcolm Wallop, the other Republican senator from Wyoming, and representatives of the agricultural and commodity groups.

While she was in Washington, Mintzmeyer says she got a call from then assistant secretary of interior Scott Sewell—technically one of Mintzmeyer's highest bosses—and he asked her to report to his office. Mintzmeyer says she was stunned by what she encountered there. "He said Sununu [John Sununu, then Bush's chief of staff] had called him and said [the document] was a political disaster and it was going to be rewritten. He was mean," Mintzmeyer says. "I've never had that kind of dressing down in my life." Mintzmeyer was amazed "because this thing was no big deal as far as I was concerned."

Sewell, Mintzmeyer says, canceled the national meeting on the vision document. However, some local meetings were held, in Riverton and Jackson, Wyoming, in Bozeman, and in Billings. Enter People for the West! and the new grass roots movement. It organized rallies and got hundreds of people out to the meetings, many of them wearing yellow armbands as a show of solidarity. This widespread show of disapproval helped sink the vision document.

As it turned out, much of the impetus for the battle against the vision document came from the Noranda mining company, which is planning the gold mine on Yellowstone's northern boundary, and which holds a seat on PFW!'s board. Fearful that a new vision for

Yellowstone could stop mining, Crown Butte Mining (a Noranda subsidiary) president David Rovig put the wheels in motion to stop the vision document, by talking to politicians in Washington and rousing PFW!

Mintzmeyer returned to Denver and did as she had been ordered: she gutted the document and canceled the remaining meetings. She was a career bureaucrat and says she was accustomed to this kind of squelching. In fact, she claims that the Park Service had long had political spies working within it to report back to high-level Republicans in Washington, D.C., on what was going on. She had been asked to change documents before, Mintzmeyer says, to fudge data and research to come up with politically acceptable conclusions that promoted development rather than environmental protection. Though she says it made her uncomfortable, she did as ordered and changed the vision document. "They tried to make it look like it was the work of the Park Service," she says. "They wanted to use the credibility and professionalism of that agency. They were using my reputation to cover up the complete subjugation of that document."

The sixty-page draft of the vision document, hardly a hard-hitting document to begin with, became a feeble ten-page paper, Mintzmeyer says. "I said, 'Let's write the damn thing up, print it and forget about it.' We just wanted to put it behind us." The report may have sunk into the swamp of obscurity, and been forgotten about, but Lorraine Mintzmeyer did not have that luxury. There were rumors that she was in trouble for lobbying, which is against the rules for bureaucrats, an allegation she denies. In 1991, Mintzmeyer got word she was being transferred to Philadelphia to manage national parks and monuments there. It's a small region and she feels she was demoted from the top of the hierarchy for regional directors to the bottom. Mintzmeyer says they wanted her out, and she believes they thought she would retire rather than move. She didn't. She reluctantly moved to Philadelphia.

In the City of Brotherly Love, Mintzmeyer says, there was none for her. Every time she asked NPS officials in Washington, including Director James Ridenour, for approval or assistance to carry out her duties, there was no answer. Her requests "went into a bottomless hole," she says. She had been recommended for a bonus of $4,500, but that bonus never came. She had become a nonentity.

Bureaucratically shunned. Finally, Mintzmeyer says, she threw in the towel. On April 3, 1992, she resigned from the agency that was her career, her whole life. But she was to suffer one final indignity.

Just a few days before her departure as regional director—while she was still technically in charge—the president came to visit Independence Center, a park service compound with historic buildings and where Park Service employees live. The president's security detail cordoned off the entire area. Mintzmeyer's photo was circulated to the Secret Service and other police agencies, which were told not to let her inside the security area, where her own home was located.

Sewell, for his part, denies that he tried to sabotage the vision document. Mintzmeyer has since filed suit against the Department of the Interior, claiming sexual discrimination.

The debate over the vision statement illustrates the enmity with which the battle between the Old West and New is being fought. The Old West got where it is with hard work and fierce determination. People adhering to the ways of the Old West will not go gently into what they see as the dark night of change; a protracted land war lies ahead. The forces of extraction and profit and jobs and status quo are aligned against the new vision for an ecologically predicated society.

The New West is in the ascendancy, a trajectory supported by the election of Bill Clinton and Albert Gore. Secretary of Interior Bruce Babbitt, a firm believer in the New West, has announced his intention to change the management of public lands to a system that emphasizes the health of biological systems. In urban centers from the East to the Far West, people shoulder to shoulder, bumper to bumper and nose to the grindstone, no closer to the West than a Marlboro Man billboard, have a stake in the West in the form of public lands, and they are moving to claim the benefits of ownership as never before. In terms of money and political power, the Old West is outgunned.

The major problem for the Old West is that the weight of scientific and economic arguments lies with those who want to change the West. There is no such thing as a free lunch, but there are lunch bills deferred or passed on to someone else. That is what scientists and economists say is happening, as taxpayers and future generations get stuck with the bill for scientifically unsound methods of resource extraction.

Some disputes are inevitable. And maybe not such a bad thing. John Folk-Williams is one of three partners in a nonprofit group in Santa Fe called Western Network, which works on environmental and natural resource conflict resolution around the West. "Conflict on a large scale needs to go on," Folk-Williams says. "There are big social and economic forces at work here, and that's how society makes decisions and keeps up with change, by slugging it out. It's my job to be as realistic as I can. People have to be realistic about what they are facing. There are market forces at work here that favor the environment and nothing can stop it. People [who want to survive the change] have to see what makes them powerful, and they have to take advantage of that." Ranchers, loggers and miners, he says, need to make their peace with a new kind of West, even take advantage of it.

The West is a land of "lasts." The American ranch, the family loggers and farmers, small miners, small towns, wildlife and wild areas, these are all things that have vanished from much of America, and are threatened in the West. At risk, in a word, is diversity. Cultural, biological and economic diversity.

Is it a fundamental loss if the cowboy becomes a marketing tool for a line of clothing? When ranches are subdivided or strip-mined or used a month out of a year for a fishing retreat and a place to wear hats and boots? When small towns that were once real and not-so-pretty adopt false fronts and look like a set from *High Noon* or are abandoned? Is it a loss when families that made a living carefully cutting trees are forced out of business by giant clear-cutting corporations? When the forests are tamed of their wild predators? When the taxpayer-owned gold and silver and platinum has been mined out in a quarter of a century, leaving nothing for mining towns to sustain themselves? When Hispanics who lived for several hundred years in Santa Fe are forced to abandon the city to the rich?

These are among the thousands of questions people of the West—and those who have a stake in the West—have to answer. Hopefully together.

"Angry as one may be at what careless people have done and still do to a noble habitat," wrote Wallace Stegner in *The Sound of Mountain Water*, a collection of essays about the West, "it is hard to be pessimistic about the West. This is the native home of hope. When it fully learns that cooperation, not rugged individualism, is the pattern that most characterizes and preserves it, then it will have achieved itself and outlived its origins. Then it has a chance to create a society to match its scenery."

Selected Bibliography

Chapter 1

Glick, Dennis, Mary Carr, and Bert Harting. *An Environmental Profile of the Greater Yellowstone Ecosystem.* Bozeman, Mont.: The Greater Yellowstone Coalition, 1991.
Haines, Aubrey L. *The Yellowstone Story.* Vols. 1 and 2. Yellowstone National Park: Yellowstone Library and Museum Association, 1977.
Reese, Rick. *Greater Yellowstone.* Helena, Mont.: American and World Geographic Publishing, 1991.

Chapter 2

Glasscock, C. B. *War of the Copper Kings.* New York: Grosset & Dunlap, 1962.
Interior Should Ensure Against Abuses from Hardrock Mining. Washington, D.C.: General Accounting Office, 1986.
Malone, Michael. *The Battle for Butte.* Seattle: University of Washington Press, 1981.
Moore, Johnnie N., and Samuel N. Luoma. "Mining's Hazardous Waste." University of Montana, 1990.
The Mining Law of 1872 Needs Revision. Washington, D.C.: General Accounting Office, March 1989.

Chapter 3

Ervin, Keith. *Fragile Majesty.* Seattle: The Mountaineers, 1989.
Franklin, Jerry et al. *Ecological Characteristics of Old Growth Douglas-Fir Forests.* Washington, D.C.: U.S. Forest Service, 1981.
Norse, Elliot A. *Ancient Forests of the Pacific Northwest.* Washington, D.C.: Island Press, 1990.
Wild, Peter. *Pioneer Conservationists of Western America.* Missoula, Mont.: Mountain Press, 1979.

Chapter 4

Atherton, Lewis E. *The Cattle Kings.* Bloomington: Indiana University Press, 1961.
Dary, David. *Cowboy Culture.* New York: Avon, 1981.
Elmore, Wayne, and Robert L. Beschta. "Riparian Areas: Perceptions in Management." Paper. Corvallis, Oreg., 1987.
Environmental Protection Agency. *Livestock Grazing on Western Riparian Areas.* Washington, D.C.: Environmental Protection Agency, July 1990.
Foreman, Dave. *Ecodefense.* Tucson: Earth First! Books, 1985.
———. *Confessions of an Ecowarrior.* New York: Harmony Books, 1991.
They Came and Stayed: A Rosebud County History. Forsyth, Mont.: The Rosebud County Historical Society, 1977.

Chapter 5

Fradkin, Philip L. *A River No More.* New York: Alfred A. Knopf, 1981.
Hunter, Christopher J. *Better Trout Habitat.* Washington, D. C.: Island Press, 1991.

Lister, Robert, and Florence Lister. *Those Who Came Before.* Globe, Ariz.: Southwest Parks and Monuments Association, 1983.
Reisner, Marc. *Cadillac Desert.* New York: Viking, 1986.
Welsh, Frank. *How to Create a Water Crisis.* Boulder, Colo: Johnson Publishing, 1985.

CHAPTER 6

Lopez, Barry. *Of Wolves and Men.* New York: Scribner's, 1978.
McNamee, Thomas. *The Grizzly Bear.* New York: Alfred A. Knopf, 1984.
Mech, L. David. *The Wolf.* Minneapolis: University of Minnesota Press, 1981.

CHAPTER 7

Chase, Alston. *Playing God in Yellowstone.* New York: Atlantic Monthly Press, 1986.
Crampton, C. Gregory. *Land of Living Rock.* New York: Alfred A. Knopf, 1972.
Hughes, J. Donald. *House of Stone and Light.* Grand Canyon Natural History Association, 1978.

CHAPTER 8

Hazen-Hammond, Susan. *A Short History of Santa Fe.* San Francisco: Lexicos, 1988.
Lessinger, Jack. *Penturbia.* Seattle: SocioEconomics Press, 1990.
Simmons, Marc. *New Mexico: An Interpretative History.* Albuquerque: University of New Mexico Press, 1977.

CHAPTER 9

Limerick, Patricia N. *The Legacy of Conquest.* New York: Norton, 1988.
Rasher, Ray, Norma Tirrell, and Deanne Kloepfer. *Yellowstone: The Wealth of Nature.* Washington, D C.: The Wilderness Society, 1992.
Stegner, Wallace. *The Sound of Mountain Water.* Lincoln, Neb.: University of Nebraska Press, 1980.
———. *Where the Bluebird Sings to the Lemonade Springs.* New York: Random House, 1992.

INDEX

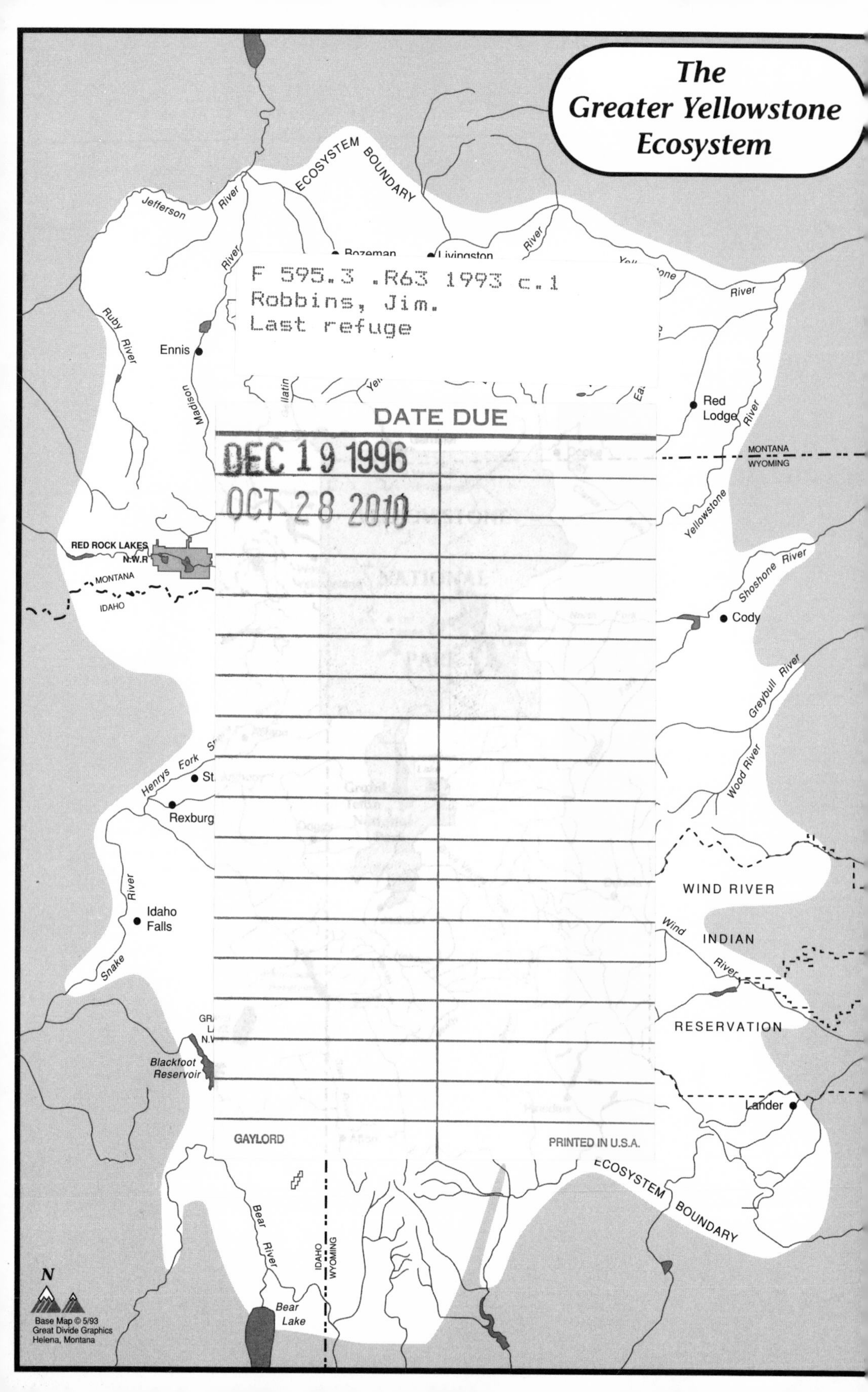
The Greater Yellowstone Ecosystem
ECOSYSTEM BOUNDARY
Jefferson River
Ruby River
Madison River
Ennis
Red Lodge
River
MONTANA
WYOMING
Yellowstone
Shoshone River
Cody
Greybull River
Wood River
RED ROCK LAKES N.W.R
MONTANA
IDAHO
Henrys Fork
Rexburg
River
Idaho Falls
Snake
WIND RIVER
INDIAN
RESERVATION
Wind River
Blackfoot Reservoir
Lander
ECOSYSTEM BOUNDARY
Bear River
IDAHO
WYOMING
Bear Lake
N
Base Map © 5/93
Great Divide Graphics
Helena, Montana